THE GREAT JERUSALEM ARTICHOKE CIRCUS

The University of Minnesota Press gratefully acknowledges assistance provided for the publication of this volume by the John K. and Elsie Lampert Fesler Fund.

THE GREAT JERUSALEM ARTICHOKE CIRCUS

The Buying and Selling
of the Rural American Dream

Joseph A. Amato
Foreword by Paul Gruchow

 *University of Minnesota Press*
Minneapolis
London

Copyright 1993 by the Regents of the University of Minnesota

All rights reserved. No part of this publication may be reproduced, stored in a retrieval system, or transmitted, in any form or by any means, electronic, mechanical, photocopying, recording, or otherwise, without the prior written permission of the publisher.

Published by the University of Minnesota Press
2037 University Avenue Southeast, Minneapolis, MN 55455-3092
Printed in the United States of America on acid-free paper

Library of Congress Cataloging-in-Publication Data

Amato, Joseph Anthony.
    The great Jerusalem artichoke circus : the buying and selling of the rural American dream / Joseph Amato.
        p.   cm.
    Includes bibliographical references and index.
    ISBN 0-8166-2344-9 (hc : acid-free). — ISBN 0-8166-2345-7 (pb : acid-free)
    1. American Energy Farming Systems. 2. Horticultural products industry—United States. I. Title.
HD9009.A58A45   1993
381′.41524′0973—dc20
                                                                                                93-12842
                                                                                                  CIP

The University of Minnesota is an
equal-opportunity educator and employer.

I will raise up for them a plant of renown . . .
—Ezekiel 34:29

The history of weeds is the history of man, but we do not yet have the facts that will let us sit down and write very much of it.
—Edgar Anderson, *Plants, Man and Life*

Contents

Foreword	ix
Preface	xxiii
Acknowledgments	xxix
Introduction: A Beckoning Plant	1
1. A Country Prophet	15
2. A Bulldozing Businessman	29
3. Buyers and Sellers of Seed	49
4. A Perfect Consultant	77
5. What Made the Company Run	89
6. Killing off the Goose That Laid the Golden Egg	106
7. Folding up the Tent	125
8. The County Attorney and His Investigator	154
9. The Lost Covenant	179
Conclusion: The Planets Went Astray	194
Chronology	203
AEFS Organizational Structure	207
Notes	209
Sources	233
Index	243

Foreword
Paul Gruchow

This story has everything: tragedy and pathos, comedy and farce, greed and piety, ambition and failure, vision and willful disregard of reality. There is even an unlikely David—a resourceful county attorney armed with doggedness and righteous indignation. If *The Great Jerusalem Artichoke Circus* were not history, it might have been a novel by Sinclair Lewis.

This is, at heart, a story of the consequences of disintegration in countryside America. The seeds of swindlers prosper in the soil of despair. There have been far greater hucksters than the small-timers who created American Energy Farming Systems in the early 1980s to peddle Jerusalem artichokes as the saving crop of the future. One of them was Earl Butz, who had been dean of the College of Agriculture at Purdue University and who served as U.S. secretary of agriculture from 1971 to 1976.[1] His tenure coincided with a period of rampant worldwide inflation, bumper American crops, famine in parts of Africa and Asia, and serious crop failures in the Soviet Union and elsewhere; world grain prices soared to sensational heights. From the bully pulpit of his office, Butz energetically fed an expansionist frenzy, urging farmers to get bigger or to get out, exhorting them to plant fencerow to fencerow, making shameless political hay out of a boomlet built upon starvation and malnourishment.[2]

By the end of the decade, social upheaval in the Middle East had precipitated an oil crisis. Petroleum prices soared, as did interest rates. Farmers were caught in the crosswinds of high energy prices, because industrial agriculture is dependent upon petroleum both as a fuel and as a source of nitrogen fertilizer, and punishing interest rates on operating loans and on highly leveraged land acquired during the brief boom. By the early 1980s, the farm economy had crashed. Land prices plummeted, commodity prices collapsed to historic levels (which have always been low), and farmers went bankrupt by the tens of thousands.[3]

It was from the cinders of this ruin that American Energy Farming Systems arose. There were, as always, plenty of economists around to aver that this latest devastation of American farmers, who had dwindled in half a century from 50 percent to less than 2 percent of the nation's population, was merely another painful but necessary "downsizing," as the cynical euphemism went, a further pruning of dead wood. But a decade later, despite the rigor of the pruning, and despite a supposedly recovered agricultural economy, farm bankruptcies are still occurring in Minnesota at the rate of ninety a week—the failure, annually, of a set of businesses with net worths of between $2 and $3 billion.

Farmers at the time also perceived, correctly, that the debris allegedly being cleared out of the agricultural system included a good many model farmers and scarcely anybody who had been discouraged by his banker or who had defied the best thinking of the experts at his land grant university or who had bucked federal agricultural policy. Farmers noticed that it was in the national interest to bail out the bankers but not the farmers. There was a brief squall of protests, marches on the Capitol in St. Paul, and tractorcades to Washington; the old Grange slogan, "It's time to raise less corn and more hell," was trotted out once again; and there was a spurt of aid to carry the political leadership through the by-elections. Then things returned to normal. Fewer and fewer farmers went back to competing for a smaller and smaller share of the agricultural economy.[4]

There was, too, in the early 1980s, much talk about structural change in agriculture. The industry's precarious dependency upon oil had finally registered; there was new enthusiasm—and during the Carter presidency, some money—for the development of alternative sources of energy. It was also finally understood that factory farms are genetically, economically, and biologically brittle. The narrowness of their genetic stocks renders agricultural commodities highly susceptible to disease and pestilence. In the intensity of their specialization, farmers are exposed to unpredictable and uncontrollable swings in the commodity and money markets. And because of specialization, they have no resiliency in the event of natural adversities—drought, untimely rains, late springs, early frosts. There was much talk in the early 1980s about rediversifying the farm economy, about finding new crops, creating new markets, and claiming a larger share of the market sector of the agricultural economy—which now accounts for two-thirds of its total revenues—for the countryside.

The Carter administration in its waning days made a fairly serious effort to carry these issues to the public table, but the Iran hostage crisis intervened, in the aftermath of its resolution the price of oil fell, and interest rates drifted downward. The appetite for the meat and potatoes work of restructuring, particularly of a small and once again nearly invisible sector of the economy, dissipated.

But among some farmers, the enthusiasm for change persisted. A great many schemes for diversification were tried, most of them scams and all of them unsuccessful. There was a sharp decline in the use of purchased inputs, particularly of pesticides and commercially produced fertilizers; this decline has persisted into the 1990s. Several methods of low and minimum tillage gained currency. And dozens of small citizen-based think tanks emerged, the most notable of which were, in the Midwest, the Practical Farmers of Iowa, the Center for Rural Affairs, the Minnesota Food Association, the Land Stewardship Project, the Land Institute, and the Northern Plains Sustainable Agriculture Society.

Their approaches varied widely: The Center for Rural Affairs set out to demonstrate practical methods of achieving energy self-sufficiency on the farm; the Minnesota Food Association sought to build an urban constituency for agrarian reform; at the Land Institute, researchers began to build the theoretical groundwork for a radically new kind of agriculture based on an ecological rather than on an industrial model. But there was, however divergent the strategies, consensus among these groups around the emerging idea that farming as it had been practiced since the end of the Second World War was not sustainable and had been socially calamitous; and there was, too, the growing conviction that the initiative for change was going to have to come from farmers themselves.

By the end of the decade even the land grant university establishment, the segment of the American agricultural community most trenchantly opposed to reform, was conceding, in a widely noticed report issued through the National Academy of Sciences, that alternative forms of farming were both viable and desirable.[5] At many leading agricultural colleges—including those in Minnesota, North Dakota, Iowa, and Wisconsin—new centers and institutes for the study of sustainable agriculture were created. At the federal level, a smidgen (about 1 percent) of the Agriculture Department's research dollars were earmarked for small-scale studies in alternative farming methods. Although major research agendas had not markedly shifted, nor, by and large, had the standard agricultural college curricula changed, and although there was a last-ditch hope, fueled by corporate research grants and a major infusion of federal dollars, that new techniques of gene manipulation might yield a technological rescue of industrial agriculture, the momentum for change was already being institutionalized.

By 1992, Earl Butz, who had sounded fifteen years earlier like a great prophet, was reduced to crooning a romantic lament for the good old days. "We simply cannot feed, even at subsistence levels, our 250 million Americans without a large production input of chemicals, antibiotics, and growth hormones," he wrote, ignoring a good deal of practical and scientific evidence to the contrary. "Our problem is that two-thirds of Americans living today never had the experience of biting into a wormy apple, seeing the wormhole, and wondering, 'Is he still in there, or did I get him?' They think that God and nature made all apples good. They didn't. God put the worm in the apple; man took it out."[6]

The point is that although American Energy Farming Systems was carelessly conceived and badly managed, and although its leaders proved, in the end, to be criminally greedy, the idea behind it was not inherently stupid, and the circumstances of the early 1980s practically guaranteed that a company like it would emerge. Professor Amato has admirably avoided the tempting, and culturally foreordained, interpretation of this sad episode as merely the story of a bunch of yokel farmers being hoodwinked by a band of snake-oil salesmen.

A kind of snake oil *was*, of course, being sold, and the farmers who got caught in the scam were naively trusting, although hardly anybody was betting the farm on its success. But there was an unstoppable trickle toward change, and there was a vacuum of leadership: the scientific establishment was still preaching business as usual; the political leadership could be interested only in short-term infusions of cash; and the organized farm groups had fallen back upon the tired litany that there was nothing wrong with farming that higher commodity prices couldn't fix. Where else was hope to be found?

Nor was there anything essentially outrageous about Jerusalem artichokes as a crop. It is a native plant, aggressive to the point of being weedy in its growth habits, and it seemed to have the merit of producing both a food with some previous history of acceptance and a biomass suitable for conversion to energy. Odder possibilities were being seriously investigated at the time, including a well-publicized study of cattails at the University of Minnesota.

And, in fact, a much more obviously unsuitable crop—corn—has since gained a niche in the energy market. Corn as an ethanol source may yield no net gain in energy, since it is energy-expensive to grow; the crop is "impressively vulnerable" to disease, as a U.S. Academy of Sciences study concluded, because of its narrow genetic base;[7] raised industrially, it is environmentally destructive; and exploiting it as an alternative energy source does nothing to diversify the economy of farming. But Archer-Daniels-Midland, the agri-industrial giant that now has a monopolistic grip on the corn ethanol market, is well capitalized and politically well connected, and it has had behind it the powerful corn lobby, financed by a producer tax. Federal subsidies to raise the corn, and state subsidies to support the market for the ethanol derived from it, have made it, although illogical, a successful business proposition.

One of the tragedies of the Jerusalem artichoke scam, and others like it, is that it gave the idea of diversification—something still urgently needed—a bad name. Our hapless dependency upon corn, in particular—a dependency exacerbated by the production of corn-based ethanol—poses a serious threat to our security. We need only look to our recent history to understand why.

A little more than a century ago, there lived on the North American prairies a people who had staked their lives and fortunes upon the buffalo. The buffalo once flourished in seemingly inexhaustible numbers. There were, perhaps, 60 million of them. When Coronado, the first European to see the prairies, traveled to what is now Kansas in 1541, a journey of several months, he reported that he was never once beyond sight of them.

If you were born into plains culture in those days, you were wrapped in swaddling clothes made of the soft skin of a buffalo calf and carried until you could walk in a papoose lined with the pulverized dung of the buffalo, which served as a diaper. You grew into an adulthood dependent in every particular upon the buffalo. The animal supplied you with food, raiment, shelter, tools, household furnishings, paints and dyes, cosmetics, and fuel. And when you died, you were buried, or raised upon a platform, in a coffin made of the hide of a buffalo. The buffalo was literally the beginning and the ending of your existence. You would have believed that the buffalo was eternal.

Then came the Europeans, whose railroad lines, fences, plows, and relentless hunting reduced the buffalo nearly to extinction. This decimation also threatened the survival of plains culture, as Americans knew. Congress passed a bill in the 1860s to protect the few hundred buffalo that still survived, out of the millions. President Grant vetoed it, on the advice of his secretary of war, who said that to get rid of the buffalo was to get rid of the Indian problem.

There arose, then, among the embattled Native Americans, a shaman who said that the buffalo had not died, that they had merely gone down into the safety of the underworld. If the people, the shaman preached, would say the right prayers and perform the right dances, the buffalo would rise up again from the underworld and the native way of life would be saved. So all across the prairies, the people danced and prayed. But Americans, despite their Constitution, outlawed the new Ghost Dance religion, as it was called.

In South Dakota, in December 1890, a group of Lakota Sioux danced in defiance of the ban. When they were ordered to desist, they quit their reservation and headed for the Badlands, where they might dance and pray in peace. Along the way, they were set upon by American cavalry and slaughtered, men, women, and children alike. The few survivors were carried to a nearby mission and laid out upon the sanctuary floor to be treated for their wounds. Above the altar, it being the Christmas season, hung a banner reading, "Peace on Earth, Good Will Toward Men." The place was Wounded Knee.[8]

This was the last battle of a long war. The buffalo were not, after all, eternal. In a way, it also marked the defeat of the prairie ecosystem.

Now we have made upon the prairies a culture as dependent upon corn as the Dakota culture was upon the buffalo. An infant born into it will be clothed in a diaper made in part of corn and fed a formula based upon corn syrup. That person will, as an adult, be sustained in thousands of particulars by products made from, or packaged in, or manufactured with derivatives of corn, from every kind of food except fresh fish to plastics, textiles, building materials, machine parts, soaps and cosmetics, even highways. And when that person dies, the laws of the land require that the body should be embalmed—in a fluid made in part from corn.[9]

We have not begun to imagine a life without corn. We have assumed, by the default of failing to think about it, that corn is eternal. But it is no more eternal than were the buffalo. In fact, because our entire crop shares a common cytoplasm, it would take exactly one persistent pathogen to devastate our culture as we know it.

We hang tenuously from another thread that ultimately threatens our security. As Professor Amato points out, scarcely anything we grow or eat comes from genetic materials indigenous to the United States. We live by the colonial appropriation of the natural wealth of other, mainly impoverished, nations. It is an odd irony that even the weeds that plague our fields have been largely imported. At the same time, the misperception persists, nowhere more vigorously than in the countryside, that it is our native flora that are alien and weedy. Literally hundreds of plant species gave sustenance and health to the indigenous peoples of this continent. That almost nothing has been made of this great biotic wealth through centuries of exploitation is one remarkable indication of how little settled here we continue to be.

"The Jerusalem artichoke is a saving weed," Fred Johnson said. The remark has, of course, as this book makes abundantly clear, its weirdly messianic overtones. But it also contains a germ of truth. Were we to begin to think of accommodating ourselves to the biota of the continent as we found it, we might well be preparing ourselves for a more stable future. The danger in continuing to build an ever more extravagant culture upon expropriated genetic materials is that the day looms when their owners will have marshaled the determination and the power to insist upon their proprietary rights. International justice, in fact, requires that that day should come. We would then starkly understand how little self-sufficient we have made ourselves. The Jerusalem artichoke scam, in its recklessness and mendacity, served at least temporarily to disgrace an idea in which there was actually a saving grace.

Professor Amato's study is keen in its dissection of two folkways of rural culture—the habit of boosterism, and the fundamentalist faith that the pursuit of material wealth, by whatever means necessary, is part of God's plan for us. To these might be added a third, born in science but embraced with a special fervor in the countryside: the trust that technological miracles will save us from the mundane labors of our days.

The altogether honorable goal of industrial agriculture, at least as it was conceived by the land grant scholars who organized to create the cooperative extension system in 1914—the equivalent of the Chinese Wall among public education campaigns—was to eradicate through enlightenment the poverty that had always been associated with rural life.[10] If only farmers, it was believed, could be persuaded to abandon the stodgy habits of tradition and to accept scientific farming practices—though it was technology, not science, that was actually being sold—then a new era of ease and prosperity might be carried into the countryside. At the same time, of course, a great many new jobs might be created for agricultural scientists. It seemed a marvelous marriage of mutual self-interests.

Indeed, better seeds and breeding stock did enormously enhance yields, and mechanization did eliminate the need for much hand labor and greatly increase the productivity per worker of American farming. By the close of the Second World

War, American agriculture had positioned itself to become the leading supplier of farm commodities to world markets.

There were glitches along the way. The breaking of marginal lands led in the 1930s to the Dust Bowl, which some environmentalists count the greatest ecological disaster in human history. Farmers would need to be taught better conservation practices. Highly bred plants and animals proved particularly susceptible to diseases and pests, and large-scale monocultural patterns of cropping and close confinement of animal herds established huge breeding chambers for them. Chemical pesticides would have to be developed. High-yielding crops taxed the natural fertility of soils. Artificial fertilizers would need to be added. These crops consumed more moisture than was naturally available. Underground reserves of water would have to be tapped for irrigation. All of these improvements required capital. The poorest farmers, unable to compete, went bankrupt by the millions. Well, there were too many farmers anyway.

Then the real glitches began to materialize. Pesticides seemed to be having a devastating effect on the diversity and stability of natural biota. Fossil fuels appeared to be a dwindling and nonrenewable resource. Pests turned out to be somewhat more agile at genetic adaptation than the laboratory scientists; as quickly as a new generation of chemical controls could be developed, a new generation of resistant pests appeared. The nitrates in artificial fertilizers seemed to be contaminating underground water supplies. The aquifers upon which irrigation systems depended proved to be surprisingly depletable. Pesticide contaminants seemed to be making their way from the field to the dining room table. Consumers seemed to think that foods like tomatoes that were bred to pack and ship well but which tasted like cardboard were not an improvement. Half a century of conservation efforts had not managed to reduce soil losses to tolerable levels. Even poverty, which had prompted industrialization, had not been noticeably eased. The poorest counties in the nation were still the most rural ones, and by the 1970s, not only individual farmers but also whole towns were drying up and blowing away, like so many tumbleweeds.

There are, to be sure, those who still see such matters as trivial, and who read the story of modern agriculture as an eye-watering triumph—the geographer John Fraser Hart, for example:

The farmer has been able to increase his yields because plant breeders have given him better varieties of crops, and he has poured on the fertilizer to take full advantage of their genetic potential. He relies on a whole arsenal of chemicals to protect his crops against voracious insects and to get rid of weeds. He can handle a larger acreage because bigger and better machines have reduced his labor requirements. He can sit in an air-conditioned cab on a powerful new machine and accomplish more in half an hour than his grandfather could do in a long, sweat-stained, backbreaking day.[11]

If people insist on seeing something wrong with this picture, Hart sarcastically suggests, then, in heavily urbanized areas, "it might make sense to treat the countryside as a museum and to pay farmers as custodians to keep it looking the way city people want it to look."[12] Modern farmers, Hart notes approvingly, are not mere tillers of soil and tenders of animals; they are money men. In 1910, they had to borrow "only" 13 percent of their normal operating capital; today they borrow 43 percent!

This is not agriculture as science or history; it is agriculture as myth. Industrialism as a practical matter may have had its technical difficulties, but the propagation of its attendant mythology has been an unmitigated success. Its characteristic features include a sense of the past as a nightmare; a vision of nature as a terror (all those "voracious" insects) against which a vigilant war must constantly be waged (the "arsenals" of chemicals); a revulsion against ("sweat-stained, backbreaking") physical labor; the glorification of bigness (the phrase is always "bigger and better"); and the conviction that our contrivances will deliver us from the tyranny of nature into a paradise of money.

American Energy Farming Systems may have been guided by an eerie brand of fundamentalist Christian dogma, but it was also acting out—albeit in an especially crude way—the myth of industrialism. If the company's officers were fatally preoccupied with the accumulation of wealth, so was the myth. If the company was founded upon grandiose ambitions, so too was the myth—what could be more grandiose than the idea that humans need not be subject to nature? If AEFS was a scheme built upon a product for which there was no demonstrated use, how was it, in that respect, different from a thousand other successful industrial products? The engine of industrialism is desire, not need, and in its mythology, people are enriched to the extent that they no longer have to sweat.

The mythology is extraordinarily unimaginative about the forms that tyranny might take. Only someone operating from some such sinecure as tenure is likely to be so naive as to suppose that freedom from sweat is of a higher order than freedom from one's bankers. It is, moreover, a mythology that places a high value on blind faith. Trust us, the technologists insist, there is no reason to be alarmed, it will all work out, and if it doesn't you can depend on us to think of something else. Don't even think of asking questions or playing the skeptic with us; we know who you are, you nattering nabobs of negativism. You hate science, you're psychologically unsuited to change (that shibboleth of modernity), you want everybody to go back to hovering in unheated hovels, picking each other's hair lice!

I have participated through the past several years in an ongoing conversation between citizens and scientists about how the new technology of genetic engineering might be applied to agriculture, what potential dangers it poses, and what safeguards, from the public's point of view, might usefully mitigate them. I remember especially two electric moments in those conversations. One night, we were questioning an ardent advocate of biotechnology about the uses she envisioned for it. She offered the example of her own attempt, since abandoned as formidably complex, to develop a better artificial strawberry flavoring. And why, she was asked, is it important to have a better artificial strawberry flavoring? She was stunned into momentary silence. The idiocy of the question was quite beyond her. She marched off to her dean to complain about the insolent rudeness of those . . . those *people*. Another night, we were in the midst of a studiously civil conversation with a public university vice president who had invested the weight of his office in an effort to derail state regulation of environmental releases of genetically engineered organisms. The man's face suddenly reddened. "Let me make one thing perfectly clear," he said, exploding with passion. "Biotechnology is one of our tools, and I will never, *never* agree to let anybody else tell me how I can use my tools!" As if it had not been established millennia ago that any tool, however splendid, can be dangerous when used carelessly, or inappropriately, or ignorantly. The message, heard so often in the countryside, was, "Don't you *dare* question my judgment."

Farmers, in the face of such authoritarianism, have, as a whole, proved compliant pupils. They embraced industrialism quickly and have marched meekly apace since, even as their ranks thinned alarmingly and it began to seem as if they were so many lemmings headed out to sea. One measure of their complacency is the degree to which they have accepted the proposition that the experts in farming are not they themselves but the people in the research institutions, who may not have had a week's experience at running an actual farm. One morning on WCCO radio, which has long had a loyal following among farmers, the arrival in Minnesota of an undersecretary of agriculture was under discussion. "So this man is an expert in soils?" Roger Erickson asked. "*No*," said the farmer reporter, "he's a specialist in international marketing, so let's give him a little respect." "Let's Stop Treating Our Soil Like Dirt," proclaims a bumper sticker the Land Stewardship Project distributes. It has the obvious conservation message, but a subtler one, too: farmers these days, so long under the spell of white-shirt experts, have to be reminded that there is nothing disreputable about coming into physical contact with earth.

One of the great attractions of industrial farming is that it requires so little independent thought. If one is able to discount the benefit in the patient and fastidious care of the land, then it is possible, even mindlessly possible, to order up the seeds one's dealer recommends, drill them into the ground at the prescribed density from the lofty heights of one's air-conditioned cab, "pour on the fertilizer," as Dr. Hart so inelegantly puts it, fire off one's arsenal of chemicals in the dosages suggested by one's extension agent, and play canasta until it is time to bring the harvest in. It is because industrial farming requires so little care that it is possible to practice it on so large a scale. It is aided by a lack of curiosity about what else is going on on one's land and abetted by a hardening of the moral arteries.

A complacent population, discouraged against skepticism, conditioned to put its faith in outside experts, inured to the daily spectacle of failure, and quickened by the often-repeated promise of wealth without labor, is one that has been prepared in every possible way to fall for such scams as American Energy Farming Systems. That is the meaning of the story Professor Amato so ably tells here. What is amazing is how few people succumbed and how quickly the whole scheme crashed.

Preface

Civilization is based, not only on man, but on plants and animals.
—J. B. S. Haldane

Few plants lend themselves to human exploitation, much less infatuation. According to David Pimentel et al., "About 90 percent of foods utilized by humans come from fifteen major crops and six livestock types. ... The crops are rice, wheat, corn (maize), sorghum, millet, rye, barley, common bean, soybean, peanut, cassava, sweet potato, potato, coconut, and banana."[1] Of the estimated 500,000 species that compose the plant kingdom, Gary Ritchie estimates that only about 1,000, 0.2 percent of the total, are used by humans for food, fiber, fuel, medicines, and other purposes.[2] Virtually every major food crop has been cultivated for at least two, and perhaps as long as ten, millennia. Disregarding the diverse uses North American Indians traditionally made of 120 native plants, including the Jerusalem artichoke, only about thirty species in the contemporary United States make up 95 percent of the American diet.[3]

The few plants that have been transformed into major crops sustain and define whole peoples and civilizations. As rice, for example, defines the Orient and wheat defines the West, so New World crops, such as the potato, introduced in early modern history into Eastern Europe and Ireland, brought both rapid expansion of population and new societal orders of small farmers.

As Sydney Mintz has shown so well for sugar in his book *Sweetness and Power* (1985), any given new crop not only transforms the cuisine and diet of consuming societies but at the same time determines the character of agriculture, the natures of class and work, and the faces of life and death in producing societies.

Plants have long shaped human cultures.[4] They have formed elemental human senses of well-being, celebration, mystery, and place. Unusual trees have universally served as markers of place, symbols of religion, and sources of healing, truth, and life, whereas selected plants have long constituted the essence of folk medicine and held honored places in folk religion.

As plants define cultures, so cultures, in turn, define plants. Folk taxonomies identify plants that cure and injure, plants that are beautiful and ugly, plants that one must cultivate and those that grow wild. Among the most fundamental distinctions made by agricultural societies is that which is made between helpful and harmful plants: helpful plants include all the plants that serve human purposes; harmful plants, known as weeds—revealingly called in French *mauvaises herbes* (bad grasses)—simply are all the plants that grow against human will and interest.

This distinction between plant and weed has not been lost in modern society. However, in the minds of most people in modern society, where cities increasingly dominate and the countryside is given over to monocultural agriculture, the greatest distinction made in the plant kingdom is that between crops and plants. Crops are understood to be economically successful plants, upon which whole societies depend; conversely, plants—in the minds of modern urban dwellers and profit-driven farmers—are assigned to more arcane realms, as are forgotten peoples, dialects, and folkways. Plants are conceived as serving what are taken to be superficial functions like tickling palates, stimulating love, filling gardens, decorating homes and lawns, or satisfying the moderate passions of botanists, hobby gardeners, landscapers, and other "less than serious people." Setting such false exaggerated notions aside, there is truth in the generalization that the names, properties, and powers of the world of plants—of which native and traditional peoples were so knowledgeable—have lost much of their immediate importance and mystery for the great majority of people in modern society.

This simplified view (particularly identified with gardenless city dwellers) is not even entirely contradicted by contemporary plant scientists who judge all plants only by their potential to serve mass consumption. Plant scientists now survey the entire germ plasm of the plant kingdom for human exploitation. While some economic biologists reexamine folklore's claims about uses and powers of a whole range of plants, others scour the world to discover beneficial plants. The greatest jackpot of all would be the discovery of a plant that would become a major new crop capable of transforming nations and redefining humanity itself.

Since the time of Columbus, history records how new plants have changed continents and peoples. For example, such Old World plants as sugar, coffee, rice, and wheat have totally altered the environments and societies of the New World, as corn, tobacco, and the potato shaped the lives and fields of the Old World. New and varied strains of plants continue to account for momentous changes in the world at large. For example, the recent history of the American Midwest is inseparable from the story of the successful hybridization of corn and the decade-long adaptation of the soybean (known as the cow of China) from a feed to a new source of oil and protein. Corn and soybeans not only rescued Midwestern agriculture but also disposed its farmers to believe in the saving powers of new crops.

The path from plant to crop is neither uniform nor predictable. Each plant has a unique history. Rye and oats were once weeds but now are crop plants; velvet leaf, Johnson grass, crab grass (a millet that came from Eastern Europe), Japanese bamboo, and kudzu, a Japanese vine, were introduced into North American agriculture as crops and now are weeds. Amaranth illustrates another path traveled by a plant. Once a major grain crop of Mayan and Aztec civilizations, amaranth was degraded, with the collapse of those civilizations to the status of a weed. There it remained until recently, when a change in North American diet (prompted by a concern for healthy foods) restored amaranth as a significant crop.

Plants move in and out of North American fields, passing from weed to economic crop, or from economic crop to unrecognized plant to weed. The elevation from minor to major crop or, more significantly, from weed to major crop, is, however, rare. Decades of experimentation must occur in laboratory, field, technological production, and market for this to happen.

One such plant that recently made a successful move from plant status to crop status is the sunflower (*Helianthus annuus*). In the 1970s, as a result of Russian efforts in the early twentieth century, the sunflower, a simple supplier of snacks for humans and feed for wild birds, became the world's second most important source of vegetable oil.[5] If plants suffered envy (which of course they do not), the Jerusalem artichoke would have died of it. Its cousin or, as analogized by some, its "stepsister," the sunflower, has proven to be one of the indigenous North American plants, like tobacco, corn, and the potato, to gain significant world recognition as a major crop, occupying a respected place in the fields of distant Russia, the Balkans, and Argentina. Sunflowers, it is argued, are the most valuable genetic resource of all North American native plants, among which are numbered the wild groundnut ("Indian potatoes"), the tepary bean, and the century plant, as well as persimmons, papaws, chestnuts, hog peanuts, serviceberries, panic grass, and others.[6]

Guayule and jojoba offer two different histories of a plant's path to establishment as a crop. In 1904, captains of industry John D. Rockefeller and Bernard Baruch established a company to extract rubber from wild guayule, a squat, gray, knee-high bush that grows in the wastelands of the Big Bend/Stockton Plateau region of Texas and throughout Mexico's huge Chihuahuan Desert.[7] In 1910, this company, located now in Mexico, furnished half the rubber consumed in the United States. By 1912, however, with the wild stands of the plant sharply depleted, Pancho Villa nearly dealt the company a death blow when he banished it from Mexico. In Salinas, California, the company barely managed to survive for the next two decades until 1942 when fate, in the guise of Japanese troops invading Southeast Asia, eliminated the West's major source of natural rubber. Scarcity created a demand. The American government promptly bought up the company and committed a thousand researchers to the plant's success and ten thousand workers to planting 12,000 hectares of guayule.[8] In 1946, with Southeast Asian rubber back on the market and the fledgling synthetic rubber industry successfully under way, guayule again lost its attraction and the company's fields were burned and plowed under. In the 1970s, interest in natural rubber (especially in its unique physical properties) rekindled an interest in guayule that has been sustained during the past two decades.

The jojoba plant has made a significant bid to gain admission to fields of the American Southwest during the past few decades. Jojoba owes its promise to the threatened extinction of the sperm whale. A perennial plant that can be developed to flourish in an arid climate, jojoba produces a liquid wax whose characteristics are nearly identical to those of sperm oil. Although scientists cautioned potential growers about the costs and problems associated with jojoba as a commercial crop, all sorts of people—including real estate speculators—jumped on the jojoba bandwagon in Arizona in the 1970s. Jojoba was advertised as a way to "save whales, cure baldness, convert unproductive desert land into jojoba plantations, provide jobs for Indians, and within four to five years repay investments in jojoba agricultural projects."[9] A jojoba fever developed against which farmers and speculators had no immunity. This new disease, according to James Brown of the Arizona Jojoba Growers and Processors, "was easily transmitted by telephone"—and it proved to be, at least for some, "a terminal disease."[10] Nevertheless, two jojoba growers associations were formed and successfully regulated the crop's development. By the end of the 1980s, jojoba appeared to be on the threshold of becoming a successful crop.

Like jojoba, the Jerusalem artichoke became popular in the early 1980s. Traditionally considered a pernicious weed by the vast majority of midwestern farmers, it was suddenly presented as a crop of great promise for the nation's farm community. It generated what Noel Vietmeyer of the National Academy of Science aptly described as "a horticultural hysteria" that reminded him of the tulip mania of seventeenth-century Holland.[11]

This book is a cultural history of this horticultural hysteria, and it is also specifically a study of the company, American Energy Farming Systems (AEFS), that marketed the Jerusalem artichoke with such phenomenal but short-lived success. In a matter of eighteen months, from the fall of 1981 to early 1983, AEFS, a new company located in Marshall, Minnesota—a small town of 10,000 inhabitants in the southwest corner of the state—sold over $25 million of Jerusalem artichoke seed to growers in thirty-one states and three Canadian provinces. Unexpected success put AEFS out of control from the very start and quickly exceeded the ability of its two owners to understand and control the company. Owned, directed, and staffed by men who were losing, or had already lost, their places in business or on the farm, the company was characterized by a desperate, frenzied, and greedy energy.

Appearing to its promoters to be both God's greatest promise and their last hope, AEFS invited a full cast of characters into the big tent of the Jerusalem artichoke circus. The cast included desperate farmers, greedy small-time speculators, unemployed ministers, charismatic salesmen, irrepressible boosters, legitimate and illegitimate scientists, a range of consultants, and a parade of attorneys, public officials, investigators, reporters, and others.

This book examines the managers of AEFS and the whole cast of characters associated with AEFS as a cross-section of American society. Also, it describes the philosophy and practices of this company, whose meteoric life ended in bankruptcy, and the complex criminal trials of the two owners and a consultant that dragged on from initial investigations in 1984 until their final resolution in 1989.

In addition to making a contribution to the unjustifiably ignored fields of business, rural, and regional history, this book is intended to serve cultural history by showing the enduring importance of plants in the thoughts, hopes, and actions of people and by examining the ideas, assumptions, myths, faiths, and passions that created a unique American horticultural hysteria.

Acknowledgments

This is a cultural history of a recent episode in national agricultural history. It examines the people, forces, circumstances, and crises, and the beliefs, passions, myths, ideas, and assumptions that in 1981 created a unique horticultural hysteria centered on the promise of the Jerusalem artichoke—a plant that up to then the vast majority of American farmers knew as a weed.

I did not want to write this book when the idea of doing so was first proposed to me. I had just finished a short book on the Belgian farmers of southwestern Minnesota and a lengthy cultural history of the changing value of suffering in the Western world. Not long before that, I had written what I found to be an exceptionally difficult book about a father and a son who, in 1983, murdered two bankers in southwestern Minnesota.

There were other reasons for not wishing to do this study. I was teaching full time, and I had only a passing interest in the history of agriculture, business, sales, cheating, and fundamentalist religion, all subjects that were at the heart of what was known locally as "the Jerusalem artichoke scheme."

One thing attracted me to this study, however. American Energy Farming Systems (AEFS) was located in Marshall, Minnesota, where I live and teach. Indeed, its main sales office was no more than four hundred yards from my office at the university. Just by virtue of living in Marshall I had heard a lot about "businessmen and artichokes"—and the more I heard about the subject, the more I believed something should be written about it.

Also, as is so often the case in the selection of subjects, I was trapped by my own arguments. As director of rural studies at Southwest State University, as history seminar director, and as a fledgling writer of regional history, I had argued that regional history not only provides viable topics to ply one's craft, but also serves as a valid way to understand the world in which one lives.

A number of people suggested I try my hand at a study of the affair. The first to do so was Mollie Person of our department of education. Also, I knew if I did a good study it would be welcomed by the people of this region.

I did not quickly yield, however, to the temptation to write this book. My wife's advice, "You can't write on everything," held firm until I accompanied one of my best 1990 senior seminar students, Rudolph Curtler, on an interview I arranged for him with nearby McLeod County investigator Jim Newes. Newes had prepared the county's case against the company's two owners, Fred Hendrickson and James Dwire, and against one of the company's key advisers, the Reverend Lowell Dale Kramer. Newes's willingness to supply us with all the sources he could—they were considerable—and his energetic and aphoristic style of speaking, proved to be the bait that hooked me.

In exploratory phases of the study, Lyon County recorder Jeanine Barker and Lyon County court administrator Van Bostrum and his personnel accommodated me to the best of their abilities. Judge David Peterson also was helpful in orienting me to the law. Pope County Historical Society generously opened its newspaper files on Kramer to me.

AEFS owner Fred Hendrickson often and generously furnished me with his personal papers, records, and opinions. He also corrected, with great tolerance, a chapter of the manuscript that at points was most critical of him. The Reverend Lowell Dale Kramer, known as "L. D.," was equally generous with his time and opinions, critically commenting on the chapter on himself. He allowed me to borrow what amounted to almost a complete set of company records (approximately twenty feet laid side by side), which he systematically and exemplarily organized and prepared for his defense. James Dwire, the company's president, allowed me to interview him by telephone, as did many other former company officers and employees, including vice president of sales Jerry Knapper, sales trainer Ron Mann, director of research Richard Spencer, and Jim Menk, executive officer during bankruptcy proceedings.

Those on the prosecution side who were equally open with their opinions included Douglas Blanke, former manager of the consumer division of the Minnesota attorney general's office, and his investigator Gregg LeCuyer; special aide to Iowa attorney general, Chuck Rutenbeck; Debra Bollinger, chief officer of South Dakota's Consumer Protection Division; Edward Bergquist, trustee of AEFS for the federal bankruptcy court, St. Paul; and Daryle Uphoff, counsel for AEFS's unsecured creditors. Blanke, Bollinger, and Uphoff allowed me access to their significant files on AEFS.

Former McLeod County prosecutor Peter Kasal; Kramer's public defender, Calvin Johnson of Mankato; Hendrickson's public defender, John Scholl of Worthington; and their defense investigator, Paul Glorvigen of Worthington, were responsive to my questions. Calvin Johnson made me at home in his office, whose basement is the repository for the complete collection of AEFS files, which Kramer so admirably assembled and organized. Jim Newes, McLeod County investigator, was kind and indispensable in guiding me to sources and an understanding of this complex affair.

With the exception of a handful of destroyed checks and twenty or so missing files taken from the company on the eve of its bankruptcy, I believe I saw most things worth seeing: I studied company organizational charts, grower surveys, sales samples, promotional and convention television tapes, ledgers and canceled checks, and all sorts of private correspondence and prayers. Furthermore, thanks to near-perfect cooperation, I examined the entire corpus of evidence created by a bankruptcy hearing, two grand juries, three trials, and many legal appeals, one of which led to the Minnesota Supreme Court.

Thanks to this study and the hours and hours of shuffling and organizing documents that were an integral part of it, I learned one near-legal truism well: murder trials lack evidence, whereas white-collar crimes abound in it.

Without nearly a hundred interviews with former AEFS employees, business and banking people, and scientists, I could never have made sense of this story. Interviews came from all sorts of people and took place in government laboratories, universities, court houses, nursing homes, food supplement plants, banks, hog farms, construction companies, barber shops, and coffee klatches. Interviews, many given confidentially and some with spontaneous bluntness, covered everything from the lives and characters of the company's owners and employees, the experiences and complaints of growers, and the arguments of lawyers to what was, for me, the entirely new and exotic territory of the history of plants and economic biology. On this latter point I am particularly indebted to Noel Vietmeyer of the National Academy of Science, especially for the phrase "a horticultural hysteria"; Tom Lukens of the Golden State Bulb Growers of Watsonville, California; John Pesek, chair of agronomy at Iowa State University; Luther Waters, chair of horticulture at Ohio State University; Daniel Putnam of the University of Minnesota; A. E. Thompson of the U.S. Department of Agriculture; James Brown of the Arizona Jojoba Growers and Processors; and James Duke of the U.S. Department of Agriculture for a fine horticultural description of the Jerusalem artichoke.

Especially valuable interviews were also provided by Ben Steensma, Luverne, Minnesota; Thomas Reichert, Edina, Minnesota; and Warren Anderson, Morris, Minnesota. Many other important interviews are acknowledged explicitly in the essay in the Sources section and in chapter notes. Unfortunately, many other valuable interviews must go unmentioned because of limits of space.

At some point in my research, only the hope of publishing a book promised to deliver me from this documentary wilderness of my own making. Accordingly, I am thankful to many people without whose help this book would not have been completed, or would have been much longer in coming.

John Radzilowski, student, friend, and critic, analyzed and researched a section of the work on growers and corrected the entire manuscript in its initial and final stages, furnishing a tentative index and glossary. Maria Markusen, aspiring history student, did valuable work organizing materials on the companies that succeeded AEFS. Chemist Robert Elaison provided a valuable glossary for my research.

Jan Louwagie lent her talents and the resources of the university's Southwest Minnesota Historical Research Center to this book. Linda Nelson, who criticized and typed much of the manuscript, and Cami Rosenboom, director of the Chippewa Historical Society, helped me complete the conditions of a generous Minnesota Humanities Commission grant that provided funds for research, preparation of materials, and the production of a major conference on the Jerusalem artichoke affair. Mark Gleason of the commission was exceptionally helpful.

Donata DeBruckeyere, former Southwest history student and assistant, not only helped with the grant but also improved the clarity of the work throughout. Dorothy Frisvold, social science department secretary, typed sections of the manuscript. Carol Schultz, history department secretary, was helpful, and Kathy Wilking of the University Word Processing Center remained keen and in good spirits while typing and retyping a manuscript in need of seemingly endless revisions. Glen Horky juggled computer disks between my system and Kathy's. Rhoda Schueller, Mary Jane Striegel, John Boden, Dicksy Howe, Sandy Hoffbeck, and other Southwest State University librarians were extremely helpful.

With his editorial skills, David Monge, friend, minister, theologian, and recent convert to history, improved the book. Kevin Stroup, friend, lawyer, and former Southwest history student, guided me through technical legal matters. Dale Sparling, colleague and geologist turned editor, significantly improved the manuscript for the mere prize of one free copy of the book, while lifetime friend Ted Radzilowski lent me his abiding good cheer and quick intelligence. Leo Langer walked me along a few ditches and through a couple of fields teaching me about plants and weeds.

Of course, there are several unnamed informants, among whom number bankers, lawyers, and people from many other walks of life, who deserve thanks. They go unthanked by name only because that's how they wanted it.

My special thanks to my copy editor, Julie Bach, and Lisa Freeman, director of the University of Minnesota Press, whose enthusiasm and intelligence I appreciated throughout the project.

My daughter Felice offered excellent artistic advice, while my three other children, Anthony, Adam, and Ethel, politely asked, with bemused smiles, "How's the artichoke book going?" My wife, Catherine, assured me a sense of place, permanence, and love as I again indulged myself in reconstructing the worlds of others.

Introduction: A Beckoning Plant

The Jerusalem artichoke is a saving weed.
—Fred Johnson

Two Swedish plant breeders have crossed the common sunflower with its perennial relative, the Jerusalem artichoke, and produced sweet sap in the stems. This gives promise of being not only good for forage, as they had hoped, but even of replacing sugar beets as a source of syrup and sugar.
—Edgar Anderson, *Plants, Man and Life*

Entrepreneurial princes emerge from time to time to court plants that have the promise of becoming great economic crops. One such prince was Fred Hendrickson, who appeared in the late 1970s as the American farm economy sagged and the nation was racked by an energy crisis. Along with James Dwire, Hendrickson in 1981 cofounded American Energy Farming Systems (AEFS), and more than any other person was responsible for the horticultural boom associated with its great initial success. Hendrickson's love was no common love. He had a mania to transform a plant that farmers had long considered a weed into a crop that would save them and the nation. The object of his passion was the Jerusalem artichoke.

A Cinderella Plant

Reaching heights of ten feet, the Jerusalem artichoke (*Helianthus tuberosus*) belongs to the genetically rich sunflower family, which includes dandelions and chrysanthemums. Since tubers are its primary means of propagation, it is a perennial that is not easily eradicated as a weed. The irregular size and shape of its tubers, significantly smaller than that of the potato, make it difficult to harvest.

Known by many names throughout the ages—including *Flos Farnesianus sive Aster Peruanus* (1616), *De Solis flore tuberoso* (1625), *potatoes of Canada* (1657), *Chrysanthemum latifolium Brasilianum* (1671), and most recently Sunchokes (c. 1970)—it is most commonly known as the Jerusalem artichoke. Common lore has it that "Jerusalem" was a corruption of the Italian name for sunflower, *girasole* (indicating it turns with the sun); "artichoke" was supposedly derived from a rough similarity of the taste between its tubers and the flowers of the French artichoke (*Cynara scolymus*). This explanation of the origin of the name was contradicted by R. N. Salaman, who argued that the name Jerusalem artichoke was established earlier than that of *girasole* and was an English corruption of the place-name Ter Neusen, where Jerusalem artichokes were introduced into England.[1]

An indigenous plant of North America, the Jerusalem artichoke probably had its origins in the Ohio and Mississippi river valleys. Capable of adapting itself to both wet and dry lands on the continent, it is primarily found on the eastern coasts of the United States and Canada and in the Midwest along a path from southern Canada to Georgia and Arkansas.[2]

While the foliage of the Jerusalem artichoke has been used for feed and its stalks burned for fuel, its tubers are perceived as its primary value. They once formed part of the diets of native and colonial North Americans and received modest acceptance in Europe, especially France. In 1605, French explorer Samuel de Champlain reported that the Indians at Cape Cod ate Jerusalem artichokes.[3] Soon after North America was settled, the plant was taken to France. There, known as the *topinambour*, it became a relatively popular food for humans and animals, especially swine.[4] Raw or cooked, the Jerusalem artichoke's tubers can appeal to the human palate.[5] Like the plant's luxuriant stems and leaves, which are rich in fats, protein, and pectin, its abundant tubers make good forage and silage. Since its food reserves are stored in the form of inulin (a carbohydrate used to manufacture fructose, found in the roots of many plants), the tubers can serve as a substitute for potatoes and starches in diabetic diets and are a potential source of levulose, used by diabetics as a sweetener. Alcohol fermented from the tubers is of better quality than that fermented from sugar beets.

In addition to its food value, folk medicine indicates positive uses for the Jerusalem artichoke. It is a gentle purgative (an aperient), a producer of bile (a cholagogue), a discharger of urine (a diuretic), a producer of sperm (spermatogenic), an aid to digestion (stomachic), and a general tonic of sorts. Folk medicine also touted it as a remedy for diabetes and rheumatism.

These strengths as an exploitable plant, however, are counterbalanced by significant weaknesses, according to alternative-crop scientist James Duke.[6] The Jerusalem artichoke produces multiple forms and stocks and lacks a well-defined classification: In USDA experiments, 1,300 selected seedlings produced 1,300 varieties. Many of the varieties produce extreme flatulence, giving rise to several of AEFS's most humorous stories.

Contradicting proponents' claims of multiple uses for the plant, Duke explains that the Jerusalem artichoke can be used either "as a crop of forage or a crop of tubers but not both. . . . Tops left undisturbed until frost to obtain the maximum yield of tubers are of little or no value for forage."[7] Also, in opposition to what early AEFS proponents argued, the Jerusalem artichoke is not immune to attacks from fungi, viruses, and bacteria. Finally, Jerusalem artichoke tubers are not easily harvested, stored, or processed. Certain soils make their harvest a formidable task. In all instances they are most successfully harvested by the slow, expensive, and labor-intensive process of hand digging. Mechanical potato pickers are not easily adapted to their harvest, especially in wet and clay soils. Additionally, Jerusalem artichokes, which bruise easily and rot rapidly, must be stored in high humidity and at a temperature of 0° C. Their thick, irregular, fibrous skins make drying and distillation exceptionally, even forbiddingly, difficult.

However, given its great yields—which approximate those of the potato—the Jerusalem artichoke offers a great prize to whoever can unlock the secret to its use. Its promise of alcohol production is considerable. This, above all else, won it attention during the 1930s and, as we will see, made it an object of a great speculative bubble in the late 1970s and early 1980s.[8] This Cinderella of crops, the Jerusalem artichoke, was again sought out, and the glass slipper of renewable fuel was tried on her foot.

The First Prince of the Jerusalem Artichoke

Approximately half a century before Fred Hendrickson was bewitched by the Jerusalem artichoke, another Fred from the Midwest—Fred Johnson of Hastings, Nebraska—became infatuated with it.[9] Under the constellation of the Great Depression, Johnson—described as craggy faced and Lincolnesque—preached the Jerusalem artichoke as the savior of the prairie in crisis. He was, in the words of his biographer, "the first messiah of the Jerusalem artichoke."[10]

As a young man, Johnson was a farmer. After graduating from the University of Nebraska, he, like Fred Hendrickson, sold real estate and practiced law. He later served in the Nebraska legislature before becoming lieutenant governor of Nebraska from 1923 to 1925. Johnson also served a single term in the U.S. Congress, from 1929 to 1931, until he and a multitude of other Republicans were swept out of office by Franklin Delano Roosevelt and the Democrats. In 1944 he returned to public service as a county judge, a post he held until his death in 1951.

Johnson was introduced to the Jerusalem artichoke by professors of agriculture at Iowa State University who had great interest in the plant's promise. His first research on the plant began in the late 1920s.[11] Johnson concluded that the Jerusalem artichoke was, in the words of his book, "the weed worth a million dollars."

Johnson centered his life around the plant. He never left his house without carrying Jerusalem artichoke tubers in the pocket of his black suit. He would stop passersby along the street and take out a tuber or two to explain the great healing and restorative powers of the Jerusalem artichoke.[12] He told farm groups, civic clubs, school children—anyone who would listen—that the Jerusalem artichoke was "a saving weed."[13] It was "the manna of the Plains."[14]

Fred Johnson had fallen in love with the Jerusalem artichoke, as Fred Hendrickson was to do fifty years later. Johnson saw the Jerusalem artichoke not only as a source of alcohol, sugar and starches, oils, cellulose, and even plastics, but as a savior of farm and nation.

For Johnson there was no end to the marvelous qualities of the Jerusalem artichoke. According to him, its yields were staggering; it grew just about anywhere; it succeeded where other plants failed; it adapted itself to all soils, except those too wet; it eradicated weeds such as quack grass from neglected soils; it continued to grow after the first frost; and not only was it a good forage, but hogs fed on artichokes had never been known to contract cholera.

Johnson took up the Jerusalem artichoke prophecy of Ralph Hixon, a chemist from Iowa State University. Hixon prophesied in the early 1930s that "the extensive use of alcohol [fuel] is bound to take place within the next five years."[15] Johnson was also responsive to the visionary work of Dr. William Hale, director of research for The Dow Chemical Company.

In the 1920s, Hale helped formulate the alcohol fuel movement, called the power alcohol vision, and was a catalyst for a movement on its behalf during the 1930s as farmers increasingly sought alternative crops to make their fields profitable. Hale contended that the age of chemistry had arrived in the twentieth century. This century heralded national energy independence on the one hand while it immensely magnified the power of war on the other.[16] As "the mechanical revolution drove men to the mines for coal and for ores from which, by metallurgical processes, they could secure metals required in machinery," so, Hale argued, "the chemical revolution," responding to the ever greater need for fuel and the scarcity of petroleum, "is destined to drive man back to the farm."[17]

In 1936, Hale wrote *Prosperity Beckons: Dawn of the Alcohol Era*. This book, which Johnson (and later Hendrickson) took so seriously, became a gospel of the alcohol fuel movement. In it Hale prophesied, "Agricultural munificence has become the nation's hope," and queried, "How long shall the inconsistencies and vagaries of purblind, wasteful men hold back the destiny of a people?"[18] He answered that chemurgy, the chemical transformation of agricultural products and wastes into industrial materials, "opens wide the door to the unlimited industrialization of the nation," and guaranteed its freedom from foreign control.[19] "Fuel-alcohol," Hale concluded, "will prove the means to stabilize agriculture. America will never need to import fuel as long as the sun shines above," and it would allow the nation to free itself from the shackles of "the triumphant synthetic petroleum industry, welfarists and damnable internationalists" and "spare it the plight of decadent Rome."[20]

Hale ecstatically wrote in his conclusion: "The door to happiness is open. . . . The password is clear. . . . : Adjust yourself chemically to a chemical world. . . . So let us grasp the hand of Nature and follow her guidance into Elysian fields."[21]

Johnson took Hale's influential belief in the emerging national alcohol and national sugar industries to heart. Johnson underlined the Jerusalem artichoke's abundant production of levulose, a sugar that according to Hale "is 50 percent sweeter than sucrose or ordinary sugar and far better than sucrose for the human system." Optimistically predicting that "a few months and a few thousand dollars, will guarantee the engineering success of the design of a commercial levulose plant," Hale rushed to a stupendous conclusion: "It means the utter banishment from our tables of all cane and beet sugar, and the direct efforts of thousands upon thousands of our farmers toward the supply of our entire need for sugar."[22]

Filled with faith, Hale, Hixon, Johnson, and others went to the 1935 Dearborn Conference of Agriculture, Industry, and Science. Sponsored by Henry Ford and his Chemurgic Council, the conference brought national leaders of agriculture, industry, and science to Dearborn, Michigan, home of Ford and the Ford Motor Company, to form what was to become the National Farm Chemurgic Council.[23]

Ford had already revealed his interest in the use of renewable agricultural products for industry. He manufactured his cars with carburetors that could easily be converted to alcohol use. He built a $5 million plant designed to convert soybeans into paints, varnishes, and plastics. He envisioned building automobile bodies from soybean mash or using it in combination with other agricultural waste.

In calling the first Dearborn conference, Ford sought to respond to what he took to be the seriousness of the hour. He aimed at starting a movement that would seek new national wealth from the soil through a "Chemical Revolution." The Chemurgic Council, of which Hale was a member, dedicated itself to "an America that would prosper by the fruits of its soil."[24] In a replica of Independence Hall in Ford's Greenfield Village in Dearborn, three hundred members of the Chemurgic Council set forth the "Declaration of Dependence upon the Soil and the Right of Self-Maintenance."[25] They pledged themselves to the search for new sources of organic agricultural materials. While international trade dissolved and societies became autarchies, while reason retreated and fascism swept across Western societies, these optimistic signers espied a new rational solution that would harmoniously join science, technology, industry, and agriculture. Their chemurgical faith—based on a chemistry that would transform plants into industrial goods—was aimed at transforming the nation to make full use of its agricultural potential.

In the words of the declaration, chemurgy "will enable the tiller of the soil to do much of the initial processing of his crops on his own farm, thus adding to the value of his own product. [It] will enable man to depend more upon current income from the soil and to withdraw less of his capital from beneath the soil, thus preserving a fair share of the treasures of nature's storehouse for future generations."[26] The nation's farmers would effect a unity between American industry and the countryside while transforming America into a self-renewing cornucopia. Sounding like environmentalists of the 1960s and 1970s, these powerful representatives of agriculture, industry, and science described themselves as mere dutiful "tenants and transients on this earth."[27]

Exciting ideas, valid hypotheses, chimeras, and outright nonsense abounded at the first and second Dearborn conferences in 1935 and 1936. The crisis of the Depression cast doubt on the voices of the established orders and opened the podium to all who conjured new orders of society. Numerous proposals for new fertilizers and insecticides were made, along with proposals for the introduction of new crops (such as cork and oak trees), for new uses of soybeans, cotton, and wood, and new plant sources for oil, sugars, and plastics. In addition, suggestions were made on improving the national sugar and paper industries.[28]

Significant attention at the conferences was dedicated to the promise of alcohol's use as a fuel, which was already anticipated in the 1920s by the search for synthetic fuels in light of an immense and unprecedented demand for oil in the United States and the world.[29] It was called "power alcohol" to avoid the lingering negative connotations associated with drink. (National prohibition had just ended in 1933.) Power alcohol promised to meet the perceived diminishing supply of national petroleum while providing a new market for the nation's impoverished farmers.

The promise of power alcohol brought the proponents of the Jerusalem artichoke to the conference podium. Johnson was one of them. Speaking as a representative of the Jerusalem Artichoke Growers at the first Dearborn conference, Johnson articulated his hope for the Jerusalem artichoke.[30] His prophecy for the plant's future would never be realized.

In June 1936, hoping to develop additional uses for Jerusalem artichokes, Johnson and fellow officers from Nebraska, Wyoming, and Minnesota formed the United Artichoke Company. Their goal was to turn Jerusalem artichoke tubers into industrial alcohol and syrup. During the summer, a limited number of investors bought hundred-dollar shares, and plans were made to build the main plant the following spring. The plant, to be built in Gering, Nebraska, was expected to employ 200 to 250 employees. It was never completed. While some excavation and foundation work was started, it, along with plans for at least five other branch plants, died on the drafting board.

The United Artichoke Company failed to pay the farmers who were under contract to grow Jerusalem artichokes. Nebraska banks, in turn, were in no mood to offer second chances. The Jerusalem artichoke's bubble burst.

Accusation and acrimony followed the failure of Johnson's company as they did AEFS's bankruptcy a half century later. Some explained the company's failure as a consequence of a giant conspiracy theory. They accused the Great Western Sugar Company of squeezing them out. The Great Western Sugar Company replied that it was too busy shoring up local banks and small businesses in the area to worry about the fate of the United Artichoke Company. It further contended that it saw no threat of competition in the plans for what it took to be a small-scale company. More realistic explanations for the company's failure included such mundane matters as undercapitalization, lack of business expertise on the part of Johnson and his neophytes, and the failure to locate an economic niche before establishing the company.

Nowhere in the 1930s did the Jerusalem artichoke show itself to be a saving crop; nor did the more general power alcohol movement establish a new source of national fuel. While Hale continued to preach the virtues of alcohol and Jerusalem artichokes, and Johnson probably still carried its magic tubers in his pocket, the majority of midwestern farmers again cursed it as a rogue weed.

The Second World War and the attendant search for national energy self-sufficiency led a handful of scientists to again cast curious glances in the direction of the Jerusalem artichoke. However, two energy crises of the 1970s—the first in 1973 and the second in 1979—occurred before the plant received another invitation to the great ball of renewable energy. Then, during the second crisis, it beguiled a new prince, Fred Hendrickson, who was singularly responsible for the creation of American Energy Farming Systems (AEFS), a small southwestern Minnesota company that spearheaded the sale of Jerusalem artichoke seed starting in 1981.

The Planets Were All Lined Up

AEFS experienced a phenomenal rise. In its meteoric existence from its founding in the fall of 1981 until its collapse in the spring of 1983, this new Minnesota company sold more than $25 million of Jerusalem artichoke seeds to farmers throughout the Midwest. Such growth can only be explained by a surprising convergence of circumstances, ideas, groups, and forces.

In 1979, a severe energy crisis swept the United States and the Western world. The crisis drove fuel prices to new heights, causing the sharpest inflationary rise of the century. The question of energy dominated national concerns. Confidence in nuclear energy had been dashed by the accident at Three Mile Island. The price of oil, which shot up by 24 percent in the month of June alone, caused double-digit inflation in the United States.

In July 1979, President Jimmy Carter announced a six-point program to the nation that set a limit on the use of foreign oil, made a commitment to conservation and public transportation, and formed an Energy Mobilization Board (modeled on the War Production Board of World War II). His program put the government—with a $142 billion plan—in support of the search for alternative fuels. The program created an Energy Security Department to produce synthetic fuels from coals, shale oil, and other sources. It also established a "solar bank" with the goal of meeting 20 percent of the nation's energy needs through solar energy by the year 2000.

The nation's concern over energy mounted as oil prices skyrocketed during the fall of 1979. It approached a near frenzy in November when Carter, responding to the Iranian seizure of the U.S. embassy in Tehran, suspended the purchase of Iranian oil.

Throughout 1980, energy remained at the center of national attention. In January, in the wake of the Soviet invasion of Afghanistan, Carter warned that the United States was ready to go to war over the Persian Gulf. National insecurity registered in the soaring price of gold, which rose from $524 an ounce in December 1979 to $835 an ounce in January 1980. The prime rate, reaching 20 percent in April, reflected the nation's economic uncertainty.

Across the nation the energy crisis licensed all sorts of amateur thinkers, tinkerers, and salespeople. They came forward to conjure their ideas, show their devices, and hawk their wares. New notions—some insightful and practical, many, perhaps the majority, bizarre, fanciful, eccentric, and outright silly—were heard in chorus across the land. The future of national energy opened the platform to everyone who claimed to have answers for the futures of agriculture, the environment, the nation, and humanity itself. Not all of these people spoke apocalyptically; however, many did convey messages about the collapse of a world based on fossil fuels.

Proponents of renewable energy preached solar power, wind power, and ocean power, as well as prospective energy from hydrogen and geothermal springs. Illustrative of the equation of energy independence and agricultural renewal was Russell Anderson's argument in *Biological Paths to Self-Reliance* (1979) that solar energy could be converted by plant photosynthesis and plant growth to biomass energy. In *Plant Power* (1979), Melvin Calvin proposed the creation of "energies farms." Citing as laudatory Brazil's national policy of converting sugar into alcohol, which, in retrospect, appears highly questionable, he speculated how in colder climates such plants as the desert shrub guayule could be used to manufacture oils. Others speculatively explored the production of methane from organic waste and from biomass, and gasohol from corn, wood wastes, garbage, and even manure, and the possible use of a whole range of new and alternative crops. Scientists at the University of Minnesota examined the conversion of cattails into alcohol.

Many people, among whom numbered the founders and early farmers of AEFS, were profoundly attracted by energy crops and biomass conversion to methane or ethanol. Like their predecessors in the 1930s, they argued that new crops pointed the way to energy independence and the revitalization of American agriculture. Such hopes, so fondly cherished in the agricultural Midwest, made bedfellows of all sorts of diverse groups that had interests in dramatic changes in U.S. energy policy.

The onset of the farm crisis that swept agriculture in the 1980s supported the call for this change. Things were not good on the farm. High interest rates, low prices for grain, and shaky land values anticipated the farm foreclosures of the middle 1980s. Auction signs for farms and farm machinery were plastered on restaurant bulletin boards throughout the Midwest. Everyone knew a farmer in trouble. Almost every town had a farm implement dealer or two who was in trouble or had failed—"gone belly up," to use the popular phrase. The price of land had tripled, even quadrupled, during the 1970s, raising the price of the best land from $500 to $1,500 and $2,000 an acre in southwest Minnesota and to $3,500 and more for the best Iowa farm land. The same land now began to decline in price and would plummet 50 percent in value in the next few years, leaving farmers without equity to borrow the money they needed to cover operations. At the same time, grain prices were depressed. As AEFS took form, farmers talked of hard times. While the full dimensions of the crisis were not fully anticipated, its beginnings were already in evidence.[31]

The possibility of new and profitable crops for America's farms was a welcome message. It was especially appealing to highly leveraged and economically strained farmers, who found themselves borrowing at exceptionally high interest rates while crop prices remained depressed. Only secure farmers could be indifferent to this promise. Hope that an answer to their economic problems could be found in a new crop rather than in market processes or government policies was not new to the farmers of the Midwest. They were familiar with a variety of important experiments with lesser crops and had benefitted immensely from the adoption of productive hybrid corn in the 1930s. The great majority of farmers were acquainted with the development of the miracle cash crop, the soybean, which had occurred in their lifetime.[32] Perhaps most of them had forgotten, or never knew, the soybean's long scientific, agronomic, and industrial history. Perhaps they knew nothing of its early genetic development at agricultural stations at the end of the nineteenth century, its first milling in North Carolina and processing in Chicago during and after the First World War, and its further genetic, agronomic, processing, and marketing history (focused in Illinois companies, experimental centers, and universities) in the 1920s and 1930s until it became the object of a single coordinated industry. Perhaps they were even unaware of the complex hurdles of finding suitable varieties, establishing farmer acceptance, constructing oil-processing facilities, and developing new products that the soybean had to clear.[33] Nevertheless, they were almost unanimously aware that the soybean had saved them as it went from being a significant feed crop in the 1920s and 1930s to a major crop in the 1940s and 1950s to America's second most valuable crop in the 1960s, when it surpassed wheat, cotton, and hay. In their own lifetime, they had experienced the benefits of this miracle crop—"which now accounts for about three-quarters of all high-protein livestock feeds and

Introduction   13

... about three-quarters of all human consumption of fats and oils."[34]

In the crisis of the early 1980s, when even soybean prices were lowered by continuous overproduction, little could have been more appealing to these farmers than a new miracle crop. Perhaps it could meet the nation's expanding energy needs while saving its farmers from bankruptcy. AEFS promised this, and more.

Fred Hendrickson and the founders of AEFS were among the boldest of those who envisioned a new, saving plant for America's fields. In the spirit of the hour, they preached to farm audiences, easily assembled during the energy and farm crises of the late 1970s and the early 1980s, that the Jerusalem artichoke—long known to farmers as a noxious weed—offered the promise of wealth and independence. Exploiting the evangelical religious sensibility of the time, the founders of AEFS prophesied that the Jerusalem artichoke was "a Providential Plant," "a Biblical plant of promise," "the plant of renown" that, Ezekiel prophesied, "God would raise up to feed and save his people."

AEFS initially promoted the Jerusalem artichoke as a new and superior source of alcohol fuel. Its representatives boosted the distillation of alcohol fuel from the tubers of the Jerusalem artichoke as the road to farm prosperity and American independence from greedy cartels and foreign nations. In their preaching, so reminiscent of that of Fred Johnson, William Hale, and others of the 1930s, AEFS's advocates joined many others inside and outside of government who heralded alcohol fuel as the answer to both the farm crisis and the national energy crisis.

As oil and gasoline prices declined sharply, however, and difficult, even insurmountable, problems surrounded the distillation and the industrial conversion of Jerusalem artichokes into alcohol, AEFS quickly preached other virtues of the Jerusalem artichoke. AEFS advertisements increasingly drew attention to the promise of the Jerusalem artichoke as a source of sucrose and insulin, a substitute for starch and sugar, making it especially useful to diabetics. AEFS also suggested a possible use for Jerusalem artichokes as human food and animal feed.

Beyond this, AEFS sold something else: It sold hope—and desperate farmers and greedy speculators bought it. In the tubers of Jerusalem artichokes buyers conjured better futures. In a market driven by the plant's imagined possibilities, AEFS sales mushroomed.

AEFS employed few full-time scientists and technicians. Sales dominated the company. Owned and run by businessmen committed to fundamental, evangelical, and charismatic Christianity, AEFS was strong in motivation and weak in product development. AEFS used the powers of direct personal sales, consciously casting an envious eye in the direction of Amway. AEFS's salespeople, who had rural backgrounds, understood the essence of selling in rural America: they sold farmer to farmer, small group to small group, Main Street coffee shop to Main Street coffee shop, country supper club to country supper club.

While AEFS did not in the legal sense (at least as defined by Minnesota statutes) create a pyramid-sale scheme, since they sold something (the tuber seed of the Jerusalem artichoke), the driving mechanism of its sales was pyramidlike: Their first-year growers (called three-year growers) intended to sell their seed to their second- and third-year growers, while second-year growers (their two-year growers) intended to sell their seed to third-years growers who would still enjoy the phenomenal advantage of getting in on the ground floor of a new American crop.

AEFS's sales exceeded its founders' wildest dreams. The planets were lined up for the Jerusalem artichoke and AEFS. Circumstance conspired with need and myth to create an unprecedented national horticultural hysteria.

1

A Country Prophet

Behold I make a covenant with you. For you shall bring forth a new day and a new season for my handiwork.... From the soil shall spring the riches of all generations. Farm the ground, for out of it shall spring living waters and behold My Glory shall be yours.
—Words of prophecy received by Fred Hendrickson the evening of Sunday, August 9, 1981

Fred Hendrickson's love for the Jerusalem artichoke rivaled that of Fred Johnson. Hendrickson loved it for everything he imagined it could be. He believed it was a gift from God that would save America, make him rich, and "provide the challenge and the thrill of making it."[1]

Born in 1935, Fred Hendrickson was the adopted son of two college-educated teachers. His father had a master's degree in education and earned his living first as a school teacher and then as a superintendent in Philip, a town of 1,100 on the Bad River in west-central South Dakota. Philip is "a dry, hot, dusty, wide spot in the road of South Dakota's flat, high, West River country."[2] Its desolate and depopulated service area reaches as much as forty to sixty miles in almost all directions. Philip, at first only a post office on a cattle ranch, then a railroad site and a county seat of Haakon County, is ninety miles west of Pierre, the capital of South Dakota, and an equal distance east of Rapid City, the gateway to the Black Hills and Mount Rushmore. Bordered on the north by the Cheyenne Reservation, Philip is about thirty miles from the northeastern entrance to Badlands National Park and about ninety miles from Wounded Knee on the Pine Ridge Reservation. For Native Americans of the region, Wounded Knee, more than any other place, is a symbol of the tragedy and the heartbreak of the coming of European civilization.

In this small town, Fred Hendrickson and a sister, who also was adopted, were brought up in a home free of strife. His Lutheran parents were active in their church. They made sure their children attended Sunday school. Hendrickson appeared the all-around American boy. He did well in his schoolwork and participated, as children often do in small rural towns, in a wholesome range of extracurricular activities, including varsity football, basketball, and track, as well as band, glee club, and speech. However, a taciturn group of older card players in a downtown Philip coffee shop, who praised the father, qualified the younger Hendrickson's accomplishments by a handful of clipped comments: "In speech, you know"; "Not much of an athlete."

By the time he was in high school, Hendrickson already took himself seriously. Thanks to the influence of some local lawyers, Hendrickson considered a career in law, conceiving of it as a means not only to make a living but also to help shape the nation. The young Hendrickson's political alliance was with the Republicans. He idealized Taft and Eisenhower, and he remained a true-blue Republican through the Reagan era. Although he did embrace Kennedy's and Johnson's social programs because they favorably affected the Native Americans of his region, he continued to believe that liberal Democrats' values were "morally unsound for the nation."[3]

While still a youth, Hendrickson formed his views about agriculture. On his family's annual trips to his adopted father's 160-acre farm in North Dakota, Hendrickson came to love the land. As a child of six he played farmer for hours on end with tractors, plows, and combines made from cheese boxes.[4] He began to learn (perhaps even more than he wished) about agricultural work when he was in the seventh grade. His father bought an existing poultry and produce business and assigned his son the job of cleaning out chicken coops. Hendrickson worked his way up to chicken feeder, egg picker, egg candler, and finally chicken plucker.

As an active member of Future Farmers of America, Hendrickson received state awards in dairy and seed judging. He looked forward to summer when he could work as a hired hand on his classmates' farms and ranches. He showed his entrepreneurial spirit early by becoming, along with a friend, one of the youngest junk dealers in western South Dakota. He bought, restored, or scrapped approximately fifty cars.[5]

In 1953, Hendrickson went to college in Huron, South Dakota, where he graduated with a degree in political science, which he complemented with concentrations in speech, English, and history. He was exceptionally active in university student affairs. Alongside his class picture is a long list of campus activities: "Alphomega [sic], Band, Board of Control, Campus Players, Forensics, H. Club, Radio Club, Student Association Vice-President, Circle K., Circle K Treasurer, World University Service Chairman, and Spiritual Emphasis Week Committee."

Hendrickson especially loved debate, through which he gained some of the skills he would subsequently bring to the promotion of the Jerusalem artichoke. He won a state oratory contest for class B high schools and placed second in the state American Legion oratory contest. Hendrickson enthusiastically joined Huron College's outstanding speech and debate team which, according to him, competed successfully against such excellent debate teams as those from Notre Dame and the University of Kansas. As a member of the college debate team, Hendrickson traveled around the nation. During these trips, he recalled, whenever he saw a complex of buildings rising out of the land he would begin to dream: "My mind would be years ahead."[6]

Although Hendrickson "didn't have a lot of friends or wasn't a group hanger on," his classmates judged him to be popular.[7] One remarked that even then Hendrickson was the kind of guy "who always had something going." He always drew others into his ventures.[8]

Hendrickson often made the dean's list, receiving the Dean's Award as a senior for his involvement in college affairs. Months after graduation, in August 1956, he married his sweetheart,

Gerri Lohner, a fellow student from a successful Aberdeen business family whose money had been made selling candy and cigarettes.

Hendrickson appeared to be on the road to success, but he never quite took root after leaving college. He explained this by saying that there was some kind of "entrepreneurial spirit in me. I was always on the leading edge," he said, using one of his favorite phrases. This spirit, he claimed, prevented him from "making money" and being successful.[9]

After one year of teaching social science and coaching debate and speech at Vermilion High School, Hendrickson returned to his alma mater to serve as director of admissions for two years before entering law school at the University of South Dakota in 1959. He finished his law studies in 1962, while at the same time completing the course work and passing the oral examination for a master's degree in government.

After passing his bar examinations that year, he began a career that was fragmented into periods of two years or less. Starting in 1962, he worked for a short time for a law firm in Huron, while also working as a special assistant attorney general for conservation in Pierre. He returned to private practice in Philip in 1963. After failing to find employment in a university in Des Moines, Iowa, Fred and his wife and two sons returned to Philip, only to return to Des Moines where Fred worked successfully in conservation and real estate affairs for the Iowa attorney general. He remained there for two years. As if two, possibly three, years marked the limits of endurance for the restless dreamer, Hendrickson went into real estate development at the Lake Okoboji Condominium Corporation in Iowa where he worked between mid-1969 and 1970. In 1970, his fourteen-year marriage, which had produced four children, ended. Since then he has had little contact with his former wife; contact with his four sons continued for another eight years.[10]

Following his divorce, Hendrickson returned to Mission, South Dakota. There he remarried and became an assistant to the director of a project for the Rosebud Housing Authority, until, according to Hendrickson, reservation politics cost him his $12,000 a year job. His new wife, Beverly, who taught at Mission High School on the reservation, was glad to leave, complaining of, among other things, living forty miles away from a doctor.[11] In 1972, Hendrickson hung up his shingle in Rapid City.

In the same year, Hendrickson underwent a religious conversion. On April 2, he believed he came to know Christ. Hendrickson reformed his life. He gave up drinking and smoking and refounded his marriage in Christ. He joined the evangelical Open Bible Standard Church, which he described as a Pentecostal church similar to the Assemblies of God.

The conversion further intensified Hendrickson's sense of being elected. This Moses-like belief colored all his thoughts. Adopted by his parents as an infant, he now believed himself to be adopted by God as an adult. In the archetypal "third age of the spirit," Hendrickson, as a prophet, would help complete God's covenant with America. Hendrickson never waivered in his belief that America was the new Israel and he was one of its prophets.

Hendrickson's newfound faith did not focus on the tragedy of the cross as traditional Lutheran faith does; nor did it dwell on irreversible historical defeats of the sort suffered by peoples like the Native Americans scattered throughout the Dakotas. Hendrickson's God spoke directly to his people, promising to heal them and to return them to His Kingdom. His God was intent on restoring America's rural people; they were the object of His covenant. Hendrickson, millenarian that he was, believed the time of Christ's Second Coming was at hand.

Hendrickson remained in Rapid City for the next nine years. There he practiced law and sold real estate, doing a lot of legal work for marginal farmers, Native Americans, and the poor. By his own estimate, Hendrickson earned $20,000 to $25,000 a year.

On the surface it appeared Hendrickson had found the stability he craved. His marriage held. His belief in God was unfaltering. He was filled with enthusiasm. Revealing how he joined faith and business in his life, Hendrickson organized the Rapid City chapter of the Full Gospel Businessmen's Association. Later, in 1978, Hendrickson served as state coordinator for an unsuccessful initiative to pass a state law against obscenity into which he sunk his energy and money.

Hendrickson remained spiritually restless, and he continued to believe a unique mission was in store for him. At a Pentecostal meeting in the Twin Cities in August 1973, he interpreted a burning sensation in his palms as a sign of God's special calling. In December of the same year, after reading the Bible, he awoke from a nap and again experienced a burning sensation in his palms. On this occasion, Hendrickson believed God was speaking directly to him: "I am your God. You are to be my spokesman to my people—a prophet for this day and age."[12]

Nevertheless, God still had not provided him with a precise calling, one equal to his talent or to God's glory—or one that provided an income fully adequate for his family's needs and wants. Hendrickson continually had ventures afoot, and his nine years of speculative enterprises in Rapid City had left him $50,000 in debt.

Even those who were sympathetic to Hendrickson during his Rapid City days judged him critically. One business associate considered him brilliant but restless, hardworking but erratic, goodwilled but short of means, weak on details but never a deceiver—dreamer, yes; schemer, no.[13] A former Rapid City business associate, who did not doubt Hendrickson's intelligence or the sincerity of his concern for the poor, described him as a religious fanatic who was continually in financial trouble because he failed to get his work done.[14] Another singularly and usually severe critic of Hendrickson claimed that Hendrickson had no discretion. "Fred," he commented, "would be the first guy to jump on a wild-ass idea."[15] This critic, who had lost a considerable sum of money on shared projects with Hendrickson in Rapid City, spared him little. He asserted that Hendrickson, broke all the time, was "a con artist at heart." When he got hold of someone, "he whittled more and more money from him." He was "smarter than hell," but he would "get into a gray area, and plunge."[16]

In 1978, Hendrickson focused on a new idea to make a dollar, to serve God, and to save the nation. He turned his restless energy and attention to the field of alternative energy and, more specifically, the on-farm, alcohol-fuel industry. His first project, which existed only on paper, was a design for a company that would grow vegetables, utilizing the geothermal energy of western South Dakota and particularly a geothermal well three miles north of his hometown, Philip.

Hendrickson devoured all the information on alternative energy he could get his hands on. The literature he read was on wind power, solar power, geothermal power, power from biomass, and alcohol power. He even confessed to having become "a great reader of *Mother Earth News*," where he encountered for the first time what he took to be the revolutionary notion that renewable fuel could save both the nation and its farmers.[17] This became the kernel of Hendrickson's vision.

Hendrickson's new enthusiasms accounted for his new letterhead, which described him as an "Agri-Business Concept Developer, specializing in Alcohol, Wind, Solar and Thermal Energy and Agri-Business Development." During 1980, Hendrickson feverishly occupied himself with a wide variety of companies and what he labeled "venture-ideas."

One company he formed, Energy Age Marketing and Management Corporation, can be seen in retrospect as the direct predecessor of AEFS. It aimed at the development of an alcohol cooperative movement and the construction of alcohol plants in the western Dakotas. In association with fourteen other alcohol-fuel proponents, Hendrickson developed a range of projects in Valentine, Nebraska, Belle Fourche, South Dakota, and a former military site in South Dakota called Igloo.

At the Igloo site, a former U.S. army ammunition dump in western South Dakota, Hendrickson conjured an ecological vision of a totally self-sufficient farming system. It resembled a biological counterpart to one of those perpetual motion machines that for so long fascinated thinkers of earlier ages. The waste from grazing cattle would be used to produce methane; steam-generated energy would be used to make alcohol. Aquaculture, fish farming, tree farming, biomass crops—including amaranth and fodder beets—all had their place on this farm.

Hendrickson never thought small. With a protractor, he circled on a state road map the tillable land in South Dakota as if to claim it for his own by virtue of his unique vision for it. Hendrickson credited the state with 66 counties, 77,000 square miles of land, and 50,000 farms, averaging 920 acres each. Of those, he had a plan for 27 counties, 27.5 million acres and more than 200,000 people. Each circle, consisting of forty smaller circles and encompassing an area of 490 square miles, would involve approximately two hundred members. Cooperative memberships would cost from $2,200 to $3,400. In return, members would receive, in addition to $500 in fuel and $500 in cash, the advantages of a cooperative marketing consortium, an experimental agricultural center, and a chain of small alcohol plants. By growing such crops as milo, sorghum, sugar beets, amaranth, and Jerusalem artichokes as well as such vegetable oil crops as sunflowers and safflowers, individual farmer members would attain food and fuel self-sufficiency. They would form cooperatives that would sell their fuel nationally. The smaller plants would produce 150,000 gallons of alcohol, one half of which would be used for straight alcohol.[18]

Characterized by a mixture of economic hopes and utopian promises, this project promised to let farmers have their cake and eat it too: It promised them self-sufficiency on the one hand, and accessibility to profitable national markets on the other. The "Igloo project," which seemed "a sure thing" to Hendrickson, fell apart in the summer of 1981 when the Small Business Association failed to guarantee his loan.

In 1980, Hendrickson's conversion to the Jerusalem artichoke followed from his newfound belief in renewable energy and alternative fuels. Hendrickson attributed this conversion to his discovery of how wonderfully six Jerusalem artichoke plants grew in the alley behind his Rapid City home. In October 1980, Hendrickson acknowledged that an article on the Jerusalem artichoke in the *North Dakota Farmer* so moved him that he proceeded to telephone every contemporary reference mentioned in it.[19] Among the experts he called were West Coast agronomist Tom Lukens, Minnesota crop experimenter and speculator Tom Reichert, Minnesota grower Vince Erickson, and Canadian agronomist Dr. B. B. Chubey. By the fall of 1980, when he wrote Chubey at the Canadian agricultural station in Morden, Manitoba, Hendrickson had already formed a company named the Jerusalem Artichoke Brokers of America. He had taken the plunge.

By the spring of 1981, in a special report to prospective customers, Hendrickson declared the Jerusalem artichoke to be "Energy Farmings' answer to OPEC." He appended to this report a collection of scientific and popular articles on alcohol's promise as a fuel substitute for gasoline, alcohol's extensive use as a fuel in Brazil, and the Jerusalem artichoke's promise as a source of alcohol fuel equal or superior to corn and other feed stocks like sweet sorghum or fodder. Arguing that the Jerusalem artichoke was "the BEST ALCOHOL FEEDSTOCK for the production of alcohol through the production thru [sic] thousands of decentralized rural based alcohol plants," Hendrickson declared it "the best road for American energy independence."[20]

Hendrickson ordered Jerusalem artichoke seed from Lyle Kilthau in Washington state and began encouraging farmers in South Dakota, Minnesota, and Iowa to experiment with it. By May 1981, Hendrickson considered himself an expert on the Jerusalem artichoke and did not hesitate to publicize its superiority to corn and other plants as a potential source of alcohol. This desperate prophet from a desperate region had found a faith during what was for Midwest farmers a desperate time.

With his newfound faith in the Jerusalem artichoke spurring him on to fresh opportunities, and with the end of any hope for the Igloo project (for whose failure some of his associates blamed the machinations of "Big Oil"), Hendrickson moved east to Sioux Falls, South Dakota. There, on the edge of corn-rich but crisis-stricken southwestern Minnesota and northwestern Iowa, Hendrickson would seek to fulfill his prophetic role.

By the time he moved to Sioux Falls, Hendrickson had exhausted his meager resources, the resources of fellow believers, and the patience of his creditors, the most formidable of which was the IRS. Unable to live by ideas alone, Hendrickson desperately needed, as he had with his past projects, a partner with cash. Also, by his own retrospective admission, he needed someone to control his endless stream of ideas. But no sooner did he acknowledge this than, almost in the same breath, he admitted that his relations with his partners always seemed to fail.[21]

Hendrickson Finds Another Partner

In 1980, Hendrickson organized a seminar on alcohol at the National College of Business in Rapid City, South Dakota. Among the speakers who attended was Al Rusk, an alcohol fuel proponent from the department of physics at Southwest State University in Marshall, Minnesota. Hendrickson next met Rusk in January 1981, in Sioux Falls, where he explained the Jerusalem artichoke to Rusk and asked him to take Jerusalem artichoke literature to James Dwire. Hendrickson had been acquainted with Dwire since he had offered to do construction work for the aborted Igloo project.[22]

In late February or early March, before Hendrickson moved to Sioux Falls, he received a call from Dwire, a call that he considered providential. Hendrickson was ecstatic when Dwire, whom he perceived to be a successful businessman, decided not just to plant one acre, but "he would take a half a semi-trailer load [of seed], enough for twenty or twenty-one acres."[23] The seed cost a thousand dollars per acre. Nearly beside himself, Hendrickson ordered a full load from Washington-state grower Lyle Kilthau and began to sell Jerusalem artichoke seeds to farmers, whose enthusiasm in many cases equaled Hendrickson's.

Hendrickson drove to Marshall to meet with Dwire. He returned home like Jack in "Jack and the Beanstalk," with magic beans in his pocket. Dwire had given him money for gas, a cash advance, and above all else, had offered him a job.[24] He envisioned himself climbing the prodigious stalk of the Jerusalem artichoke out of his lackluster everyday life up into a magic kingdom of wealth.

Hendrickson rubbed his beans hard, for he was at the bottom of his financial barrel when Dwire offered him a month's salary to do a feasibility study on building an alcohol plant in Lynd, Minnesota.[25] Located six miles southwest of Marshall, Lynd was the home of Dwire's road contracting business. Hendrickson gratefully accepted Dwire's offer. With nothing but his beans in his pocket, Hendrickson returned to Dwire's office in Lynd, where he worked by day and slept on the company's couch by night. "I was flat broke," Hendrickson recalled. "For three weeks I slept on his couch, designing 'the web system.'" The counterpart of the circle system that covered South Dakota, the hexagonal "web system" divided the whole of the continental United States into sales areas.[26]

Dwire listened enthusiastically to Hendrickson. He too saw a need for cheaper and alternative fuels for his energy-intensive construction business. He had already experimented in his home and office with wind and solar power. He also nodded in agreement when Hendrickson prophetically proclaimed that unless something was done, and done soon, the Christian farm was doomed and the nation would be lost. Dwire shared Hendrickson's conclusion that the Jerusalem artichoke was the answer for America and its farmers. He had no doubts that Hendrickson was knowledgeable about the lofty matters of which he spoke and that he had practical knowledge about building alcohol plants.[27]

Hendrickson and Dwire convinced themselves that they were destined for each other: Hendrickson had the ideas, and Dwire had the means; he owned a company generously estimated to include seventy-five employees, twenty vehicles, and capital.

Hendrickson and Dwire found other grounds for mutual acceptance. They considered each other fellow Christians in the popular rural church, fellow Americans, and fellow believers in the family farm. Moreover, they were both self-proclaimed businessmen, Republicans, boosters, and in the spirit of the hour, entrepreneurs. They candidly confessed they were not averse to making a buck. "We feel," Hendrickson remarked, "we have been given a Christian calling as well as a business opportunity." In the margin of an article on Amway, which Hendrickson used to prepare AEFS promotional materials, he revealingly wrote, "AEFS is not just interested in marketing Jerusalem artichokes to farmers for the sake of 'making money,' but its founders, James Dwire and Fred Hendrickson, are the first ones to admit that those farmers who initially participate in the Jerusalem Artichoke Growing Program will make a lot of money." Hendrickson underlined a passage of the article that noted the greatest single reason for Amway's phenomenal success as a direct sales network: "the lure of wealth." He also underlined the words of Amway cofounder Richard DeVos that it was no coincidence that "so many Amway distributors are openly patriotic and religious." DeVos commented that he had "a hard time motivating unreligious people."[28]

Regionally well-known radio evangelist "Pastor Pete" — Richard Peterson — confirmed and blessed Hendrickson's and Dwire's proposed venture. Pastor Pete, a defrocked Lutheran minister turned radio evangelist, was especially important to Hendrickson. Pastor Pete's ministry, called Prayer Power, blossomed in the middle and late 1970s. It encouraged people to believe in baptism by the Holy Spirit and to pray for all the miracles they desired. He considered his ministry a constant intercessory prayer for rural America. His local critics, including fellow Lutherans, unsympathetically judged his ministry to be a sham. According to them, Pastor Pete reduced religion to a supplier of a steady stream of miracles, and his ministry was an opportunity for him to indulge what one fellow minister described as his medically diagnosed megalomania, which manifested itself in a taste for flashy suits, antiques, and other goods. Whatever the truth of these opinions, Pastor Pete's fusion of nation, farmers, and miracles anticipated the essential tenets of AEFS. He laid his hands on Hendrickson and the new company.

Pastor Pete encouraged Hendrickson to think of himself as a prophet bringing a saving crop to the nation. On the basis of Pastor Pete's confirmation, Hendrickson was confident that AEFS and the Jerusalem artichoke answered the prayer ministry of Pastor Pete, and he predicted, "It will produce the sugar and protein that will feed the two billion people the Lord will add to this planet in the 1980s and 1990s."[29]

Hendrickson so wholeheartedly accepted Pastor Pete's ministry and providential view of things that he interpreted Pastor Pete's altogether unexpected death in the fall of 1981 as part of God's plan for him and the Jerusalem artichoke. On the first anniversary of Pastor Pete's death, Hendrickson explained to his widow, Rose Mary: "The hand of God took Pastor Pete from our midst on September 8, 1981. . . . I believe the end of that segment of God's plan for rural America necessitated the physical death of Pastor Pete." Hendrickson, who would help get Rose Mary and her son John jobs at AEFS, further consoled her: "The fall of 1981 was the birth of the Jerusalem artichoke growing program in America. . . . [It] was the answer to all your prayers at Prayer Power."[30]

Hendrickson interpreted everything as part of God's providence. In one instance, he wrote Dwire that God had guided them to the right accounting firm; in another instance, he wrote Dwire that only God could have led him to make a visit to a fructose-processing plant.[31] He declared that Oral Roberts was God's chosen servant.[32] Agreeing with an idea on Jim Bakker's

PTL (Praise the Lord) ministry, which he supported, Hendrickson concluded that a new age was upon humanity, and he declared to Dwire his intention to form a Christian Farmers Association to organize all American agriculture around God and the Jerusalem artichoke. The new association would fight the international bankers and the much feared Trilateral Commission, a consortium of eminent private American, European, and Japanese business leaders whose goal is to foster economic cooperation. The commission was interpreted by a large part of the American political fringe, especially in the countryside, where conspiratorial theories historically abound, as the secret and real source of world economic dominance.[33]

No Ordinary Partner

In deciding to form a company in October 1981, Dwire had selected no ordinary partner. Under Hendrickson's influence, the company would be called the American Energy Farming Systems; it would be based in Marshall, Minnesota. Dwire would be president and chief financial officer, while Hendrickson would serve as secretary and vice president of research. Their original plan was to market seed to only two hundred growers in a six-state area, rather than the four hundred and fifty growers scattered throughout the Midwest who, beyond Hendrickson's and Dwire's greatest expectations, flocked to their new company as if it were an answer to their prayers.

Dwire's brother-in-law, the Reverend Jerry Knapper, who became head of sales for AEFS, captured Hendrickson's unique position in the company when, at the first growers' convention, he said, "Fred is an amazing person, who means many things to many people, whose body has to work hard to keep up with his constantly moving mind, a man of deep conviction who won't give up, who will in time be applauded as one of the family farm's great friends."[34]

At this convention, Hendrickson summarized the views that led him to found AEFS. He declared it was the task of Jerusalem artichoke growers to save America and the family farm from Arabs, who were villainized as controlling the world's supply of oil and seeking to destroy Israel and Christendom. For him, the Jerusalem artichoke was indeed "the weed that whips OPEC."[35]

Hendrickson trod a path he had worn smooth during the preceding three years—a path he walks to this day—arguing that the key to the salvation of the Midwest and America was energy self-sufficient farms. For Hendrickson, energy self-sufficiency included the fashionable ideas of windmills, solar heat, tree farms, fish ponds, and above all else, small alcohol plants for the conversion of Jerusalem artichokes. Hendrickson hypothesized that possibly the steam from these plants could be used to produce good vegetables, unlike the contaminated, sewer-fed vegetables from Mexico. He conjectured that Jerusalem artichoke alcohol would provide cash for new technologies and would pave the way to the creation of new farm energies. Farmers, with or without the oil companies, could help America, and even China and Japan, with their energy needs. Farmers could even sell $45 billion a year of Jerusalem artichokes, he conjectured. Reconciled with President Reagan's destruction of Carter's energy tax credits, Hendrickson boosted himself and growers: "Reagan has cut us free from dependency by denying us tax credits for energy experimentation. We must now forge our own destiny, free from government, and universities. Only we, the industrious, entrepreneurial, independent farmers of America, can save ourselves and the nation."[36]

In his promotion of the Jerusalem artichoke, Hendrickson, to use a French expression, "turned every stick into an arrow." He borrowed ideas from earlier periods in American agriculture, especially the 1930s. He often cited William Hale's 1936 book, *Prosperity Beckons: Dawn of the Alcohol Era*. He rallied to his cause the opinions of experts who agreed with him, and did not overlook in his pitch all the money that could be made from the Jerusalem artichoke (as fuel, sugar, food, or feed). Hendrickson told the doubting Thomases in his audience that if they found no immediate use for their Jerusalem artichokes, the plants could be stored in powder form for great lengths of time and later reconstituted with water.

Hendrickson concluded his talk by beckoning growers to "gear to a whole revitalization of America." There is, he encouraged, "a whole world to be changed. We must venture ourselves."

2

A Bulldozing Businessman

I was a real believer in the artichoke and I seen [sic] it as an opportunity to get into business and help a lot of farmers.
—James Dwire, at Fred Hendrickson's trial

Dwire may have believed he'd save the farmers, but deep down he knew he was screwing everybody . . . like another Jimmy Bakker.
—A local acquaintance of Dwire's

James Dwire thought—and to this day still thinks—Fred Hendrickson was "a real idea man."[1] He believed Hendrickson not only could build him an alcohol plant and put him in contact with the alcohol fuel movement but was, in truth, a kind of prophet. Dwire had hardly heard Hendrickson's pitch before he decided to make him his partner. Dwire didn't bother to check on Hendrickson's background. "I sized him up," Dwire recalled, "as we in the Midwest do: by his word and a handshake." He didn't even bother to make a few telephone calls to Rapid City to find out why his prospective co-owner and director of research was no longer practicing law and was broke.

As sole financier and president of AEFS, Dwire catered to Hendrickson's needs. He allowed Hendrickson to locate his office in Sioux Falls where he had his home and he allowed company money to satisfy Hendrickson's modest but steady stream of special requests. He okayed Hendrickson's requests for company money to buy a car (a $12,000 Chrysler) for company business; to start up two new companies, Rural Data Corporation and Rural Freedom Capital Corporation; to pay rent on a summer cottage; to cover his moving expenses; to make a down payment on a house; to pay for legal fees for past and pending services and settlements; to meet an IRS lien; and to repay money Hendrickson had borrowed from the Igloo project to pay for his Rapid City office.[2]

Hendrickson, for his part, respected Dwire immensely. He perceived Dwire to be a successful businessman. Not unexpectedly, Hendrickson thought their meeting was providential. Why look a gift horse in the mouth? Priding himself on thinking big concepts, he took little interest in what he disdainfully called "the everyday affairs" of the company. Even in the initial phases of the company, when if ever a co-owner should take interest in its affairs, he did not bother to examine AEFS's books, to scrutinize its hiring, or to examine how and on what terms Dwire's companies worked for AEFS. Hendrickson trusted Dwire and Dwire trusted Hendrickson, and their trust was not free of self-interest.

Two Brothers

Compared to Hendrickson, James Dwire had a difficult childhood. He was the fourth child in a family of six children. His mother, Caroline Wild Dwire, and his father, Allen Dwire, both had only grade-school educations. In the early years of their marriage, they worked hard to keep their family off public assistance. The children, who were never indulged by their parents, were forced to go about in holey underwear no matter how much they complained.[3] In 1945, when James was four, his mother committed suicide. The mother's death separated the children. James went to live with an uncle and aunt until he was eleven, while his youngest brother, Donald, who was three months old when his mother died, lived almost his entire childhood with others.[4] Relations between James and his siblings were not close. When the family was together, shouting matches and displays of temper were common. Relations between the siblings further soured as James, clearly the father's favorite and his chosen successor, received more and more of the benefits of Allen's prospering contracting business, Dwire, Inc., which James eventually took over. The other children believed James received the lion's share of their father's estate. Allen's ignorance of his own net worth, which clearly reached into the millions, his failure to keep records, and his penchant for using a shoe box as a safe did nothing to allay suspicions, and lack of a missing will and emptied saving accounts fueled misunderstandings between James and his siblings.

The rivalry between James and his older brother, Richard, made the family's dispute public. James, who began doing a full day's work when he was in the eighth grade, grew up working in Allen's construction company. Conversely, Richard, who discovered his mother dead at the side of her bed, strangled by a necktie attached to the headboard, wanted to get out of Marshall and be free of Allen.[5] He and "the old man," as Richard disdainfully called Allen, never really got on. Richard considered his father capable of almost anything, and he frequently challenged Allen, who responded by severely punishing him. On one occasion, Allen hauled Richard away from home, tied him, and left him outdoors all night. Later, seeking to escape the old man, Richard left home and joined the army.

Richard had spent ten years in the paratroopers and was considering staying on to retirement when his father wrote him in 1960, asking him to come home to help him in the company because he was short of laborers. Richard returned home and had been working for Allen for only a week when "the old man says, 'I don't need you.'"[6] Richard, by then married and now without employment, had to go to work for minimum wage at Swifts, a local meat processing company, while his father and brother ran the successful "family" business. Later, Richard returned to work with his father and brother only to experience another falling out. This time Richard responded by starting his own gravel-hauling company.

At one point James, who was then heading Dwire, Inc., and Richard, who headed his own company, began cooperating, but they ended up warring.[7] Richard believed that "the old man" did what he could to see to it that the local bank denied him credit, and that James sought to put him out of business by creating a competing local gravel company with an employee of Dwire, Inc.

James was by far the better contractor of the two. One of Richard's harshest critics said, "He was simple as soup. He figured his job estimates on matchbooks, and then he threw the matchbooks away as he left the site."[8] Richard himself, who died in 1992 in a motorcycle accident in California where he lived, more or less conceded the truth of this, acknowledging, "Jim could outtalk me and do everything I couldn't. . . . He was a sharper and a better contractor than me." Richard even took a certain pleasure in remembering James's cunning and in reciting James's favorite quote: "He'd always say, 'I could sell a dumb farmer anything.' "[9] However, Richard's concessions that James was a better contractor than he was did not stop him from believing that James cheated him out of his share of the "old man's" estate. In Richard's opinion, James was not only "spoiled by the old man," but also started to help himself to Allen's money and assets long before he died, despite Allen's occasional complaints. James put one of the company's buildings in his name, and he used company money to buy what he wanted. According to Richard, James put their father out of his home and let him back in on the condition that he give James money. Richard estimated that in this manner James took as much as $40,000 at a crack.[10]

Richard, who really came "unglued" when he was angry, was publicly critical of James. Long familiar with Richard's bitterness, people in Marshall were not at all surprised when, in the immediate aftermath of AEFS's eventual declaration of bankruptcy, they saw Richard going about town wearing a T-shirt whose bold letters proclaimed, "I am not James."

A Bull of a Man

James resembled his father more than Richard did. Allen was hot tempered, hard pushing, and hardworking. He was a kind of crazy man who would throw a tantrum in a store one day and then return the next to pay his bills and order thousands of dollars worth of new merchandise. He worked like "a wild man," said one of his former employees.[11] Another acquaintance of Allen's said, "He would work as much as twenty-four hours at a crack. Once when he bought a crusher that needed to be run twenty-four hours a day to make a profit, he made sure that it was run twenty-four hours a day." This acquaintance added, "He was the older kind of boss and foreman who believed that you got to chew ass to get things done."[12] He fired workers at the drop of a hat.

No one took Allen for anything less than shrewd. Richard literally believed that "the old man could smell gravel a mile off. He just knew—he knew it by instinct."[13] Allen walked around with all his affairs in his head, which later got him into big trouble with the IRS. He priced things on the spot, discounting and augmenting bills according to his estimate of a customer's willingness to pay. He cunningly turned companies that normally would have been his creditors into his debtors by paying them in advance. These companies, one of which even paid him interest, were always left scrambling to provide good services to their creditor, Allen Dwire.

Many local people believe that Allen could both outthink and outwork his competitors. Certainly, he had the gift of gab. Richard Dwire proudly recounted one instance when his father talked the council members of Browns Valley, Minnesota, into paving not just some but all of their streets. "Browns Valley ended up broke but happy," Richard commented.[14]

Some speak of Allen as a fair and generous man who did what a contractor should. He made sure a job was done right, he paid his bills, and he didn't exploit his employees. One former Dwire, Inc., employee considered one of Allen's few vices a harmless vanity that led him to be an usher at church so he could wear a boutonniere.[15] Others, repeating common gossip, sketch a portrait of Allen as a womanizer and drinker, who was intent on screwing, in one way or another, whomever he could out of ten dollars. One distant relative of Allen's wife vividly remembers him as a cruel bully. He recalls how Allen responded to the condolences he tried to extend at the time of the accidental death of one of his employees. "The dumb son of a bitch deserved it," Allen shot back. This relative is not alone in believing that Allen drove his wife to suicide.

Allen's will was never in question. By all accounts, he was a forceful man who pursued his own ends. In one telling instance from a construction work site, a telephone cableman parked his three-quarter-ton truck over a cable to protect it against Allen's construction crew. Irate, Allen hopped on a large loader and simply moved the truck.

Some acquaintances, without evidence, conjecture that Allen himself committed suicide in 1973 by intentionally driving his car into the path of an oncoming truck. He did this, they suggest, to avoid facing the outcome of an ongoing IRS investigation for not paying taxes—something Allen determinedly and consistently avoided doing. He believed the investigation would eventually result in his imprisonment. While the contention of suicide is extremely unlikely, Allen, having recently been remarried, was upset over the IRS investigation, which eventually resulted in his estate paying $240,000 in back taxes.[16]

"Like father, like son," is the most common phrase used to describe James. Like Allen, James Dwire was uniformly known to be an incredibly hard worker. From his youth, James always worked hard at his father's construction business. While attending high school, from which he graduated in 1959, he frequently skipped classes to work. The only activity in which he participated in school was four years of varsity football. Some of his old-time Marshall friends, when they picture him, still see him seated on a machine. "He could make a machine talk. He was good, real good," one former classmate said. He remembered a story about just how good an operator of heavy machinery Dwire was. At a local Caterpillar exhibit a salesman coaxed a coy and reluctant Dwire to take a test drive of a piece of heavy machinery, only to see Dwire mount it and make it run and purr as few men could. When Dwire dismounted, he informed the awed salesman that he had not only driven the machine before but was its owner. He had lent it to the company for its exhibit.[17]

Dwire took on the responsibilities of adult life early. In 1961, he married Peggy Fredrichs of Mankato. She, like her husband, had a high school education. They had four children. Aside from work and family, James Dwire had a few hobbies, including boating, deer and pheasant hunting, tinkering with mechanics, and reading self-help books, an increasing number of which dealt with alternative energy. He never traveled far nor served in the military. His life turned on family, friends, church, and work.

In contrast to Hendrickson, Dwire's work record is remarkably consistent. Beginning in 1954, before starting high school, he worked, helped run, and then managed his father's construction company, Dwire, Inc. In 1972, Dwire became proprietor of his father's company. His father gave him stock in the company and sold James the remaining shares for $210,000 to be paid up in 1993 at 6 percent interest.[18] Dwire remained proprietor of Dwire, Inc., until 1986, enjoying, on the whole, a reputation equal to his father's as an honest, intelligent businessman. He served one year as president of the Minnesota Association of Builders and Contractors and was a member of its board of directors for five years.

Like his father, Dwire was known to attack life. One former employee said, "He was a worthy son of a bitch."[19] Another acquaintance said, "Dwire and his old man were the God-damnest renegades you ever saw. They'd fire guys right and left. They ran their machines wide open. On one occasion," this acquaintance went on to say, "Dwire, who frequently took over the job of a slow employee, pushed one of his drivers off a loader only to mount it and, out of haste, immediately proceeded to misshift it, sending the loader up and over his pickup truck."[20]

Prior to his involvement at AEFS, Dwire's only crimes, predictably, were speeding tickets. His flying was equally reckless, and, as one might guess, many people were afraid to fly with him. He piloted his planes aggressively. On one occasion, he nearly caused the deaths of several people. Disregarding the advice of an airport manager, he ordered an AEFS pilot, who couldn't fly by instruments, to take off in foggy darkness at three o'clock in the morning. The pilot no sooner got up than he was forced to return to the ground. Unable to find the runway, the pilot crashed in a nearby farm field, perilously close to a major drainage ditch. Fortunately, there were no serious injuries.[21]

Once in control of Dwire, Inc., James pushed the company ahead. He had a unique gift for leadership. He got the most out of his workers by believing in them and, thus, calling forth the best from them. While he was quick-tempered like his father, he didn't hold grudges and quickly forgave even those who contradicted him. He presented workers with unrequested raises in their salaries, and he even spontaneously paid for their vacations.[22] One former employee said, "He was as good a guy as you could ask to work for. You never had to ask for a raise." He continued, "If you did good work, you got one."[23] More significantly, Dwire offered his loyal workers new responsibilities and opportunities. In some instances, he ventured his capital to form small, but successful, companies with employees. Two examples were D. and G. Excavating Inc., the initials of which stood for Dwire and local contractor and partner Dave Gruhot, and Lynd Redi-Mix, Inc., which he started with former employee Warren Severson. Other former employees, such as Walter Maeyaert and Al Roos, acknowledge their standing indebtedness to Dwire for their start in the construction business.

Dwire was never afraid to spend his money. He proved the aphorism "Inherited money spends easily." He is an example of how the second generation learns to spend money better than to make it. He took the parable of the talents too seriously. Doing throughout the 1970s what he repeatedly did later at AEFS, Dwire accepted the advice of a "business expert" who counseled, "It takes money to make money." He made Dwire, Inc., far bolder than it had ever been under his father. He bid more jobs, did more jobs, and significantly increased the size of the company without adding a penny to its profitability.

Dwire lacked the financial acumen of his father. This defect proved deadly when combined with his impulsive personality. He was subject to buying frenzies. They seized him especially when he had a new project in mind. They made him a common participant in auctions, whose increasing numbers, as much as anything, revealed the sagging fortunes of rural America. They resulted in his purchasing large and expensive construction equipment that "he loved far more than simply work tools."[24] These frenzies meant, time and time again, that he bought stuff he neither needed nor could afford. Once, for example, he bought a generator without examining it. He took it home only to discover a large hole in its side from the rod it had thrown.[25]

Dwire was labeled "a plunger," by more than one Marshall acquaintance. "A-hundred-and-ten-percenter! A head-over-heels guy!" was the comment of another Marshall businessman.[26]

Dwire's tendency to go whole hog was evident in the new country home he bought in 1979. He used his earth-moving machinery to divert a small stream, which he transformed into a small lake that fronted the house. Motivated by the bountiful survivalist literature of the hour, as represented by such magazines as *Rough Times*, which he read regularly, Dwire created a walk-in vault below his house and stocked it with dried fruit, guns, and other goods.[27] Anticipating a need for costly and scarce fuel, he had one twelve-thousand-gallon and two ten-thousand-gallon fuel tanks buried in his yard. Also, fearing the onset of a prolonged drought, as the weather patterns of the late 1970s suggested to him, he purchased, but never installed, an expensive irrigation system. Realizing the great changes he believed were at hand, Dwire built an earth home and experimented with windmills and solar energy devices.

Even Dwire's closest business associates couldn't restrain him. He kept trying to bull and buy his way through the world. Try as they did, they couldn't get a drag chain around him strong enough to hold him back.[28] Dreams, infatuations, and spending money were closely associated in Dwire's personality.

The year 1979 was a crisis year for Dwire. His two most important employees, accountant Walter Maeyaert and job foreman Al Roos, decided to start their own construction company. Realizing they could never constrain Dwire, they were determined to go it alone.[29] Their decision angered and embittered him. Earlier in the year, on far more amicable terms, Dwire had started the aforementioned partnerships with former employees Gruhot and Severson, but now his two most trusted employees were leaving him, and they wouldn't even take him along. Dwire felt betrayed—he had a need to show them he didn't need them.

But 1979 was a terrible year to try to show anyone anything. This was especially true if one needed to borrow money to prove his point. The economy was turned upside down. Fuel costs soared. Interest rates reached the high teens and then momentarily breached the 20 percent mark. In fact, Dwire and Gruhot paid 20 percent interest on money borrowed to purchase two pieces of large machinery.

As in 1975, in 1979 Dwire again lost his bonding—his capacity to insure his own jobs.[30] In the same year, he got stuck on a losing job near Blackduck in Beltrami County in northern Minnesota. It was a big job, he had bid it low, it was a long way from home, and it began to rain and rain. His profits were soon washed away as his debt swelled.

Circumstances were squeezing Dwire out of the construction business, and he was losing his inheritance. One local electrical contractor had to go to court to get him to pay for work done on his home. Dwire needed a way to make money—and fast.

He Needed Cash

Despite what Dwire claims, his need for cash seems to help explain his infatuation with the Jerusalem artichoke. On the eve of the founding of AEFS, Dwire belonged to that large and growing national family of highly leveraged contractors, farmers, speculators, insurance companies, savings and loan companies, and banks of the late 1970s. Not unlike countless other contractors across the nation, Dwire was caught up in the difficult economic times.

In his financial statement for 1979, Dwire represented himself as being worth almost $700,000: He indicated that his total assets were approximately $950,000, while his liabilities were $250,000.[31] However, upon examination one discovers his assets were composed primarily of his companies and recently acquired real estate. Approximately $500,000 of his assets were stocks in Dwire, Inc; another $300,000 was in real estate. He had less than $25,000 in cash, savings, and bonds; his annual income of $80,000 a year depended largely on a $50,000 salary from Dwire, Inc., and $20,000 from rental properties.

His 1980 financial report testified to Dwire's increasing dependency on real estate. He now estimated it to be worth more than $400,000.[32] In that year Dwire increased his appraisal of Dwire, Inc., stock to $650,000. His paper assets were increased to more than $1.3 million, while his debts from mortgages and payable bank notes approached $450,000. Despite his $20,000 a year income from rent and an enhanced salary of $75,000 (improved for no apparent reason by 50 percent), Dwire's liquid funds sunk to $15,000. Dwire was cash starved. He could, to use gambling lingo, only bet on the come.

A consolidated ledger for Dwire, Inc., for 1979 and 1980 (read separately from his two financial statements) could also be interpreted to portend disaster. Even though his liabilities had depreciated greatly—they were down by approximately $700,000—his assets also depreciated from $2.2 million in 1979 to $1.5 million in 1980. It could be conjectured that Dwire was trying his hand at the highly speculative business of real estate investment to compensate for his failing construction company.

Prior to 1979, Dwire owned only a small farm, his homestead, and his Lynd shop with its adjacent land. From 1979 to 1981, Dwire purchased eleven pieces of real estate for rental purposes. The purchase cost of these eleven properties, which included houses in Marshall and farm land in Lyon, Lincoln, and Murray counties, exceeded a million dollars. In a personal financial evaluation report of August 1982, he acknowledged owing almost $700,000 on these properties. Among other things, this suggests how little money he had put down on them. Like so many farmers who went broke in the late 1970s and early 1980s, Dwire was betting his fortunes on the continued inflating value of land.

An examination of Dwire's 1982 financial evaluation report (drawn up by his consultant, the Reverend Lowell D. Kramer, when AEFS was exactly one year old) confirms his clear financial dependence on real estate and, in turn, his dependence on AEFS cash to make the payments due on that real estate. According to this evaluation, Dwire now owned a thousand acres of farmland and had more than $5 million in assets, with less than $1 million in liabilities. His wealth hinged on the liberal estimate of his assets. These included half a million dollars of Jerusalem artichokes planted on newly acquired land; a half-million-dollar house whose value had somehow appreciated 300 percent in two years; $1.5 million worth of other real estate; and $3 million worth of companies. (Dominant among these companies were Dwire, Inc., and AEFS, as well as Jim Dwire Construction and a handful of smaller partnerships with friends and former employees, including D. and G. Excavating, Lynd Redi-Mix, and SL&C Partnership. SL&C joined Dwire with his local attorney and local accountant, brothers Jim and Duane Anderson. Also, he co-owned Blue Water Harvester, Inc., with AEFS consultant Wayne Dorband.) However, aside from his assets, he still had only $20,000 in cash. Dwire was an economic Humpty Dumpty, vulnerable to a quick and great fall.

Where he sat, if rents from his lands rose and if his properties and companies retained, or increased, their value, Dwire would be fine. If things went badly—that is, if interest remained high, if real estate lost its value, and above all, if AEFS ran out of cash—Dwire would crash to the ground and the cleverest accountants wouldn't be able to put him back together again. Without AEFS cash his whole economic kingdom would disintegrate: he would lose his property; he would no longer have his handsome AEFS salary; there would be no work for Dwire, Inc., or his other companies; he would lose the preferential rent of two hundred dollars per acre he received from AEFS on his farm land; his Jerusalem artichoke seed would not command a premium price; and, furthermore, he would be unable to meet the numerous annual and balloon payments he owed on his property and payments on debts owed his brothers and sisters on the settlement of his father's estate.

Dwire quickly got hooked on AEFS cash. It was his goose and it was laying golden eggs. Even before AEFS's first board meeting on November 9, 1981, he had already borrowed $10,000 from the company, with which he purchased a small farm from the family of his friend and Dwire, Inc., employee, Richard Skorczewski. Between September 1 and December 31, Dwire, Inc., did $90,000 worth of work for AEFS and Jim Dwire Construction did more than $100,000 worth of work for AEFS. The following spring, Dwire used AEFS money to repay two $100,000 loans that he had taken out in 1981.[33]

Within months of its creation, Dwire's success and AEFS's success were linked. Dwire and AEFS would rise or fall together. There was no retreat for him. His need for cash drove him forward, and it turned Dwire, a "blade man" and a construction company owner, into a salesman. He would have to sell Jerusalem artichoke seeds to farmers, or he would fall off his wall.[34]

He Believed Too

A need for cash married Dwire to Hendrickson and to AEFS. The Jerusalem artichoke meant a chance for him to make a buck—and that was precisely what he needed to do, according to Kim Boe, his accountant at Dwire, Inc.[35]

Yet a need for money alone doesn't explain Dwire's quick embrace of Hendrickson and his ideas. First, there was a genuine religious affinity between them, even though Dwire's recent conversion to fundamentalism didn't square entirely with Hendrickson's miracle-laden charismatic faith. They both believed God would bless them, meet their needs, and guide them to great things.

Many doubted the authenticity of Dwire's conversion. They read his newly found faith as a mask from behind which he could sell Jerusalem artichoke seed. Some skeptically remembered how Dwire made his large, clumsily obvious Sunday donations at the church, while others remembered him as a hard-drinking, hard-swearing son-of-a-gun, who had no place in a Bible-touting crowd. One of his associates remembers Dwire telling him how glad he was to escape the pious crowds of AEFS so he could let his hair down and swear a little.[36]

Yet, as so many testified, Dwire did undergo some sort of conversion in the late 1970s. Brought up as a Methodist, he became a born-again Christian. He joined the new Marshall Evangelical Free Church where he professed his newfound faith. Dwire regularly attended Bible study and made church attendance a central part of his life. He no longer drank; he took the television sets out of his home; he prayed before his meals even when out in public; and he openly incorporated faith in God into his speech.

Dwire believed, as did Hendrickson, that their meeting was providential. Although Dwire differentiated his brand of Christian fundamentalism from Pastor Pete's charismatic Prayer Power, he nevertheless may have subscribed to his prophecy that the Jerusalem artichoke was a saving crop. Dwire had no doubt that he and Hendrickson were establishing a Christian company.

Dwire also believed, as Hendrickson did, that the big powers of oil and government controlled the nation and were destroying the social and moral fabric of the nation and rural America, which for him were one and the same. Dwire was not surprised when Jerry Knapper, his brother-in-law, recounted how John Block, U.S. commissioner of agriculture, had told Knapper that it was his intention to eliminate 65 percent of the nation's farmers.[37] Like Hendrickson, Dwire saw the farmers and the people of the Midwest as besieged by alien forces.

Dwire identified with the main tenets of the survivalists, and he believed energy independence was the key to saving the nation's heartland. Arguably, Dwire's search for energy independence, more than anything else, explains why Dwire was willing to join Hendrickson in creating AEFS. At the very time he met Hendrickson, Dwire was preoccupied with finding an inexpensive alternative to the diesel fuel used by his companies.[38] On several occasions in the past, once in 1973 on a bid for interstate highway 90, and again on bids in 1976 and 1978, he had lost considerable sums of money because of precipitous rises in fuel costs.

Dwire's interest in alternative energy was wider than alcohol fuel production. Before meeting Hendrickson, Dwire had already begun to study and to read on the concept of total energy independence, and he had even read an article on the fuel potential of the Jerusalem artichoke. A self-taught amateur like Hendrickson, Dwire threw himself headlong into whatever interested him. He looked into windmills for energy production, experimented with solar panels and other energy-saving devices in his home, and built an earth home for an office.

Dwire believed that Hendrickson knew precisely what he, Dwire, had been grappling to learn. The blind led the blind. Dwire believed Hendrickson knew the important people in the field of alcohol fuels, understood the technology of fuels, and foresaw the alcohol fuel promise of a whole new crop, Jerusalem artichokes.

On one count, Dwire and Hendrickson were remarkably similar. They were both plungers. No sooner did they get an idea than they were ready to convert others to it. Both rushed ahead to start companies that, rather than being deliberate projects, consecrated newly formed ideas and enthusiasms.

In fact, on the eve of forming AEFS, Dwire was initiating his brother-in-law, underemployed Jerry Knapper, from nearby Maynard, Minnesota, into the dream of energy independence. (Knapper was to become head of sales for AEFS.) Even prior to meeting Hendrickson, they were considering the formation of an energy consulting company whose goal would be evaluating farms for energy independence.[39]

Dwire didn't take a back seat to Hendrickson as a plunger. "Dwire spent money like water, almost as if it didn't matter," one former employee said.[40] "He would start a company, with almost anyone, at the drop of a hat," the same employee noted.[41] His local accountant, Duane Anderson, perceived him to be like so many other entrepreneurs. "He believed the American dream. He thought that everything would work out in the end; that his scheme would have a great, happy, and rich ending."[42]

All this prepared Dwire—Christian, patriot, enthusiast, and entrepreneur—to meet Hendrickson. Amateur Dwire was ready to meet the king of amateurs, Hendrickson.

In testimony at Hendrickson's trial, Dwire described the circumstances that led to his meeting with Hendrickson. He and Al Rusk of Southwest State University in Marshall, with whom he had formed a company, were initially interested in looking at building energy digesters. According to Dwire, Rusk himself was "real involved in the alcohol movement . . . [and he kept] telling me about this crop with a tremendous potential. . . . You wouldn't have to replant it and the conversion factors looked real good for making alcohol, and corn was $3.00 a bushel." Rusk further advised Dwire to call Hendrickson if he was interested in the promise of the Jerusalem artichoke. Dwire did. "Subsequently over the phone, I bought, gee I don't know, I think it was six or ten thousand pounds of artichokes from Fred."

With the planting and growing of those artichokes, a dream grew up between them. "By fall the foliage was so thick you could hardly walk through the field," Dwire further remarked in his testimony, "and the crop literally sold itself to the farmers." As if describing a religious conversion, he went on to say, "We literally stood out in the field one day, and I looked at Fred, and I said, 'You know what we ought to do, we ought to market this crop' 'cause there was nobody marketing it, and I seen [sic] it was an opportunity too—I was a real believer in the artichoke, and I seen it as an opportunity to get into business and help a lot of other farmers."[43]

Sales, Not Science

Predictably, any company Dwire and Hendrickson started would be more about promotion and sales than science and technology. Without a formal education beyond high school, Dwire was impressed by people with college degrees. He revealed the limits of his understanding of science by actually believing that Hendrickson could be responsible for the company's development of alcohol plants and other research.[44]

If Dwire were not infatuated with ideas, he might have suspected Hendrickson's knowledge. What sort of science could be expected from a person who frequently heard voices? (Dwire and Knapper unsuccessfully argued with Hendrickson that the voices he heard were not God's but those of angels or lesser principalities.) Another clue to the limits of Hendrickson's capacity for research was his proclivity for immense visions, grandiose explanations, and gigantic, megalomaniacal selling schemes.

If Dwire himself had had even a minimal knowledge of crop science, he would have realized from the outset the folly of what Hendrickson proposed. There was simply no way an outcast plant could be transformed into a major crop for the production of fuel in a three-year period. Common sense and agricultural knowledge dictate that to turn any plant into a major crop requires years, even decades, of laboratory, genetic, agronomic, and market work. Among many other required conditions, there must be real promise within the crop, a potential niche in the market, means of industrial processing, a large buyer, faithful and risk-taking farmer-suppliers, tenacious and entrepreneurial developers, and luck itself, which might give the crop an initial start as one product but eventually reveal a use altogether different. All this is shown by the soybean's four-decade development from a small and growing feed crop to a major oil crop.

Despite the soybean's full importance to the agriculture of southwest Minnesota and the Midwest, Dwire knew little of its history in particular, or the nature of crop development in general. In effect, he was ill-prepared to recognize Hendrickson's folly. Dwire had no basis to identify Hendrickson and those whom Hendrickson identified as his allies in the alcohol fuel movement as amateurs dabbling with a dream rather than a group of men on the verge of changing America's farms and fields. Dwire should have been suspicious that Hendrickson's primary allies were old cronies from the failed South Dakota alcohol fuel project—including local dreamers and tinkerers whose sincere desires to lead the alcohol fuel revolution were insufficient to turn their prototype distilleries, carburetors, and cars into an energy revolution.

With a rudimentary understanding of crop development, Dwire would have realized that a handful of reputable scientists in the United States, Canada, and Europe saying the Jerusalem artichoke had promise either for alcohol-fuel or as a source of sugar did not span the great divide between laboratory and market. Nor was a significant effort to bridge this distance made by having AEFS issue a handful of small grants and contracts (usually less than ten thousand dollars) to scientists such as L. T. Fan in chemical engineering at Kansas State University, Al Rusk and Richard Spencer at Southwest State University, or Wayne Dorband and Larry Tieszen at Augustana College in Sioux Falls, South Dakota.

Sometime during the first six months of the company's existence, it finally dawned on Dwire that Hendrickson was "all talk and little show." Dwire also became aware how much of AEFS's scientific research depended on a single scientist, namely, Wayne Dorband. Dorband, an assistant professor at Augustana College, was himself as much an entrepreneur as a college teacher or scientific researcher. When Hendrickson hired him he was president of six small commercial research companies, and within months of joining AEFS he affiliated himself with Dwire in forming other small companies to carry out commercial ventures. (After AEFS's bankruptcy, Dorband joined Dwire in selling Amway products.) Knapper commented that AEFS tried to use Dorband "to cover for Hendrickson. Freddie couldn't do anything."[45] Knapper added, "Dwire wanted the meat from Dorband that Hendrickson didn't have. Dorband continuously sidetracked Dwire with his schemes."[46]

Dorband's credentials did not fit the fundamental scientific and technological needs of AEFS. Dorband had received his Ph.D. in fisheries resources from the University of Idaho in 1980. Prior to earning his doctorate, he had done some work on alcohol fuel as well as on limited agronomic research projects on wetland areas. In 1975 he started his primary company, Aqua-nalysis, Inc., which specialized in aquatic environmental research. Before going to work for AEFS, he had no knowledge of the Jerusalem artichoke and little or no knowledge in specialized fields associated with crop development.

As Dwire knew, what Dorband essentially did for AEFS was "wear a white coat." He provided a quasi-legitimacy for a company of amateurs. Dorband, who received more than $200,000 in wages and expenses in the course of AEFS's brief history, did try to carry out some legitimate projects. He gathered a large collection of articles on the Jerusalem artichoke. He carried out preliminary evaluations of the feed value of the plant. He offered a set of proposals "of different sorts of research programs to give the company research credibility with their growers and the scientific community."[47] Also, he undertook a large but essentially uninstructive literature search, devised a very primitive survey for collecting field data from growers, supervised AEFS's experimental acres, and offered agronomic advice on weeding, harvesting, and pesticides.

Crossing the line between sales and science, Dorband led sales seminars for AEFS. Also, he wrote a significant, if not the greatest, portion of the company's more important sales literature. This literature later was at the center of the Minnesota attorney general's investigation of AEFS.

In the early months of the company's existence, Dwire looked to Hendrickson and Dorband for agronomic research. Preoccupied with getting AEFS off the ground, Dwire had little choice but to trust Hendrickson and Dorband to critically examine thirty varieties of the plant and take the first steps to prepare the Jerusalem artichoke for national markets.

Certainly Dwire and Hendrickson knew next to nothing about crop development, yet some, if not most, of their efforts to develop the crop were sincere. For instance, they identified some prestigious scientists who studied the Jerusalem artichoke; entered into a lease-purchase agreement for the use of a local alcohol plant; started a dehydration project; approached a few large companies about research on and purchase of the Jerusalem artichoke; and took a trip to France to see what positive use the

French purportedly made of the Jerusalem artichoke. However, none of their efforts were part of a thoughtful plan; they were instead, like dice thrown on a table, a mixture of helter-skelter initiatives aimed at somehow hitting pay dirt—or at least providing the necessary appearance of legitimate research.

Dwire and Hendrickson passed off their efforts as part of company research. They justified the farms they bought for themselves as research labs necessary for conducting experiments to discover new forms of energy self-sufficiency. Dwire testified that they intended to use one farm to make terraces, develop a fish farm, grow artichokes, and build a small energy plant; another farm was intended to be the site of a fish farm, an alcohol plant, and a methane digester for cattle waste.

Hendrickson's and Dwire's initial efforts were at best those of clumsy amateurs who did not understand the science of crop development. At worst, their endeavors were merely part of the artifice to make their company appear legitimate. Whatever the case, they were dreamers and entrepreneurs, enthusiasts and plungers—the kind of men who delude others as they delude themselves.

At the founding of the company, both Hendrickson and Dwire were justifiably giddy with success. More farmers wanted Jerusalem artichoke seed tubers than they had ever imagined. Money rolled in. Hendrickson believed he was leading the nation and himself to prosperity. Dwire was equally enthusiastic. He was making money. AEFS provided work for his companies. He met his payrolls, hired his friends, and started to purchase new properties. Now was not the time for either of them to question their creation.

Throughout the company's history, ignorance and naivete protected the consciences of Dwire and Hendrickson. On one occasion, Dwire fired AEFS's accountants rather than heed their warnings about his large borrowings and the company's serious cash shortage. Dwire explained his action by saying that the accountants didn't classify seed contracts paid to AEFS as income until the seed had been delivered. "So you know, one is a debt and one is a credit, and I don't understand the two terms that well, but they were saying it was a loss and actually we had this money in the bank and by my private projection we were a profitable organization. We were basically a cash basis organization. Actually, we were a cash rich company."[48]

AEFS, Dwire argued, made $2 million in December 1981 and $6 million in January 1982. He anticipated that AEFS would soon be making $10 million a month. "So," Dwire concluded, "I [thought that] there would be more than enough money to always pay and they call that robbing Peter to pay Paul but it is a continuation of business, and that describes it."[49]

Dwire conducted his business largely to keep Dwire, Inc., afloat, and to boost his ego. Meanwhile, AEFS boomed. In fact, AEFS boomed so much that Dwire himself later explained its failure as a case of being overwhelmed by success. In the beginning, the company planned on having only eight or nine salesmen. It ended up with eight or nine regional salesmen and thirty or forty state representatives. (With the exception of one woman who sold Jerusalem artichokes for a short time, all the company's sales representatives were men.) Its employees were exhausted by the company's wild growth. Dwire used the example of employee Kim Boe, Dwire, Inc.'s, accountant, who went from being "a sharp young vocational school graduate [who was] very confident [and] a very detailed bookkeeper [to being], probably the last year and a half, just almost literally out of his mind." Dwire confessed of himself, "I was burned out. We were working literally eighteen hours a day. I'd jump in an airplane, we'd fly to meetings at night. . . . I was always in meetings and literally the pilot would fly me back, I'd sleep in the airplane, get home sometimes five, six in the morning, change clothes, shower and go into the office."[50]

At first Dwire rushed about believing that he had discovered a magic money tree. Then he rushed about out of desperation as early euphoria gave way to anxiety as oil prices fell, public interest in alternative energy waned, and the likelihood of finding a viable market for Jerusalem artichokes grew remote. Without a market for their product the company, increasingly resembling a pyramid-sales scheme, lived on sales and more sales.

3

Buyers and Sellers of Seed

Anoint me with artichokes and set me on fire.
—Don Sheenan, AEFS sales staff

A fabulous deal, if only half true.
—A South Dakota artichoke speculator

At AEFS we are a family of believers. We believe in God, we believe in America, we believe in the farm family and we believe in the Jerusalem artichoke.
—AEFS corporate philosophy

A local Marshall barber said of AEFS's sales, "It took a lot of skill to sell weeds to farmers." In truth, it took more than skill to sell the Jerusalem artichoke to more than 2,500 American farmers. It took an energy crisis and a farm-credit crisis in combination with a resurgence of affirmation about the uniqueness of America, its land, its countryside, and its farmers. In fact, without recourse to profound myths and metaphors about the nation's covenanted greatness, AEFS could not have sold the Jerusalem artichoke as the God-appointed "plant of renown."

Boosting and Boasting

Boosterism, the spiritual breath of the American countryside, had long prepared the soil for the buying and selling of Jerusalem artichokes. From colonial times, Americans had been in the habit of boosting the New World, not as it was, but as they wished it to be. Boosterism habituated Americans to enthusiastic exaggeration, and on this count both Dwire and Hendrickson were real Americans.

Boosterism has a set of telltale synonyms. They include Barnumism, baloney, blarney, bullshitting, horn-tooting, heisting, and hot-air making.[1] Boosterism is also associated with bubbles, extravaganzas, gushing, puffery, hullabaloo, grease jobs, back-slapping, soft-soaping, leg-pulling, talking-up, vainglorification, and other darker connotations (to be heard in the language of AEFS's critics and prosecutors), as well as enticements, allurements, inveiglements, come-ons, bamboozling, getting one's meat hooks in, and lying, theft, fraud, and swindling. (At carnivals and circuses to boost means to shill: to shill is to use planted buyers to drive up the price of auctioned goods.)

More benignly, boosterism can be defined simply as the necessary exaggeration that accompanies human endeavors. Without boosterism, it can be argued, very little could be accomplished in mass society. As defenders of AEFS contended, there surely would be no development of new crops without a sufficient application of boosting. Defending boosterism, historian Daniel Boorstin draws a distinction between boosters and speculators. The former, he suggests, invest themselves and their money in the outcome of their chosen civic enterprise; the latter simply exploit new economic activities for maximum profits.[2]

The moral fence of sincerity between these two types of exaggerators has probably never been as high or impassable as Boorstin suggests; it was almost nonexistent in the case of AEFS. It certainly did not sequester the speculators and boosters who settled and defined the great prairie. Settlers themselves, for all sorts of reasons, confused making a dollar and establishing a home, and founders of the smallest towns promoted their towns as the great cities of an advancing civilization.

Exaggeration—at which the staff at AEFS was so good—formed the first language of self-definition on the newly settled prairie and it has remained inseparable from the expression of its civic patriotism and economic development. As the official language of expansion, boosterism assembles citizens and business leaders into enthusiastic communities beaming with confidence about the future.

With no, or very little, room for doubt or skepticism in these communities, there has always been the constant temptation (one to which AEFS personnel repeatedly yielded) to assume that belief alone determines the outcome of things, and to go on to conclude, as illogical as it is, that the more hopeless a project appears, the more it requires belief to succeed. This belief in belief—the essential dogma of every booster—is where such far-fetched and desperate faiths, like that proposed by AEFS, are bred.

Especially during bad times speculators, gamblers, miracle makers, con artists, and other dark cousins of the boosters appear. And so they appeared during the 1980s. In southwest Minnesota, the home of AEFS, people looked for oil and gold where it never would be found, tried new crops where they wouldn't grow, and sold all sorts of speculative insurance and investment schemes that could only end badly. To the west of Marshall, in impoverished Lincoln County, a handful of desperate marginal farmers fell for the scam of buying mushrooms from a parent company that allegedly would buy back all the mushrooms they grew. To the north of Marshall, in Boyd, Minnesota, "a savior" appeared: He came in the form of an English gentleman who claimed to be an heir of the patrimony of King Charles I. He promised to reestablish the failed local bank. He promised his new bank would offer loans at exceptionally favorable rates, and furthermore, it would provide free college tuition for its customers' children. Many local people found him to be their best and last hope until this "royal heir" disappeared from town in his Rolls-Royce in a flurry of bad checks. Fittingly, he left behind a lot of disappointment and one broken-hearted lawyer from the Twin Cities, who had believed all too much in Prince Charming.

AEFS was at home in the early 1980s. It fit right in with a nation whose dominant metaphors are opportunity, promise, and hope, whose economy preaches risk, speculation, and reward, and whose technology rests on the premise, "Where there is a will, there is a way."

Evangelical Christianity also proved an important medium for AEFS staff's boosterism of the company and its miracle product. Experiencing a great resurgence in the 1960s and 1970s and emerging into the national limelight during the Reagan presidency, evangelical Christianity provided an enthusiastic faith that was so singularly important for the birth of AEFS. More than anything else, it accounted for the energy and infatuation of its owners, Hendrickson and Dwire, the fervor and salesmanship of such company officers and consultants as the Reverends L. D. Kramer and Jerry Knapper, and the faith of many company employees and Jerusalem artichoke buyers.

In the 1970s and 1980s, evangelical Christian ministries sprang up across the nation. Evangelists took to television; Christian athletes filled campus locker rooms. Jerry Falwell carried on an "I-love-America" campaign. Jimmy Swaggart successfully swaggered, with his ministry's income topping $60 million in 1982. Tammy and Jim Bakker, whom AEFS consultant Kramer and his family knew from earlier days at a Minnesota Assembly of God church, talked their PTL (Praise the Lord) ministry to national renown. Oral Roberts, to whom Fred Hendrickson donated money as AEFS prospered, oversaw the successful expansion of his ministry to the building of a university. Giving a new twist to the argument that belief in God loses one nothing and might gain one heaven, evangelists went further. They asserted that heaven and earth can be won by the same faith. They believed material wealth is God's way of blessing those who put Him first.

Unmistakably, AEFS belonged to the emerging phenomenon of a new kind of direct sales organization, described by Nicole Woolsey Biggart in a recent work as "charismatic capitalism." "In direct selling one can work and serve God and country at the same time. ... Direct selling ... is a quasi-patriotic activity: God and the nation are served by the pursuit of direct sales. In this way the American ethic contributes to a generalized desire to go out into the world and make money."[3]

Christianity, especially in its evangelical and charismatic forms, nicely converges with boosterism and the principles of sales.[4] It identifies faith and confidence with enthused conviction, and it affirms that God will respond to such faith with miracles. Additionally, it defines the church as a community of enthused believers. Without established doctrine, sacraments, and lines of authority, evangelical churches rely on fervent sermons, energizing revelations, conversions, and miracles, all things that have their counterpart in good sales and a good sales team.

When this type of faith is put in the service of business, as it was in the case of AEFS, sales become a matter of enthusiasm. The buyer's decision to buy becomes a test of faith; at stake in every purchase is not the quality of the product but the sincerity of the buyer's faith, which will be rewarded by God. Exemplifying the merging of religious faith and sales, AEFS sold Jerusalem artichokes as if they were a special invitation from God and part of God's promise to save America and its farmers.

The First Convention

Boosterism was the spiritual sinew of AEFS. Dwire and Hendrickson spun the company's corporate philosophy out of American myths and metaphors. This philosophy affirmed, as farmers love to hear, that all wealth comes from the land and that the family farm is America's moral greatness. AEFS supporters dedicated themselves (in the same spirit as Populists a century before) to saving the countryside from the nation's swollen cities and foreign dependence. They asserted that their own calling was "a calling beyond and above commerce." AEFS was not just a company but a "family of believers" who believed in God, America, the family farm, and Jerusalem artichokes.[5]

AEFS's first National Growers Convention in June 1982, in Marshall, Minnesota, revealed the boosterism that underlay the company. The convention was titled "Energy Freedom for the Eighties." More than a thousand AEFS growers, salespeople, and prospective buyers attended the convention.

The convention hosted a variety of lectures, show-and-tell sessions, and small alcohol fuel demonstrations, suggesting how the Jerusalem artichoke would be commercially transformed into fuel and feed. Free hot dogs and lemonade were given out, but the main gratuity was long-winded talks. One South Dakotan, James Fish, recalled, among other things, being moved by one of the presenters who described how she had died and spent time in heaven before returning to this earth. Approvingly, he said the meeting was like a real Bible conference.[6]

Hendrickson offered his vision of the Jerusalem artichoke. Scientists such as Wayne Dorband and L. T. Fan spoke about present research, fructose production, and agronomic practices pertaining to the crop, while Dr. B. B. Chubey, head of the horticultural science and new crops section at the Canadian government's Morden, Manitoba, research station cautioned that recent interest in Jerusalem artichokes may be outpacing research.[7] Others addressed more applied concerns. For example, Dr. Wendell Peden, a friend of Hendrickson's, spoke of the Jerusalem artichoke as animal feed; Lyle Kilthau, a large grower, entrepreneur, and AEFS seed supplier from the state of Washington, discussed planting and harvesting; Rodger Seratt, an author and an active promoter of alcohol fuel, discussed the conversion of vehicles and alcohol plants; and Robert Soleta, a real estate dealer and a member of the National Gasoline Commission, spoke about alcohol and alternative fuels. Bonnie Laidlaw, a friend of Kramer's, introduced the future believers to her cookbook, *Jerusalem Artichoke for all Seasons*.

The three-day program contained a variety of motivational speakers. Evangelical minister Jerry Knapper, Dwire's brother-in-law, struck AEFS's main pitch in a talk called, "Straight to the Top with a Brand New Crop." After talking about his "calling to the crop," he suggested that the Jerusalem artichoke was potentially a new soybean or sugar beet. Don Sheenan, a member of AEFS's sales staff and author of a pamphlet called "Shut Up and Sell," spoke about motivation. He started his talk claiming that "He [the Lord] had never denied me one thing in my life." He suggested that "sales was the key to the 1980s" and concluded with a novel appeal to the Holy Spirit: "Anoint me with artichokes and set me on fire."

Kramer, who played such an important role in AEFS, gave a motivational speech in the spirit of his ministry's motto, "Dedicated to Serve God and Man." Using his favorite rhetorical devices, he introduced himself by elucidating the anagram EVANGELIST: "E = Energetic, V = Vibrant, A = Anointed, N = Notable, G = Great, E = Electrifying, L = Lively, I = Innovative, S = Sensational, and T = Terrific." After explaining how we all like and need money, and how effectively Mary Kay Cosmetics has used the gift of a Cadillac to reward its successful sales personnel, he spelled out the anagram MONEY: M means God is for me; I must live in his plan. O stands for the opportunity provided to me by the Jerusalem artichoke. N expresses the necessity of surrendering ourselves to God. E equals the energy within you. It is greater than all OPEC's power and it will serve your God, nation, and generation. Y is for you, the one who must apply his faith. The message was clear: Trust God, buy Jerusalem artichokes, and become rich.

AEFS convention planners did not forget the farmers' wives. Mary Jo Clark, a counselor and instructor at Trinity Bible College in Ellendale, North Dakota, preached being gentle and non-blaming, cheerful and supportive. Esther Zink, also from Trinity Bible College, offered a similar message in her two sessions at the convention. She spelled out "the ideal wife's duties": accept your husband, don't compete with him, praise him, and make him your hero.

Another evangelically inspired presenter was Betty Maiz, author of *My Glimpse of Eternity* and *Prayers That Are Answered*. She also appeared regularly on PTL and the 700 Club. Donna Fargo, a well-known gospel melodist who was to be the convention's main evening attraction, didn't show.

The convention connected Jerusalem artichokes with myths of good country living and full-gospel sincerity. It was a revival meeting of a sort.

Cal Maxwell, a farm machinery salesman from nearby Montevideo, Minnesota, underwent a conversion at the convention. Cal described his conversion: "I almost feel like a fellow who has fallen out of an eighteen story building and hit the sidewalk. After working with agricultural machinery for twenty-four years and observing the recent farm situation," Maxwell explained, "I became convinced that somebody has to do something for farming.... Stranded in Marshall in January, I visited AEFS headquarters, and I was excited to see that something was happening (people were coming from all over the United States, and there were people who either had been researching the artichoke ... or were interested in processing the crop), and I just wanted to be part of it." Maxwell continued, "I went home and I told my wife 'I think that it is going to be an important factor for the American farmer.'"

Although his wife was skeptical, he finally convinced her to go to the first national convention where she saw all of the people there who were growing Jerusalem artichokes. "I thought to myself, 'Lord, if you really want me to make this change help to change my wife's attitude,' " Maxwell said. During the convention that change of heart occurred: "I saw her willing *to risk the go.* . . . My wife kept saying, 'Somebody has to do something for the farmer now. You've got the opportunity.' " With his wife on board, Maxwell culminated his own conversion: "I made that decision . . . and I have real peace of heart."[8]

The Pitch

Euphoria grew as money rolled in. "When a million dollars would come across the desk," said Jerry Knapper, "the only one you would hear say anything is Fred and he would say, 'We don't have to worry about anything now.' "[9] As initial successes grew, Hendrickson extended his megalomaniacal drawing of circles and hexagons to enweb—at least on paper—nearly the whole nation in AEFS's sales network, while Dwire rushed across the nation in one of the nine planes he bought and piloted to make Fred's dream a reality.[10]

In his annual progress report in 1982, Hendrickson expressed his grandiose vision. He called for a Marshall Plan for American agriculture. In ten years it would result in a hundred million acres of Jerusalem artichokes. (Of these acres, Hendrickson estimated, a million acres would be edible food; 10 million acres each would be used for fructose sugar source, flour, livestock feed for domestic purposes, and livestock feed for export purposes; 30 million acres would be used for fuel and industrial feedstock; and another 30 million acres would be exported for edible food purposes.) Tying his plan to a projected growth in world population of two billion people in the next twenty years, Hendrickson claimed that the "Jerusalem artichoke could be the crop that supplements existing worldwide acreages of corn, wheat, rice, potatoes, etc."[11]

AEFS "Corporate Philosophy" (formulated under that name) bore the mark of Hendrickson's colossal vision. First, the Jerusalem artichoke would help achieve long-sought-after parity—an equality of exchange between agricultural and industrial goods. In addition, "it would help farm families, through research, organizational and legal aids, provide the technical guidance whereby farm families can organize, build, and operate and manage their own biomass-to-energy processing plants and marketing system." Committed to a vision of "a nationwide system of small farmer-owned-and-operated biomass conversion and marketing facilities," AEFS would help "stabilize the farm families," "establish new hometown industries," "reduce population pressures on congested cities," "eliminate tax-paid farm price supports," "eliminate so-called crop surpluses," and "encourage full production, agriculturally and industrially." Moreover, this cure-all magic plant and its advocate, AEFS, would not only help reduce the national debt but also would secure a national food and fuel reserve.

AEFS offered the buyer of Jerusalem artichokes a chance not just to make a profit but also to enroll himself in a "spiritual" family, a veritable movement, a kind of church. Buyer and grower alike, the pitch ran, were joined together in a project pleasing to self, nation, and God (see figure 1).

AEFS used other promises to attract growers. Its salesmen commonly used the specific promise of an escrow account to make AEFS seem as much an investment as a purchase. They promised that for every dollar spent on seed, fifty cents would be kept back so the company would have the resources to buy growers' seed. (The promise of an escrow account is not uncommon in a seed development project, but it also can be a useful artifice in a sales scheme, as it was in three recent midwestern scams involving in one case mushrooms, in another worms, and in a third case, mold for cosmetics.)

Integral to AEFS's pitch was the notion that growers were at the forefront of an important but risky undertaking; if it worked out, they would receive the generous reward they deserved. This sales principle of well-rewarded risk is identified in scams such as the "Spanish-prisoner scheme," whose come on is "Give us a little money now, and you'll get a lot of money later."[12]

Like any good pitch, AEFS's pitch had many tones and variations. It could appeal to the buyer's sense of urgency, greed, or altruism; his wish to grow the crop; or even a desire to become a

Figure 1. One of the many marketing and sales brochures developed by Dwire and Hendrickson.

7 complete reasons to grow Jerusalem Artichokes

Join others who are becoming energy conscious by planting Jerusalem artichokes.

1. America's number 1 alcohol fuel and fructose sugar crop!

The Jerusalem artichoke is a high sugar crop. The sugar, fructose, is an edible sugar and can be converted into ethanol or N-butanol alcohol. Each ton of plant matter at 16 percent fresh weight yields 22 gallons of 200 proof alcohol (ethanol). The Jerusalem artichoke *will* lead America's farmers into the age of self-sufficient energy farming!

2. High protein livestock crop!

The Jerusalem artichoke, a versatile crop, offers forage value with up to 17 percent protein, dry weight. The protein is high in amino acids, especially lysine. TDN value is high with a feed value comparable to early bloom alfalfa. The total plant is high in essential nutrients. Cattle, dairy cows, horses sheep, poultry and pigs all like the Jerusalem artichoke.

3. Easy to grow!

The Jerusalem artichoke grows from a seed tuber, like the potato. One pound of tubers can be cut into 16 to 20 pieces. One thousand pounds of seedstock tubers yields between 10,000 and 14,000 plants per acre.

The seed tuber allows the plant an early start over weeds and grasses. The crop is frost resistant in the spring and reported to survive drought periods. The tubers form in August and develop through late September and October. The crop matures in about 105 days and can grow into the late fall, resisting frost.

4. A "double portion" crop!

Plant growth above ground is matched by underground growth. This "double portion" growth distinguishes the Jerusalem artichoke from most other sugar and protein crops. Total per plant yields are between 4 to 8 pounds of tops, 3 to 6 pounds of tubers and 1 to 2 pounds of roots.

5. Tubers are winter hardy!

Tubers can be harvested in the fall or left in the ground for winter storage and spring harvest. Tops, roots and tubers can be stored as harvested or can be dried or dehydrated. Harvest time and storage techniques will vary, depending on the plants' use as FUEL, FOOD or FEED.

6. "Goodbye" to expensive fertilizer, herbicides and insecticides!

The Jerusalem artichoke, member of the sunflower family, takes only a small percentage of its required nutrients from the soil. Ninety percent of its growth comes from air, sunshine and water. With proper cultivation practices, repeat crops can be grown on the same fields without exhausting soil nutrients. The plant is not affected by insects and is resistant to disease. No herbicides are necessary because the plant acts as a weed eradicator by crowding out weeds and grasses.

7. The number for completion!

Growers only need to purchase the tuber seedstock one time. From the initial crop, farmers will have an abundance of seed tubers for acreage expansion. Since some tubers always remain in the ground at harvest time, next year's seed crop is already planted. WHAT A PERFECT WAY TO COMPLETE A CROP SEASON!

© 1982 America Energy Farming Systems, Inc.

The Jerusalem Artichoke

The Jerusalem artichoke (*Helianthus tuberosus*) is not from Jerusalem and it is not an artichoke. What is it? It is one of 90 species of sunflowers (*Helianthus*) that grow worldwide. However, this species of sunflower has agricultural and nutritional characteristics, which make it the most versatile of the sunflowers.

America's original export

The Jerusalem artichoke is native to the central regions of North America. Like the common sunflower (*Helianthus annus*), the artichoke was used as food by several North American Indian tribes prior to the arrival of European settlers.

The Jerusalem artichoke found its way to France from North America with the explorer Champlain as early as 1605. A young lawyer, Marc Lescarbot, who returned with Champlain is credited with establishing the artichoke in France. Soon after Lescarbot's introduction, the plant became widely accepted as a human and livestock food and by the mid 1600's, the artichoke's usage spread throughout Europe and England. In contrast to Europe, the artichoke was not cultivated in the United States during the 1600's.

Naming the Jerusalem Artichoke

In France and a few European countries, the artichoke is called *topinambour*. It is believed that French merchants appropriated the name "topinambour" to capitalize on the advertising value of six Brazilian natives, who came to Paris in the early 1600's and became popular with the French aristocracy.

The name "Jerusalem artichoke" (*Helianthus tuberosus*) has numerous explanations. The "*artichoke*" part of the name is simple; early explorers thought the tubers' taste resembled that of the Globe artichoke.

There are three plausible explanations for the name "*Jerusalem.*" One of the accepted theories is that Jerusalem is an Americanized twisting of the Italian word for sunflowers, girasol.

Another is that the popular 17th century European gardener Petrus Hondius of Ter-Neusen, Holland, distributed his garden grown tubers throughout Europe as "artichoke-apples of Ter-Neusen." This name followed the plant back to England and then to the United States where Ter-Neusen was modified to Jerusalem, a name having more meaning.

The third explanation is that North American pilgrims, who ate the artichoke along with corn as a staple, thought of their new home as a "New Jerusalem." Since the artichoke was a new food in a new land, the name Jerusalem was fitting. The Jerusalem artichoke was one of the foods eaten at the first Thanksgiving feast.

The 20th century artichoke

Jerusalem artichoke cultivation as a crop in Europe has increased steadily since its introduction. Currently there are over one million acres in production in France and probably as much as ten million acres in the Soviet Union. Jerusalem artichokes are cultivated worldwide from the tropical rainforests of the Philippines to the cold, unpredictable steppe region of Russia.

In the United States the native Jerusalem artichoke has been almost totally ignored by the farmer. Optimistic estimates place the total United States acreage at less than 1,000 acres. Interest in the plant did occur during the depression days of the 1930's. Dr. William Hale, a consultant for Dow Chemical Company in the 1930's, stated in his prophetic book *Prosperity Beckons* (1936):

"The Jerusalem artichoke will undoubtedly become our greatest crop as far as widest distribution and acreage is concerned. It will afford us our main supply of levlose, which is to be our principle sugar (sweeter than dextrose and sucrose) and, of course, will lead directly into that greatest of all activities, the alcohol industry . . . our fermentation industries in supply of agricultural alcohol will require the cultivation of at least 100 million acres of land within 20 years."

This statement reflects the goals of America Energy Farming Systems, Inc. who has recently renewed the interest in Jerusalem artichoke cultivation.

America Energy Farming System's cultivation program

America Energy Farming Systems, Inc. has chosen the Jerusalem artichoke, after exhaustive research, as the energy crop for the American prairies. America Energy Farming Systems, Inc. has developed a major cultivation program to establish the versatile Jerusalem artichoke for the North American farmer.

America Energy Farming Systems, Inc. is dedicated to the philosophy of establishing economic independence and energy self-sufficiency for the American farmer. The company feels that dependence on petroleum resources for gas, diesel fuel and fertilizer, as well as chemical based pesticides and herbicides is destroying the independence of the American family farm system. During the 1980's the energy farming industry beckons as a new era for the *survival* of the American family farmer.

Jerusalem Artichokes...

the fuel, food and feed crop bringing farming and research together

AMERICA ENERGY FARMING SYSTEMS, INC. (AEFS) is the nation's leading agri-business company in the development of the Jerusalem artichoke as a multi-purpose farm crop. A service oriented corporation, AEFS is assisting farmers in growing and processing this versatile high sugar and protein plant. AEFS is dedicated to making self-sufficient energy farming a reality throughout rural America.

MARSHALL, MINNESOTA is America Energy Farming Systems, Inc.'s national headquarters and business office. AEFS's marketing program is centered in Minnesota, Wisconsin, Iowa, Nebraska, North and South Dakota. Jerusalem artichoke marketing is now expanding nationwide and to Canada.

THE GOALS AND OBJECTIVES of America Energy Farming Systems, Inc. are to establish:

- ten million acres of Jerusalem artichokes in five years and at least thirty million acres in five to seven years and
- thousands of decentralized fuel, food and feed processing plants in rural areas.

Through these goals and objectives, the co-founders of America Energy Farming Systems, Inc. will show America's farmers how to:

- become energy self-sufficient through alcohol fuels and
- grow a crop that will bring them new wealth and economic independence.

Through such a program thousands of new employment and business opportunities will be created throughout North America and Canada.

SIOUX FALLS, SOUTH DAKOTA is the location of America Energy Farming System's research and development office. Through contracts with Aquanalysis, Inc. of Sioux Falls, AEFS is conducting research on the Jerusalem artichoke's:

- agronomic development;
- food crop potential centered around its levulose sugar quality and protein value;
- high yielding livestock feed value; and
- use as an alcohol (ethanol and butanol) for vehicle fuel and in industrial applications such as plastic, manmade fiber and pharmaceutical manufacturing.

DR. WAYNE DORBAND OF AQUANALYSIS, INC. is one of the foremost Jerusalem artichoke research scientists. Aquanalysis, Inc. is conducting private research to assist Jerusalem artichoke growers in farming techniques and in the development of its use as a fuel, food and feed crop. Dr. Dorband has established a program of information exchange with universities, industry and individuals who are researching the potential of the Jerusalem artichoke.

DR. L. T. FAN, head of the Chemical Engineering Department of Kansas State University, has worked extensively with the Jerusalem artichoke for 10 years. America Energy Farming Systems, Inc. has retained Dr. Fan as a consultant to conduct research on fructose sugar and butanol alcohol production from the Jerusalem artichoke. Kansas State University is nationally recognized as a leader in biomass energy and agri-business development.

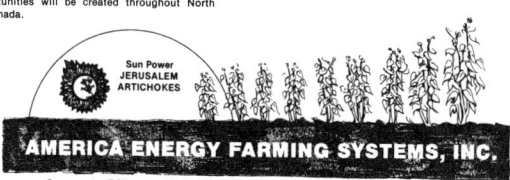

Corporate Offices: P. O. Box 176, Marshall, MN 56258   507/865-4488
Research & Development Office: 1416 South Kiwanis Avenue, Sioux Falls, SD 57105   605/335-6374
© 1982 America Energy Farming Systems, Inc.

salesman. Some AEFS sales staff preferred heaping on "hard numbers" about yields and returns, while others set prospective growers' imaginations awhirl with the Jerusalem artichoke's promise to be the new soybean, the most recent crop in memory to transform, even save, midwestern agriculture. Yet others gushed with spirituality.

One common AEFS sales line was the "train-is-leaving" pitch, which was inseparable from the buying hysteria that surrounded the plant. In the spring of 1982, vice president of sales Jerry Knapper informed the press, "This thing is going like wild fire," as he pointed out that in less than a year the company had hired forty full-time sales staff and three hundred to four hundred part-time staff.[13]

Some AEFS advertisement was puffery of a high order. One of its more notable ads had French farmers growing more acres of Jerusalem artichokes than there were acres in France, when, in fact, there were fewer than 20,000 acres of Jerusalem artichokes under cultivation in France at the time.[14] Other ads repeatedly suggested that industrial uses of the Jerusalem artichoke for sugar and fuel were imminent, when the opposite was true.

Some AEFS sales techniques appeared to be deliberate deception. For instance, one regional sales representative encouraged his salesmen to take along on sales trips such Jerusalem artichoke products as spaghetti, pellets, and jars of alcohol and fructose (in crystal form). The intended implication: The jars contained products made from Jerusalem artichokes, which they were not.[15]

Attorneys general from several states contended that AEFS falsely pitched the Jerusalem artichoke when it claimed the plant was drought-resistant, disease-free, and in need of no more fertilizer than potatoes. They further charged that AEFS falsely suggested that, since the Jerusalem artichoke was a perennial, it did not need future seeding and that it was easy to harvest. These claims, the attorneys general contended, suppressed the fact that the cost of seeding could run as high as $300 an acre, and harvesting, especially in muddy fields, could prove to be a nightmare, a nightmare made all the worse by the difficult tasks of cleaning, sorting, and storing the irregular-shaped, easily damaged, and highly perishable Jerusalem artichoke tubers.

Additionally, AEFS's sales literature failed to inform growers of many important facts, such as that there are many varieties of Jerusalem artichokes and that tremendous amounts of research were needed before it would be possible to identify the best varieties of the plant for different agronomic conditions. In addition, there was not a single alcohol processing plant in the nation prepared to extract fuel or sugar from the Jerusalem artichokes.

Also, according to the Minnesota attorney general's office and other attorneys general's offices, AEFS's standard mathematical pitch was patently false. AEFS contended that it takes a thousand pounds of seed tubers (at a dollar a pound) to seed an acre, but each acre yields, they most exaggeratedly claimed, forty-five to sixty-five tons of tubers. On this basis, conservative estimates would lead a grower to believe that ten acres (the average acreage of growers) would net nearly half a million dollars a year. If AEFS attained its goals, which included selling 20 million acres of Jerusalem artichokes in the next five to seven years, phenomenal growth and profits lay ahead. For instance, according to the AEFS publication, *Record*, the nearly five hundred artichoke growers who had contracts for the first three years with AEFS and who were located in the six-state area of North and South Dakota, Minnesota, Iowa, Nebraska, and Wisconsin, would produce (at a 30 to 1 ratio) by 1984 enough seeds to supply the seed needs of 450,000 additional farmers, more than double the total number of farmers in North and South Dakota and Minnesota combined.[16] If these 450,000 additional farmers grew seed tubers in similar amounts, North America itself would be inundated by seeds. A euphoric and megalomaniacal vision of the Jerusalem artichoke's future kept AEFS's phones ringing off their hooks throughout 1982.

To take advantage of this "wonderful offer," which allowed farmers to make more than $40,000 an acre, they needed only to accept AEFS's standard three-year agreement. The grower, the pitch ran, would buy seed for ten acres for $12,000 — which was calculated at 1,000 pounds of seed per acre at the cost of $1.20 a pound. For its part, AEFS would become the grower's exclusive marketing agent for the following three years. AEFS would receive a marketing developer fee of 50 percent of all gross sales of the seed tubers harvested in the fall of 1982 and the spring of 1983 and a 40 percent fee on all crops grown for the following two harvests. In addition to promising the development of machinery to harvest the artichokes and furnish custom planting, AEFS promised to make its "best efforts to market the grower's crop . . . to develop a program of research on improved strains . . . and of use of [the crop] as an alcohol-fuel crop, a fructose sugar crop, an edible plant for humans and a livestock and poultry feed."[17]

While many fish jumped right into the boat, AEFS used whole tackle boxes of lures to catch others. AEFS used quasi-institutional ads to convince the growers that it had significant research under way to unleash the potential of the crop and to establish its best varieties. It invited its growers to participate in the agronomic study of the crop. AEFS tried to make the growers believe they were joining a family: AEFS celebrated growers' birthdays and anniversaries. It sponsored contests for the tallest plant and the best school speeches on the artichoke as a future crop. It solicited recipes from growers' wives and involved them in trading Jerusalem artichoke recipes, an experience AEFS promoters shamelessly labeled "Breaking Loose." AEFS supplied growers with a chance to win recipe books, to obtain free samples of pelletized Jerusalem artichokes and Jerusalem artichoke flour, as well as to purchase Jerusalem artichoke T-shirts and Jerusalem artichoke buttons, one of which announced "Jerusalem Artichokes could keep you in farming." In Minnesota, AEFS drove a large bus from farm to farm to sell Jerusalem artichokes and it used an alcohol fueled car for the same purpose.

AEFS issued numerous publications. Most noticeable was *Freedom News*, which was under the editorship of Larry Gauthier and was headlined with such AEFS standbys as "Farm Alcohol Is the Road to Independence" and "Save the Family Farm, Grow Jerusalem Artichokes." A September 1982 issue carried the headlines, "Dr. Fan Predicts Major Role in Growing Fructose Industry," "Ford's 'Better Idea' [alcohol fuel] Finds Home in Brazil," and "Chokes Beat the Hail." A special edition in the spring of 1983 was headlined "Artichoke Market Development Takes Big Steps." The front-page photograph featured Dwire, Hendrickson, and three visiting Yugoslav dignitaries interested in alternative energy smoking "an authentic peace pipe" from the nearby Pipestone National Monument. It also featured an article on "The French Connection," which argued that the Jerusalem artichoke (the glorious *topinambour*), once a delicacy for royal buffets in Europe, had become distasteful to the French since World War II when, according to AEFS's new head of research, Richard Spencer, "they were forced to eat Jerusalem artichokes when the Germans took all of the potatoes." While the French supposedly showed superior scientific research and significant industrial concern for butanol from artichokes and fodder beets, Spencer candidly acknowledged that the number of acres currently under cultivation in France were not at all near the number originally identified by AEFS.[18]

AEFS's bimonthly *Communicator* mixed "Historic Events," such as Al Rusk's boostering announcement that "the fermentation of the hydrolyzed mash far exceeded any of our wildest predictions" and Andy Van Zee's announcement that his Jerusalem artichoke fields formed a "gusher," with run-of-the-mill matters on tests of the crop, equipment news, and lists of field coordinators, plus Jerusalem artichoke recipes for pie, cookies, chocolate cake, and stew.[19]

Beyond its standard publications, AEFS issued numerous special publications, took out ads, and put out special press releases. These materials promoted successful growers and the scientific uses of the plant and called attention to what AEFS took to be a mounting industrial interest in the plant. One promotional used by AEFS showed the tops of the plant being utilized for mulch and fertilizer, feed, silage, and bales, while its tubers provided food (raw, cooked, canned, and pickled), sugars (fructose), fuel (ethanol and butanol), feed (pellets, silage, feed whole), and flour (bread, pastries, and noodles). Predictably, AEFS literature called growers to the high road of freedom from foreign dependence. It challenged them to take a risk. "Risk," one AEFS flyer quoted Samuel Adams, "is the price you pay for opportunity."

Those Who Sold

It fell to Jerry Knapper, more than anyone else, to formulate AEFS's first sales program. After a brief stint as a salesman for the company in the fall of 1981, Knapper was appointed to serve as national sales director from December 1981 until July 1982, when he was "kicked upstairs" to become a director of public relations.

Knapper was typical of the salesmen and top personnel hired by AEFS. He lived in the nearby small town of Maynard, Minnesota, and was hired because he was a good salesman, he was Dwire's brother-in-law, he was interested in alternative energy, and he needed work. He also fit the religious motif of AEFS. A self-educated clergyman, Knapper was an ordained minister of the Evangelical Church of Lions. His preference was for an evangelical Christianity in which personal prayers were answered by miracles.

Like the majority of AEFS employees, Knapper came to the company in need of work. The gods of economic opportunity had not smiled kindly on him in the past. His employment record included a stint as a motorcycle repairman, owner of a small music store in Montevideo, work for a Bible institute in Missouri, and operator of a computer dealership in Grove City, Minnesota. For years before coming to AEFS he served as a pastor of a small Baptist church in Maynard. In addition to preaching, which by his own admission didn't support him and his family, he was always selling things, including pots and pans, at night.

Knapper believed God had led him to AEFS. "One day," Knapper wrote, describing his circumstances when he received his calling to AEFS, "I was coming back from the Lac Qui Parle County Fair and I just started to ask the Lord, how can you help me succeed so I can provide for my family? I didn't realize it at the time, but over in Marshall, Minnesota, there was a fellow [Jim Dwire] praying also. He was saying how can I get these artichokes sold."[20]

The next day Dwire called Knapper and invited him to supper. Providence had joined them. The purchase of a $127,000 house, with new carpeting and furniture, which he acquired soon after joining AEFS thanks to a good salary and commissions, no doubt confirmed his faith in the providential character of his calling.

Like the great majority of employees who came to AEFS, Knapper had neither significant business experience nor any scientific training in agronomy. What he lacked in experience and education, however, he made up in enthusiasm. He sold as much as 670 acres, netting himself $67,000 in commissions. While speaking to his salesmen, he made himself a motivator. He preached the necessity of unquestioning faith in oneself and one's product as the key to successful sales.

In one of his motivational sales talks, Knapper offered the story of how, on his way to visit a prospective buyer, he was seized by doubts. He pulled his car onto the shoulder of the road and prayed to the Lord for unquestioning faith, for he knew every percent of missing faith would result in a corresponding loss in his commission. He deduced from this experience the truth that "Selling is transferring your beliefs into [your buyers'] minds."[21]

Such faith allowed Knapper then and at other times to profess the most wondrous things about the Jerusalem artichoke. In his presentation at the first annual AEFS convention, called "Straight to the Top with a New Crop," he forecasted that Jerusalem artichokes could become a 30 million acre crop. He believed the potential of the Jerusalem artichoke to be greater than that of soybeans or sugar beets, and he suggested that farmers could expect immediate returns from Jerusalem artichokes of $6,000 per acre until it settled down to the wonderfully high return of $1,000 or $2,000 per acre. (At this time, a soybean or corn farmer would have profoundly welcomed $100 per acre profit.)

To the doubting Thomases, Knapper promised, as did his salesmen, that half of their money would be held in a separate account. The promise of an "escrow account," which was used against AEFS defendants in subsequent criminal prosecution, allowed Knapper and his salesmen to assure growers that AEFS itself would—and did—have the means to do research, find markets, and buy growers' future crops.[22]

Ron Mann, who took over the job of training salesmen in the summer of 1982, represented another type of employee who served in AEFS sales. Before coming to AEFS, he had taught shop at Marshall High School for two years prior to his job as a training administrator in an electronics company in nearby Redwood Falls. He was recommended to AEFS by one of Dwire's sons. Mann brought to AEFS his interest in alcohol, mechanical-industrial knowledge and, according to Mann himself, "an ability to organize training sessions around doable tasks."[23] Mann—who was paid approximately $25,000 a year—quickly met his assignment by setting up a two-day sales program that explained the scientific aspects of the plant, indoctrinated the sales representatives with motivational skills, and provided technical information on the forms, contracts, and communications of the company. Himself a believer in the Jerusalem artichoke, Mann shared the dream of a nation run on alcohol and bought his own ten acres of Jerusalem artichokes.

Mann believed "AEFS had a tiger by the tail."[24] He explained that the pilots of AEFS's fleet of small planes were often worn out from flying all over the nation to bring a parade of prospective buyers to the firm's headquarters. On their descent to Marshall, he noted, some visitors were deceptively shown the large Marshall corn processing plant as belonging to AEFS. Once on the ground, the visitors were given a tour of AEFS's main sales building and its displays, company headquarters, Dwire's fields of artichokes at nearby Lynd and, on occasion, a local alcohol plant that AEFS was negotiating to purchase. At the end of the tour, after giving prospective growers a chance to sign on the dotted line, AEFS provided them with a smorgasbord of fresh artichoke foods before their return trip home. This last snack occasioned many a sly smile on AEFS employees' faces. They knew their "windy fruit's" power would exert itself before the prospective buyers completed their flight home.

Mann was not entirely uncritical of AEFS's activities and management. He saw the company under great pressure. He, like others, saw Dwire as power hungry, commenting that Dwire had a near constant "need for a whipping boy." Above all else, he said that he and his sales staff were concerned by the paucity of scientific materials they were given. "We were constantly begging for data . . . for scientific research," he noted.[25]

He described the men he trained in groups of ten and twenty at a time to be an odd lot. Aside from the growers themselves, the majority of prospective salesmen were unemployed or underemployed. They came knowing nothing, or next to nothing, about the crop. Some came to this program having sold other products, especially agricultural crops. At one sales-training seminar held in Marshall in September 1982, there were in attendance a fertilizer salesman from Winona, Minnesota; two growers from St. Paul who together owned thirty acres of Jerusalem artichokes; another grower from Beltrami County, Minnesota, with thirty-six acres of artichokes; a sales representative from a North Dakota company that sold alcohol stills; a former Braniff pilot from Missouri; a vocationally unidentified individual from Texas; and a crop duster from Kansas.[26]

A few men in his classes, Mann recalled, were "true believers" who knew little of the crop except that it was a God-given and Christ-appointed savior of the nation. None of the salesmen Mann trained became employees of the company. They were retained as independent contractors who sold on commission—making 5 percent on their first sales and 10 percent on subsequent sales. Having earned fifty dollars a day for two days of training, the majority of prospective independent salesmen returned home never to sell a single acre of artichokes. (According to the bankruptcy court's estimate, independent sales representatives accounted for only one-sixth of the company's total sales. Their commissions equaled only $336,000 of approximately $1,736,000 in total commissions.[27])

Belatedly, in February 1983, AEFS sought to articulate a rational, national sales program. They identified regional managers and state managers. In addition to standard commissions on their own sales, regional managers were to receive two thousand dollars a month and a half percent of the gross sales in their region; marketing agents were to be paid at the rate of one and one-half percent of gross receipts. This national scheme was never implemented. The selling of Jerusalem artichokes was never put on a schematic or rational basis. Just as the crop lacked a science, so too did the AEFS sales plan lack order.

There also was an absence of discipline in the ranks of their salesmen. Although cautioned against interjecting religion into their sales pitch, many AEFS salesmen did so anyhow. They couldn't quite help themselves, explained AEFS' most successful salesman, Gregg Bittner, who wrote the Minnesota attorney general saying, "I believe the Lord brought this crop to the farmer for a reason." Bittner did confess, however, that Fred's literature, "which was too bad to get out," did get out.[28]

Bittner was typical of AEFS in other ways too. As Knapper's son-in-law, he exemplified a kind of nepotism that characterized much of the company. Suggesting the strong company connection between images and sales, Bittner, who originally had worked with video materials, moved to sales, taking over for Don Sheenan as motivational trainer. Bittner, a shining light at sales, also revealed how quickly one could make money at AEFS: He made more than $100,000 in commissions.[29]

Grow 'em and Sell 'em

AEFS was aware that its first buyer-growers would prove to be its best salesmen. The company put this common sense insight into effect. It not only offered the growers 50 percent for AEFS's pooled sale of their crops, but also offered them an additional 15 percent for all completed sales they made from their own fields. This 15 percent surpassed the commission offered company salesmen themselves.[30] In the country restaurant world, where future growers penciled big numbers on little napkins, 15 percent meant that the grower-sellers would make an additional $3,600 over the standard contract. This contract provided for the sale of ten acres of artichoke seed tubers at a thousand pounds an acre for $1.20 per pound; it meant, with just a little more figuring, that three standard sales would pay for their contracts and still leave them with thirty thousand pounds of Jerusalem artichoke seed left for future sales. Other sorts of special deals also were common inside and outside the company as growers and company employees shared among themselves, and with others, common acres and split contracts, traded planting and harvesting services, and paid in future seed.

Illustratively, in his bankruptcy deposition, Hendrickson clarified AEFS's relationship with its outstanding grower-salesman, Andy Van Zee, a South Dakota farmer. Van Zee was a first-year grower who had planted forty-three acres of Jerusalem artichokes (at the cost of $43,000) on marginal lands. According to Hendrickson, AEFS agreed to pay Van Zee his 50 percent, plus a 10 percent commission if he brought in more than one hundred thousand dollars, and if he would be responsible for the delivery of the seed tubers. This Van Zee did, and a lot more. After some tough wrangling, he got two AEFS checks totaling at least $500,000.[31] With much fanfare, Van Zee received the checks at the first National Growers Convention, and he gladly allowed himself to be featured in AEFS's *Freedom News* under the headline, "I never had a million dollar crop before" (see figure 2).[32]

Figure 2. *Left to right:* James Dwire, Fred Hendrickson, and Andy Van Zee, who received a check for approximately $500,000 at the first convention

A handful of growers envisioned great profits to be made by supplying AEFS itself with its seed. Two such growers were Les Van Dyke and Ben Steensma of Chandler, Minnesota. They jumped in after considerable initial hesitation arising from their belief that anything with which Dwire was associated wouldn't be on "the up and up." "We went full hog," Steensma said.[33] He explained that Dwire had really found religion and that the company would keep its promise to limit first-year sales to approximately 1,800 acres. (This promise to Steensma meant there would be a maximum of 180 growers, instead of the actual 540 original first-year growers there turned out to be.)

Van Dyke, Steensma, and Van Dyke's brother Larry, along with Steensma's brother, Fred, and his brother-in-law Wendell VanderBroeck, a banker in Chandler, formed a five-person partnership. They purchased eighty acres of seed for $76,000; their intentions included selling their seed not only to future growers but to AEFS itself. According to Steensma, they put up another $88,000 for two harvesters and more than $10,000 for other equipment that they used to haul, plant, and harvest seed for AEFS—seed for which they were never paid.[34] Proving their full commitment to the dream of a new source of energy for the American countryside, Steensma, Van Dyke, and their partners purchased, in association with AEFS, a $100,000 alcohol-corn processing plant in Sherman, South Dakota, which ended up costing them another $50,000 for a tangled court affair in which they were charged with false representation. Even after AEFS filed bankruptcy, Steensma contended, they continued to harvest, clean, and deliver for AEFS Jerusalem artichoke seed tubers worth an alleged $850,000, for which they received no compensation.[35]

The Buyers

There was no mystery about who bought the Jerusalem artichoke seed. Other than company officials and employees who speculated in the seed in a variety of ingenious ways, the approximately 2,500 growers can be divided into seven types.[36] Of course, any one grower might fit one, two, or even three of the following classifications.

First, there were those who believed in the Jerusalem artichoke. Numbered among this group were Hendrickson's associates in South Dakota and believers in renewable energy, farm self-sufficiency, alcohol fuel and American energy independence. Growers of this sort constituted a significant majority of the 450 three-year growers who bought Jerusalem artichokes the first year.

Second, there was a small and early group of growers who saw this as an excellent chance to get in on the ground floor of a lucrative venture. This category included farmers and small rural businessmen.

Third, there was a group of farmers who believed in new crops, and inspired by what the soybean had meant for midwestern agriculture, judged twelve thousand dollars to be a small risk when weighed against great possible gains and the fact that they could take any expenses and losses as tax deductions.

Fourth, there were many farmers for whom Jerusalem artichokes represented their last gamble. They were small farmers, not well established on the land, and usually not members of successful, conservative, ethnic farming communities. A handful of those taking their last roll were by all measures bad credit risks.

Fifth, there were those who bought Jerusalem artichokes lest they miss a good deal. The power of "me-too-ism," which should never be underestimated even in normal times and in suspicious rural communities, was radically operative throughout AEFS's history.

Sixth, there were individual religious believers and communities of religious believers. In addition to a rush of charismatic Christians who joined the company in the spring of 1982, there was a community of Hutterites in South Dakota, a community of Amish in Pennsylvania, a community of Catholics in North Dakota, and a community of Mennonites in Kansas who bought Jerusalem artichoke seed. There were also individual believers like Hubert Bietz of Mitchell, South Dakota, who planted thirteen acres and expected to net fifteen to twenty thousand dollars an acre and wrote, "We know the beautiful artichoke is here to stay because I believe God wants it so."[37]

Many of these religious believers stuck with the crop and with the company to the end. Reacting to the legal investigation of AEFS's sales claims for the Jerusalem artichoke, one such believer, Thomas Sanger of Mankato, Minnesota, wrote to Jerry Knapper that the Jerusalem artichoke was an answer to a prayer and AEFS itself was an agent of God's providence. "[At a prayer meeting] a woman in attendance visioned 'lots of sprouts coming out of seeds all over. These seeds are in a field planted solidly in rows and these rows are reaching down.' My wife and I simultaneously looked at each other and said, 'Jerusalem artichokes.' I experienced such a peace and joy that I actually cried with joy. Praise the Lord. . . . [God] purposely chose what the world considers nonsense in order to shame the wise and he chose what the world considers weak in order to shame the powerful. . . . [W]hat no one ever saw or heard, what no one ever thought could happen, is the very thing God prepared for those who love him. Whoever wants to boast must boast of what the Lord has done." Showing that his faith was not entirely innocent he added, "I also have some thoughts and ideas about forming a co-op or an association that would remove the concept of us being a 'pyramid type selling scheme.' "[38]

Finally, there was a small group of speculators whose single and unadulterated interest in the Jerusalem artichoke was cash. This small group, which probably numbered less than a couple dozen, was mostly composed of nonfarmers and even company employees. They saw the Jerusalem artichoke as the road to prosperity.

Another way to survey growers is geographically. The 1982 company report on growers per state noted that strongest concentrations existed in four states: Minnesota, with 509; South Dakota, 288; Iowa, 255; and Wisconsin, 246. Significant concentrations existed in Kentucky with 92; Missouri, 90; North Dakota, 81; Indiana, 75; Illinois, 70; and Nebraska, 58. Minor numbers existed in other states.[39]

In conformity with AEFS's claim to serve the small farmer, the average unit of sale throughout the nation was ten acres. AEFS sold approximately $25 million of seed to 2,500 growers, as evident in a state by state analysis.[40] Approximately four out of five sales were for ten acres. However, a notable number of sales of less than ten acres were counterbalanced by a significant number involving twenty and thirty acres. A very small number of sales exceeded thirty acres.

The Hopeful World of If

A preliminary draft of a company memo, from the fall of 1982, revealed how much a euphoric vision dominated the company and its sales. The memo—awkwardly titled "Marketing Bulletin on the Marketing Techniques Involving Total Acreage to be Developed into Jerusalem Artichokes in [the] Next Three to Five Years and Urgency of the Sale[s] Technique and Approaches"—foresaw the Jerusalem artichoke as a crop redefining the agricultural destiny of the United States: "By the end of the 1980's there could be 100 million acres," the memo predicted. A hundred million acres (an area roughly twice the size of Minnesota if it were planted from border to border) would produce—at the modest yield of 20,000 pounds per acre—an annual yield of 2 trillion pounds, which would be roughly four times more than the annual yield of rice in China and well over twice the annual yield of corn in the United States.[41]

If this dream were realized, it would make the United States truly energy independent, because the proposed annual yield of 2 trillion pounds of Jerusalem artichokes each year would exceed, by a thousandfold, the combined annual crude oil productions of Saudi Arabia and the United States in 1980. Never again would the lowly Jerusalem artichoke spend a single jealous day as an outcast weed.

The dream astronomically exceeded reality. "Each grower," the starry-eyed memo continued, "will assure reaching our maximum goal acreage . . . *only if* each grower is directly responsible for ten new growers." Big numbers like these were part of the horticultural hysteria. (Pat Derner, friend of Fred Hendrickson's and AEFS's head of market development, noted that any supplier of the crop had to convince a potential industrial user that it could furnish a large and steady supply of its product, so that the company could risk dedicating a significant portion of its industrial capacity to the processing and distribution of the new crop.[42])

This memo amounted to yet another enthusiastic burst of felicific calculation of the world of hopeful ifs. If a farmer, so the memo proposed, could recruit three new growers, he would recover his seed costs. If he could convince eight other farmers, this "will result in $96,000 of gross sales (if the price stays at $1.20 a pound) and his 50% share of that will be $48,000." The memo calculated, "if at least one half of that amount [were] invested into a bio-mass yard or into a group-owned . . . processing plant, that farmer will be on the way to becoming an Energy Farmer and getting paid full price for his crop (100% of parity) rather than [being] just a farmer securing a food and feed price for [it] like he does for corn and beans." Bearing the clear stamp of its author, Hendrickson, the memo concluded in bold type with a call "TO HAVE BETWEEN 75 AND 100 MILLION DOLLARS WORTH OF SALES BY DECEMBER 31, 1982."[43]

Such visionary allurement was enhanced by an array of bonuses. They included cash, seed tubers, free crop planting, and prizes like a vegetable processor or juicer and free trips to Marshall. Finally, however, it was faith that sold Jerusalem artichokes and made AEFS run. It was faith that made Hendrickson a prophet, joined him and Dwire together to create AEFS, and motivated Knapper, Bittner, and others to sell. It was faith that made them all believe that the Jerusalem artichoke was good fortune smiling on them. Not to believe was to bite the hand that fed them. They believed and money came in—that was what they knew, and that was all they needed to know to be in the big tent.

4

A Perfect Consultant

> No one I know has this man's heart of love and deeds of action. ... L. D. is ... perhaps one of the greatest men in Christendom.
>
> –Arenia C. Mallory, president of Saints College, Lexington, Mississippi, upon bestowing L. D. Kramer with an honorary doctor of humanities degree

When a former employee of the Reverend L. D. Kramer read that Kramer had been hired as a consultant for AEFS, he remarked that Kramer would be "a perfect consultant for Jerusalem artichokes."[1]

Kramer came to AEFS flat broke, yet he was never short of energy or intelligence; he brought a kind of vitality to whatever he did. Also, Kramer had business, financial, and personnel skills that both Hendrickson and Dwire lacked.

In his middle forties, Kramer, a former televangelist of the Assemblies of God, had developed a $30 million nursing home chain called Challenge Homes. As its CEO, Kramer had developed the nonprofit Challenge Homes from scratch in Glenwood, Minnesota. In the course of the 1960s and 1970s it grew from a single nursing home to a multistate chain of more than thirty nursing homes.

Kramer did not come to Glenwood rich. He belonged to that growing legion of young evangelical and Pentecostal ministers who struggled to make their living by preaching. He climbed the ladder of success that commonly led from preaching in revival tents for a percentage of the gate to becoming the pastor of an established church.

Kramer was filled with the restless energy of his own fast-growing gospel-inspired church, the Assemblies of God. While the Assemblies of God's seventieth anniversary in 1989 was tarnished by revelations from "Gospelgate" and the all-too-visible plights of its two most visible evangelists, Jim Bakker and Jimmy Swaggart, it remained America's fastest growing church. As orthodox and more traditional churches struggled to stay even, the Assemblies of God grew from 8,500 churches and more than half a million members in the mid-1960s to 11,000 churches, 2.5 million U.S. members, and a worldwide membership of 18 million in 120 countries.[2]

The history of Kramer's family is inseparable from the church. Kramer followed in the footsteps of his father, an ordained minister of the Assemblies of God. His mother also took her turn at professing the faith from the pulpit. For Kramer's parents, Ivan and Beatrice, church meant community. When Kramer was young, his parents ministered to small congregations in Iowa and Minnesota, staying longest in Cedar Rapids, Iowa, where they helped found a new congregation that grew from a handful of families who met in a garage to a successful and well-established church.

Born in Walker, Iowa, in 1934, Kramer was the only child in a poor family of seven children not to graduate from high school. Yet he radiated intelligence and energy. While in high school he played track and basketball and ran his own construction company. He began to preach at age fourteen. Dropping out of high school in his senior year for medical reasons, he went on to attend the Central Bible Institute in Springfield, Missouri, the headquarters of the Assemblies of God church. He graduated four years later, having taken a lot of correspondence courses and supported himself by itinerant preaching. The only other formal education he received was through business correspondence courses from the American Management Association.

Kramer was ordained in Duluth, Minnesota. His father pastored a small church in International Falls, which Tammy Bakker once attended. In 1953, at age nineteen, he married Ruth Bonstrom in Minneapolis. After serving small parishes in Minnesota, the Kramers, now with two sons, Dale and Timothy, went at their church superintendent's request to serve a very small parish in Glenwood, a town in west-central Minnesota with a population of 2,500 people of predominantly Scandinavian ethnicity. Kramer was paid $35 a week and provided with a residence, eggs, and produce from farm parishioners. These were better than the benefits at his previous position at Springfield. Kramer found Glenwood an open playing field for his energy. His first move was to start a radio station in the basement of his church. Monday through Saturday, 8:00 A.M. to 8:30 A.M., he transmitted a program called "Songs of Praise and Words of Life." He supplemented his show with materials from church headquarters. He followed a two-hour Sunday afternoon program with clips from Oral Roberts, whose tolerant optimism was opening "the way for Pentecostals to move into middle class life without losing their faith."[3] Kramer transformed his radio ministry into a successful television ministry that by the middle 1960s was carried by at least ten television stations. By the 1970s, that number had grown to 120 with, Kramer estimated, a viewing audience of 3 million people. Kramer is still proud that he was one of the nation's first televangelists.[4] He admired and identified with Billy Graham, Bishop Sheen, and Oral Roberts. His program, like that of Oral Roberts's ministry, received only small donations from viewers, running on advertisements rather than solicitations from viewers, which could net less than $10,000 a week and average only $1.50 an envelope.

He enthusiastically took the Christian gospel to the world. On Christmas Eve 1959, only two years after arriving in Glenwood, Kramer—builder that he was—boldly talked the members of his church into purchasing a local residence for a nursing home. By 1963, he had resigned from the church to dedicate himself full time to the nursing home. By 1968, he headed the burgeoning new Assembly Homes.

Soon separated from the local church, Assembly Homes became the largest single-corporation nursing home organization in the United States. It employed nearly one hundred people from the Glenwood area and 1,500 in the nation. In operation, under construction, or on the planning board were thirty-six Assembly Homes, with approximately 2,500 beds, in ten states, including Minnesota, the Dakotas, Texas, Arkansas, Florida, and Louisiana.

In 1968, Kramer announced even more growth for Assembly Homes. He announced a second addition to their headquarters, situated in Glenwood on the banks of Lake Minnewaska, and the opening of a home for the mentally retarded in Austin, Minnesota. He also started construction on "his longtime dream" of a Challenge Chapel, a small roadside chapel.[5]

For Kramer, life became an expanding series of opportunities as he entered enthusiastically into middle-class society. An ardent pilot, he flew everywhere. (Nicknamed the "Flying Pastor" or the "Circuit Rider," he claimed to have logged 200,000 miles for Assembly Homes and his gospel ministry.) In an article in the *Pope County Tribune*, Kramer talked of his life as a matter of future plans and challenges.[6]

In the article, Kramer set forth a five-point plan. First, he intended to minister to as many elderly people as possible. Second, he wanted his television program to reach every state in America. Third, he intended to publish a booklet a month for the next five years. Fourth, further developing his social ministry, he wanted to open homes for the trainable mentally handicapped in every state where he had a nursing home; eventually he hoped to branch out, working with unwed mothers, dope addicts, minority groups, and alcoholics. Fifth, he planned to carry his ministry to a new place in the United States every week, while preparing for two foreign crusades. His first crusade was scheduled for Brazil.

Kramer emerged as Glenwood's most important citizen. He spoke for God, industry, jobs, growth, and town spirit. He fused well the national trinity of religion, business, and civic affairs. In the spirit of John F. Kennedy, Kramer attached the word "challenge" to each of his projects.[7] His presence was felt everywhere in Glenwood. He offered tours to the Holy Land, which he called The Challenge of the Holy Land. He started a boys' ranch in Glenwood Township called Challenge Ranch. He initiated Dial-A-Meditation, sent out what he called Challenge Ministry Teams across the Midwest, and held weekend Challenge Revivals.

Even people who didn't like Kramer couldn't ignore him. He

was a member of Glenwood's Rotary Club, Jaycees, and Civil Air Patrol. He even served temporarily as mayor.

Religion didn't inhibit Kramer from having a good time. He belonged to two horseback riding clubs, which he enjoyed immensely. He snowmobiled and was a member of the Minnewaska Golf Club.

Glenwood recognized its favorite son. As early as 1961, he was recognized by the Junior Chamber of Commerce as an Outstanding Young Man of America. In 1964, Kramer won the Jaycee's Distinguished Service Award.

Kramer played a prominent role in Glenwood's most important annual event, Waterama. (Waterama, a tourist event started in 1955, is a three-day celebration at the end of July that features parades on water and land and fireworks.) He began the ten kilometer race that circled Lake Minnewaska. He added the morning Galilean church service in 1965, and he presided over the service in 1966. The *Pope County Tribune* described the second Galilean service in these terms: "The musicians and instruments, along with Pastor Kramer and his workers, will conduct services from the decks of a giant pontoon boat.... In keeping with the Centennial theme of Waterama—for both Pope County and Glenwood celebrated their 100th anniversary this year—Pastor Kramer is to come as a 'missionary pioneer preacher' and will be paddled out to the platform boat by an Indian in a canoe."[8]

Kramer received a steady stream of honors during the sixties and the early seventies. In 1974, a small black school, Saints College in Lexington, Mississippi, granted Kramer a doctorate. Its president, Dr. Arenia C. Mallory, noted upon conferring the degree that "no one I know has this man's heart of love and deeds of action for his fellow man. L. D. is a wonderful, dedicated person—perhaps one of the greatest men in Christendom."[9]

The year he received his honorary doctorate, Kramer announced to the bewilderment and dismay of Glenwood that he would move the headquarters of Challenge Homes from Glenwood to Dallas, Texas. The move could be rationally explained in terms of the evolving configuration of the nursing home chain, which had only nine homes in Minnesota and twenty-five in Texas, and plans to acquire another twenty homes elsewhere in the south. However, troubles soon engulfed Challenge Homes.

Within two years of leaving Glenwood, the company—which had a board of directors and in which Kramer owned no stock—came under investigation by the Securities and Exchange Commission (SEC) and filed for bankruptcy. Kramer was forced to resign.

What happened during those two years between leaving Glenwood and filing for bankruptcy in Dallas is still a contested matter along Glenwood's main street. The view of one prominent businessman, commonly held, was that "Everything was fine until L. D. got swindled by those New Yorkers in Texas."[10]

A woman who worked closely with Kramer for years believed that he had simply gotten in over his head in Texas. She acknowledged that Kramer was vain: He wore a lot of jewelry, spent a lot of time in front of mirrors, and had an inordinate liking for fancy things, including shoes, suits, airplanes, and offices. But she considered this flaw—a flaw common to those from lower classes who overcome their humble origins—slight when compared to his virtues. His faith was sincere. Workers, she noted, came to his prayer service at work to start the day, even if they weren't members of his faith. He was tolerant of others. He had true empathy for the underdog, and his empathy crossed racial lines. Kramer found time to visit the old, and he had a special way with them. He was always fair to his employees. He offered them health insurance, vacations, and retirement benefits, which was unusual in rural Minnesota.[11] This secretary also pointed out that Kramer worked hard. When he was in town one could hardly ever pass his office without seeing his car there. (That's why he had a kitchen in his luxurious office that overlooked the lake.) In her opinion, Kramer would have succeeded in Dallas if disloyal company officers, who were against the move, had not reported him to the SEC and thus precipitated the investigation that caused a loss of confidence in the company.

Less kind views of Kramer can also be found in Glenwood, where "Revenue Kramer" is his common nickname. One employee affiliated with the nursing homes judged him to be unbearably vain, incapable of taking advice, and not responsible to his family or the company and its board. He often complained about his wife, and he was not home enough for his family. He dismissed those who were critical of him as being motivated by jealousy, and he confronted discipline with strong outbursts of temper. On one occasion, he literally jumped up and down, one informant said, when for economic reasons he was denied further use of the company-leased Lear Jet. (Kramer disputes this, saying he himself was in favor of giving up the Lear Jet.) The informant concluded that he was a petty tyrant who directed the company capriciously, which Kramer denies, insisting on the authority and autonomy of the board under whose direction he served.[12]

Another employee who worked for Challenge Homes in 1974, when "everything went wrong," depicted Kramer as a fine preacher and good boss but also "a braggart," "a show-off," and "a fast talker" who was not above talking people out of their estates.[13] Unlike his wife, who stayed home and minded her own affairs, "he was showy"—and he ran around, this employee believed. According to the employee, Kramer bought his clothes at Nieman Marcus, and he let people know he had a Hollywood hairdresser. Kramer responded that he got his suits for ten dollars apiece as a reward for wearing them on his TV show.

A business acquaintance of Kramer's, who intimately knew the economic operation of Challenge Homes, saw its history as two intersecting lines: The rise of the nursing home chain was crossed by the decline of Kramer's character. The bigger his business got, the more unruly his vanity and spending became. As he spent lavishly on himself and his office and went from health-food fads to the most recent self-help notions, the nursing homes fell into more and more trouble. Money had to be shifted back and forth between the individual homes as necessities and emergencies arose, and individual homes received warnings from state departments of health. "Nursing homes were going without vital supplies so he could indulge his growing ego, and that's what got me mad," the interviewee said.[14]

As a 1976 complaint of the SEC made clear, there were other problems at Challenge Homes that anticipated problems Kramer would have at AEFS. Challenge Homes was marred by nepotism. Kramer made his father an administrator of the nursing home in Barnesville, Minnesota, and he lent company money to his brother, Steve, to start a necktie company, which was financed by the Pope County State Bank. Kramer also worked out deals for his friends. As if preparing himself for his role at AEFS, Kramer created a variety of corporations that served Challenge Homes as well as other enterprises that involved him in the ownership of cafes, furniture stores, and construction companies, and in the building of apartments.[15] As a former mayor and prominent citizens of Glenwood painfully discovered—at the cost of thousands of dollars—some of Kramer's schemes were disastrous.

A professional in town who knew well the history of Kramer and Challenge Homes judged him to be a marvelous promoter and a man of boundless enthusiasm. For every scheme, idea, and impulse he implemented, he discarded twenty upon the advice of his Glenwood lawyer, Norvell Callaghan. Callaghan was the only person who gave Kramer advice until his move to Dallas. On one occasion, he followed Callaghan's advice to ease his father out of his administrative role at one of the nursing homes. On another occasion, he followed Callaghan's advice to go on a world crusade as a way to let things cool off in the company. Although this informant did not judge Kramer to be malicious, he had no doubt that Kramer took what he wanted in perks from the company and handsomely supplemented his income by serving as a consultant for the establishment of new nursing homes. He summed up Kramer as a person of sheer exuberance and energy who at times got swept up by "a frenzy to have things."[16]

The move to Dallas, in this informant's opinion, followed the logistical needs of Kramer's growing nursing home empire, but it contained built-in problems. Dallas' labor costs were higher. "He went from [paying his workers] $2.00 an hour to [paying them] $6.00 an hour." In addition, he lost the skill and the loyalty of Glenwood's work force. More significantly, Kramer took his worst problems with him in the form of his closest consultants. As Challenge Homes grew, the almost total absence of wise counsel caught up with him. Engaging in a kind of evangelical nepotism—similar to what happened at AEFS—Kramer surrounded himself at the top with fellow ministers and evangelicals who were not competent businesspeople. Their knowledge of nursing home administration and finance was as slight as their hunger for money was great. Once in Texas, they turned against Kramer. Excusing himself, Kramer argues that the nonprofit Challenge Homes were run by a powerful and autonomous board made up of district superintendants of Texas and Minnesota sections of the Assemblies of God and five other superintendants, who met once a month.

Almost as soon as Challenge Homes moved to Dallas in 1974, its affairs were in disorder. According to Kramer, faced by delinquent accounts, Challenge Homes found itself unable to borrow money. Money, he explained, was being lent at 14 and 15 percent interest, but Texas had a usury law that forbade lending money to nontaxable agencies for more than 10 percent.[17] According to the SEC, Kramer and his various companies formed a maze of questionable economic transactions involving millions of dollars and his personal wealth. In a signed statement in February 1975, Kramer indicated he was worth $2.5 million, with an annual income of $220,000. However, he told SEC examiners that this was simply a projected income meant to impress bankers. It did not conform to his income tax filing for 1974, in which his adjusted gross income was $26,864.[18]

Additionally, his $2.5 million net worth contained a completely useless note for $1,250,000 from a Texas con woman. Claiming to be a doctor of medicine, a registered nurse, a concert pianist, a professor at Rice University, and a millionaire to boot, she promised Challenge Homes from $1 million to $11 million, once her pending divorce was settled. Kramer gave her $30,000 to help her through what she described as her "present troubles."[19] Callaghan, who had checked around in Texas, couldn't convince Kramer that, although she may have been a talented woman, she wasn't worth a plug nickel. Kramer contends that the sum he lost was only $3,000, and the con woman, who met with his board of directors, was a doctor, did play the piano, and was the daughter of oil money.[20]

This swindle of Kramer amounted to little when compared to the maze of transactions and the amounts noted in the SEC complaint against Kramer, his two associates at Assured Funds, and several of the nonprofit Challenge corporations, including Challenge Homes, Challenge Homes of the Dakotas, Challenge Child Care, Challenge Evangelism, New Challenge Homes, and Challenge Ministries. Each of these corporations, except Challenge Evangelism, had the same board of directors. The SEC complained that Challenge Homes, which failed to pay bills, had "outstanding 15 series of debenture bonds amounting to $1,587,850 as well as more than $1,400,000 in time payment certificates and call payment certificates." Challenge Homes and Challenge Homes of the Dakotas had outstanding securities totaling more than $3,400,000, which had been sold to more than 1,500 investors residing throughout the United States.[21]

The SEC charged that Challenge Homes' securities were made attractive by offering investors a chance to put their money in the service of improving and building nursing homes and the promise that 20 percent of the amount of all outstanding securities of Challenge Homes and Challenge Homes of the Dakotas would be held in reserve. In addition to having utilized funds from a promised reserve for operating expenses, another $200,000 of $410,000 raised by one of Kramer's associates was spent on undesignated ends.

The SEC further charged that Kramer "[had] diverted several hundred thousand dollars from Challenge Ministries, Inc. and its affiliates to his own ... Assured Funds, Inc."[22] (McLeod County would later level a similar charge against Kramer for his activities at AEFS.) Kramer used these funds for investments and loans to various Assured Funds enterprises, which numbered approximately fifteen and, in many instances, had absolutely nothing to do with the goals of Challenge Homes. His Assured Funds investments, as indicated by the SEC and reported by the *Minneapolis Tribune*, went to such companies as a motor home manufacturing company, a commercial leasing company, a construction company, and a decorating firm, all of which worked for Challenge Homes; an aircraft leasing company, which probably rented to Kramer's ministry; a commercial collection agency; a men's discount clothing chain; a Bible and record store; a sales scheme to promote organic foods and vitamins, called Good Life; and a firm to market hair preparations that Kramer said, "will come in a cartooned container that looks like a big circus to be called 'Hair Fair.'" (Hair Fair, Kramer predicted, "will catch on real big in a year and a half, since it designs the hairstyles on my show.") The most colorful of Assured Funds' investments was a drive-through pantyhose store. Kramer bought the pantyhose store to help out the son of a friend. He described it as "looking like a great lemon, sitting in a parking lot of a shopping mall. . . . It had palm branches all around and looks like it's out on a little island."[23]

According to a newsletter of the securities division of the commerce department of the state of Minnesota, "All of the corporate defendants, along with . . . Kramer, have entered into a Consent order without admitting or denying allegations in the complaint. The order provides that a new board of directors will be appointed for all the corporations."[24] The new board filed bankruptcy under Chapter Eleven for purposes of reorganization under the order.

The eventual consequence of the reorganization was that at the end of 1978, Challenge Homes bondholders received 100 percent of their money back, thanks to the purchase of Challenge Homes by Anta Corporation, an Oklahoma-based nursing home operator. Kramer remarked, "God worked a miracle to let these homes sell for enough to pay off the bondholders. I have always felt that a person shouldn't lose money invested for God's work. This is wonderful."[25]

In May 1976, however, in the wake of the SEC investigation, Kramer had been bitter. He'd been chased out on the streets by the representatives of a $30 million to $40 million business he had founded and developed. He believed that the origin of the SEC complaint was two former Challenge Homes employees, and that he had been stabbed in the back by them and a lot of other ungrateful friends.

Kramer left Texas, but he didn't return to Glenwood. He and his wife tried unsuccessfully to reassemble their lives in Edina, Minnesota. He continued to preach but found no steady work until four months before he joined AEFS as a business consultant. At that time he began preaching at Evangel Temple in Minneapolis. During this five-year unemployment, he was occupied with numerous Challenge Homes civil suits. Legal fees led him to declare personal bankruptcy in 1980. In the same year, he and his wife formally separated without seeking a divorce because, according to Kramer, it would be inappropriate for him as a minister of the church to initiate a divorce. His wife was reluctant to divorce because her family would disapprove.

Shortly after coming to AEFS in the fall of 1981, Kramer described himself in his resume, as a business consultant. He featured himself as "an aggressive proponent . . . of 'whole man' care service to the underprivileged and the unfortunate of society. I formed my own consulting firm after many years of service as both a minister and a chief executive officer in a national ministry organization." He added, "[for] fifteen years I was featured each week on the national gospel television program, 'Challenge of Truth,' which was aired on more than 125 million outlets with an estimated audience of 3 million viewers." At the top of Kramer's resume, he spelled out the word "evangelist," attributing the following characteristics to himself: "*E*nergetic, *V*ibrant, *A*nointed, *N*otable, *G*reat, *E*lectrifying, *L*ively, *I*nnovative, *S*ensational, *T*errific."[26]

Kramer seemed to fit the needs of AEFS. He was an enthusiastic, evangelical Christian who knew business. He could preach and he could calculate. By experience he had learned about managing a company and its finances, and he had learned a lot about the many-sided relationships of government and business. At least in general terms, Dwire and Hendrickson knew about and discussed Kramer's problems at Challenge Homes. In fact, Hendrickson had represented clients who held Challenge Homes bonds. Yet they chose not to investigate Kramer's background.

Right from the start, Kramer and Dwire hit it off well. At their first meeting, Dwire hired Kramer on the spot. The only question remaining was which of the talents of their new consultant would they put to use in their new Christian company.

5

What Made the Company Run

Down in Appleton there, guys went down to get their seed and they were big shots . . . and there was nobody, there was no organization, everybody was passing the buck. . . . There was a guy that was supposed to have $250,000 in this thing and he just sat there for two days waiting for his seed, and it was just like *a doggone circus*, and he went home . . . and he took his money out. It was just mismanagement. . . . They had some flunkies in there, didn't know anything! I guess they got them off the street or something.
–A Jerusalem artichoke grower from southwestern Minnesota

American Energy Farming Systems defined itself as a Christian company and made religious faith part of its sales pitch. Its first sales list was the membership list of Pastor Pete's radio ministry, Prayer Power. The first employee AEFS hired was John Peterson, Pastor Pete's son. The Reverends Jerry Knapper and L. D. Kramer were hired because they could preach; Richard Spencer, the head of AEFS's research team, attended Dwire's church, the Marshall Evangelical Free Church.

AEFS dressed itself in Christian trappings. Its meetings began and ended with prayer. The workday often began with a prayer service and organ music. Prayers were used to express special wishes. Carried away with the power of prayer to serve self-interest, one AEFS official prayed for the failure of the corn crop so farmers would be led to find their way to the true crop, the Jerusalem artichoke.

Christianity was the essential and the common language of AEFS. In a letter of Christmas greetings for 1982, Fred and his wife, Beverly, wished "Jim and Peg Dwire and all the AEFS Corporate Family" a joyous Christmas and then reminded them that Christ the King was born to a virgin in a stable, and "We are all a part of AEFS because we feel that our purpose and mission is to bring a new farm crop to America's family farmers.... Isn't it odd," Fred asked, "that the Jerusalem artichoke heralded by some as the Plant of Peace and the Plant of Promise, really is just a lowly weed?"

Religious language also served the medium of criticism. In a memo to Dwire, Kramer used the voice of religious exhortation to express his concern about bad morale, the pervasiveness of gossip, the absence of coherent leadership, and the tendency to spend more than one had.[1] On one occasion, Hendrickson wrote Dwire criticizing two of the company's most important managers, Paul Skrien and Bob Messersmith, for not having "the same heart and the same desire to do good and serve God that you and I do."[2]

More than faith alone ran the company, however. AEFS was promoted as a once-in-a-lifetime chance to get rich. Fueled by greed, AEFS was stunningly successful, and it advanced in a breakneck and topsy-turvy fashion. Not having a valid product to sell, AEFS increasingly resembled a fly-by-night company that survived by selling hope to desperate farmers. Almost from its beginnings, AEFS was driven by the need to respond to public warnings and adverse legal actions.

Warnings and Accusations

Warnings and accusations about the crop and the company came quickly. As early as October 1981, a University of Minnesota Agricultural Extension Service memorandum to regional agents in Southwestern Minnesota cautioned, "A firm in Lyon County promoting the growing of Jerusalem artichokes as a crop overestimates the yields of the plant as well as the plant's potential for conversion to alcohol fuel and sugar, and even human food." In April 1982, the Extension Service in another memorandum cautioned that the much-touted claim that the

Jerusalem artichoke got 90 percent of its nutrition from air, sunshine, and water was true not only for the Jerusalem artichoke but for all plants. AEFS's second claim that the plant was drought resistant was simply false.[3]

Already in December 1981, Minnesota commissioner of agriculture Mark Seetin openly charged that no research in the past fifty years supported AEFS's claims about the yield of the Jerusalem artichokes, and he announced his intention to ask the Minnesota attorney general's office to examine AEFS as being engaged in pyramid sales. The attorney general's office favorably responded to Seetin's request and began an inquiry into AEFS's business practices in light of possible pyramid schemes, monopolies, and fraud.[4]

Criticism soon surfaced in the press. On December 9, 1981, the Sioux Falls *Argus Leader* bannered its state section with the headline, "Jerusalem Artichoke Production Question." The paper quoted the bemused state director of energy policy, Charles Vanderziel, who found the contrast between the ten-dollar-an-acre cost of seeding corn and the thousand-dollar-an-acre cost of seeding Jerusalem artichokes ironically worthy of AEFS's motto, borrowed from Sam Adams, "Risk is the price you pay for opportunity."[5]

In January 1982, a critical article was published by *The Farmer*, an influential agricultural paper of Webb Press in Minneapolis. Its author, Jim Ruen, labeled the Jerusalem artichoke a highly speculative venture in light of the fact that there were no existing new markets for the crop. He quoted one of the nation's most knowledgeable artichoke advocates, Tom Lukens, who claimed that markets for the crop were several years away by even the most optimistic estimates. He also quoted Jerusalem artichoke advocate, developer, and speculator Thomas Reichert, who suggested that AEFS might be growing the wrong variety of Jerusalem artichokes; the earlier-maturing Columbian variety might prove more appropriate in northern climates, which have shorter growing seasons, than the French Mammoth White sold by AEFS. Anticipating investigations into possible monopoly charges against AEFS, Ruen pointed out the profound price discrepancies between the $1.00 and $1.20 a pound charged by AEFS for Jerusalem artichoke seed tubers and the 18 cents to 23 cents a pound it sold for in many fresh produce markets and the 40 cents to 50 cents a pound being paid for tuber seedstock in Washington state. Ruen concluded his article by quoting Wayne Olhoft of Herman, Minnesota, a grower and Minnesota state senator, who believed that he and his friends had purchased Jerusalem artichokes with their eyes wide open. "I don't think any of us are under any delusion. . . . It [the Jerusalem artichoke] has a very speculative future."[6]

Far more menacing for AEFS than newspaper articles were government investigations. Fortunately for AEFS, the criminal division of the U.S. Department of Agriculture and the postal inspectors dropped their early investigations of the company. However, the South Dakota Division of Securities and the Minnesota attorney general's office did not.

South Dakota securities concluded its review, which had begun in December 1981, with the finding that AEFS was selling securities. In March 1982, the state of South Dakota, in an order to cease and desist, prohibited AEFS "from making any future sales or offers of Jerusalem artichoke tubers" until it properly registered itself in the state.[7] While South Dakota lifted its ban in July 1982, it required the company to offer its South Dakota growers a chance to rescind their contracts. AEFS agreed. As was the case in subsequent rescissions in Iowa, Nebraska, and elsewhere, its growers—much to AEFS's pride—were not interested in the offer. Only one South Dakota Jerusalem artichoke grower out of approximately thirty took advantage of the rescission offer. At the meeting between growers and a representative of the consumer division, the majority of growers, according to Dwire, literally laughed at the consumer division representative.[8] They told him to get his nose out of farming. South Dakota continued its investigation into charges of fraud, as did several other states, including Minnesota and Iowa.

In December 1981, Minnesota Attorney General Warren Spannus began an investigation of AEFS. The owners of AEFS believed the investigation to be part of a conspiracy against them. Hendrickson suspected—and still suspects—that behind the attorney general's investigation were the world oil cartel and the world's giant grain merchants.

The Minnesota attorney general's investigation focused on three possible areas of misconduct. First, it examined AEFS as constituting a pyramid-sales scheme. Minnesota law proscribes sales offering rebates and values to a buyer on the condition the buyer make future sales. Minnesota statutes also outlaw sales whose inducement is not the product itself but profits to be made from referrals or the holding of distributorships.

At the same time, the attorney general's office scrutinized AEFS for possible violations of antitrust laws. The company's own lawyer, Louis Ainsworth, acknowledged this possibility, conceding that AEFS's present contract could be understood to fix the prices of the crop ($1.20 per pound) independent of the market.[9] Ainsworth, of Wiese and Cox, Ltd., cautioned that the attorney general might find additional antitrust practices in AEFS's attempts to have complete control of its buyers' future sales of Jerusalem artichoke seed, even when they had obtained the seed from sources other than AEFS.

The attorney general's office pursued a third investigation into product misrepresentation or, put more strongly, fraud. This massive investigation focused on the whole range of AEFS claims about the scientific and economic possibilities of the plant and the company's ability to market the crop. The Minnesota attorney general's concerns, which Iowa, Wisconsin, and ten other states shared, were multiple. They involved the fields of chemistry, agronomy, technology, industrial production, medicine, economics, and marketing.

As early as December 1981, the Minnesota attorney general's office asked whether AEFS's information was derived from actual field research or amounted to mere laboratory hypotheses; whether there existed any market other than a seed market for the crop; and whether the company's literature implied that markets already existed for fuel, feed, sugar, and other uses. At the same time, it investigated growers' complaints about AEFS's inconsistent sales pitches and raised questions about its research capacity and the existence of processing facilities.

With the help of its scientists, Wayne Dorband and Richard Spencer, AEFS produced a mountain of literature in response to the attorney general's inquiry. While they did convince the attorney general's office that AEFS was not an outright scam, they did not satisfy questions about the legitimacy of the crop or the company.

Failing to convince the attorney general's office of the existence of any significant markets then or in the near future, AEFS sealed its fate. Even though the company was judged to be neither a pyramid scheme nor a monopoly, it was judged to be selling something useless: a seed that had no other purpose than to produce more seed to be sold. A product of dubious value does not gain value by infinite production.

In response to the demands of the attorney general's office, and upon the advice of its attorneys, AEFS rewrote its literature, altered its contracts with buyers and growers, and designed and redesigned its multiple programs with growers. It also abandoned its effort to define itself as a shared enterprise, since not to would have made the company subject to the laws regulating securities. Also, it rewrote its contract to avoid being judged a monopoly. It had to restrict itself to selling seeds to its buyers, without seeking to control the future stock, sale, or price of seed. It could no longer attempt to limit markets, regulate competition, control the future seed sales of buyers, or demand that buyers become AEFS members.

Additionally, AEFS had to alter its basic sales strategy if it were not to be judged a pyramid-sales scheme. It could no longer link the benefits of purchasing a seed contract to future sales of the seed, sales of salesmanships, or the sales of distributorships, all of which, as Ainsworth pointed out, are "hallmarks of a pyramid-scheme or multilevel distributorship."

Furthermore, AEFS had to show that the value of Jerusalem artichoke seed was not predicated on infinite sales or, to use Ainsworth's phrase, "an infinity of participants."[10] Ainsworth argued in a December 20, 1982, memo to AEFS that "If the seedstock market is the only viable economic market, then by mathematical certainty the later growers, whose numbers would dwarf the earlier growers (451 in 1982, 2,000-5,000 in 1983, 8,000-50,000 in 1984), would be unable to earn money from the sale of seedstock since the acreages sown with Jerusalem artichokes would, at a (conservative) estimate of twenty-fold per year, [result] in 5,000 acres (1982), 100,000 acres (1983), 2,000,000 (1984), and 40,000,000 (1985)." Noting that U.S. corn acreage was presently 100,000,000 acres, Ainsworth added, "to expect Jerusalem artichoke sales to come close to corn would be unrealistic and would tend to show that a straight pyramid scheme was operating."[11]

AEFS's legal dilemma persisted. If it were to satisfy the attorney general's office that it was not a security, it had to sell tuber seed and tuber seed alone. Yet if it were to avoid being a pyramid scheme, it had to demonstrate that Jerusalem artichoke tuber seed had a value. The question of the plant's value confronted AEFS with one insurmountable problem. While hypothetically AEFS could satisfy the law by showing that it was not to be a security, a monopoly, and a pyramid, it could not—try as it would—identify a market for its product. This failure meant that in the end all AEFS had to sell was the blue sky.

AEFS could not escape its day of reckoning with the attorney general. It futilely prepared itself for the fatal hearing that lay ahead.[12]

The company's mounting legal preoccupations displayed themselves in multiplying attorney's fees. (Bills to prepare AEFS for the attorney general's hearing totaled, minimally, $228,400—the lion's share of which was received by the company's lawyer, Louis Ainsworth.) The search for a market expressed itself in a range of efforts that were often hastily conceived. For instance, AEFS leased a small alcohol plant in Marshall that never succeeded in processing more than a cup or two of alcohol. Also, the company tried, unsuccessfully, to turn a failed Marshall food processing plant into a Jerusalem artichoke processing plant. The impure and fibrous Jerusalem artichoke, as one worker noted, defied the processing plant driers as much as it did the stills of the alcohol plant.[13] Following the fashionable concept of biomass conversion, Hendrickson started an offshoot company, Bio-Markets of America, whose purpose was to convert the Jerusalem artichoke into an energy source.

There are reasons to suspect that months before the conclusion of the attorney general's investigation, Dwire, Hendrickson, Kramer, and others started to prepare for the day when AEFS's great tent would be hauled down. Yet, more than fear of the law and vague religious aspirations moved AEFS in its topsy-turvy eighteen-month history. The company also marched to the quickening rhythm of expanding greed and the growing need to sell more and more seed to survive at all.

"Hyper-Growth"

In the aftermath of AEFS's bankruptcy, Dwire publicly explained the failure of the company as a problem of "government interference, bad press, employees, and hyper-growth." Dwire claimed that AEFS had the potential to earn $20 million a month and that the Minnesota attorney general's rescission would not have been an insurmountable problem for the company if the attorney general had not "put it [the rescission] out all over the place." "The corporation," Dwire concluded, "would have been a viable business entity today yet."[14]

Dwire liked to explain the failure of AEFS in reference to "hyper-growth." "We were," he told the court, "two million dollars in December 1982, six million dollars in January 1983. . . . [By March we would be] twenty million dollars a month. With fifty percent to the farmer we would be generating ten million dollars a month. So I [believed that] there would be more than enough money."[15]

Dwire knew that attributing AEFS's failure to hyper-growth, which was the title of a then fashionable book about a failed computer company in Silicon Valley, would lend an air of respectability to AEFS by equating it with this celebrated California firm.[16] It also exempted AEFS from such run-of-the-mill explanations for its failure as incompetence, stupidity, and greed and contradicted the charge that the company was a typical, short-lived pyramid scheme.[17]

Aside from rationalizing AEFS's bankruptcy, the notion of hyper-growth also explained things Dwire couldn't fathom about the phenomenally rapid growth of his company. It explained why he, Dwire, had to serve as "a troubleshooter," flying from place to place, straightening out mess after mess.[18] It clarified for him why the company never seemed to be on an even keel, why it lacked order and direction, and why replacing, shifting, and hiring new personnel never solved the company's underlying disorder. Finally, hyper-growth explained for Dwire why the company itself outgrew the competence of its employees and management.

"Just a Horseshit Operation"

In the aftermath of the company's bankruptcy, AEFS employees joined Dwire in assessing reasons for the company's failure. Wesley Buchele, a longtime field agronomist for Iowa State University and an acquaintance of Hendrickson's and AEFS's, was the clear exception when he almost uniformly defended them. He argued that the development of a new crop demands a rare breed of entrepreneurs and carries with it a high chance of failure. These are things for which neither university scientists nor government attorneys have understanding or sympathy.[19]

If few employees adopted this generous interpretation of the company's failure, none of the many interviewed believed the company had been organized solely as an elaborate scheme to defraud buyers. And while a few employees viewed failure as an inevitable consequence of a confused and incompetent management, none pointed their accusing fingers at themselves.

Mark Hughes, an agronomist, was as critical as any former AEFS employee. He considered the company flawed in conception and practice, and he believed that company officials either knowingly made false claims about markets for the Jerusalem artichoke or were stupendously stupid. The production of alcohol from the Jerusalem artichoke wasn't yet feasible even from an engineering point of view. According to Hughes, while Larry Tieszen's research on photosynthesis was valid, Wayne Dorband was just a scientific front for the company. Richard Spencer, who took over control of the company's research, had responsibility without power. Pat Derner, Hendrickson's colleague who was expected to help create markets, lacked a chemical engineering background and had little knowledge about processing. According to Hughes,

> No one stopped to think twice. They had no foresight. The seed program was a sham and the seed should not have been spread all over the country. There was no disease control. . . . They just didn't know agriculture. They knew they were spreading

sclerotina, a plant disease which is found in beans and sunflowers, and they did nothing about this.

"The company was a disaster," Hughes claimed. Greed, ignorance, and zealousness alternately ran the company. The managers of a seed company did nothing about the rotted, diseased, and poor quality seed in their possession. They used religion as a selling point. Indeed, Hughes considered them to be crooks under the guise of religion. His assessment of the owners and directors was equally strong: "There were yes men on the board of directors. . . . Dwire ran the whole show, and . . . Fred sat on the sidelines." He judged Dwire to be a ruthless and dishonest man who manipulated and intimidated people and who was interested only in taking care of Dwire, Inc. Sparing none, Hughes conjectured, "There was a strong possibility that the farmers, too, were greedy."[20]

Dwire's personal secretary and administrative assistant, Linda Julian, who co-owned a company with Dwire (D & J Enterprises), observed no wrongdoing at AEFS. In her opinion, the company moved too fast. Many employees were incompetent and failed to do their jobs. "I've seen people on the street who have produced more than these directors we had," she said. With some bitterness, she commented that the male directors would not take her, a woman, seriously. Despite her efforts to implement directives, she explained, things were simply not done when Dwire wasn't around; even when he was, he was too softhearted to fire the incompetents. Furthermore, Julian said the company was marked by "fighting and backstabbing," anything but Christian. She saw herself as the victim of a lot of this "Christian backstabbing," especially for all the time she spent with Dwire. In contradiction to other employees such as Ron Mann, head of sales training, who saw Dwire as constantly in need of a whipping boy, Julian contended, "it took a lot for him to fire someone or tell them to go to hell." She defined Dwire, like Fred, as an idea man, someone who was ahead of everyone but who never stuck with his ideas and didn't pay attention to details.[21]

Richard Skorczewski, Dwire's old friend, denied the charge that there was any conspiracy at AEFS to defraud anyone. Skorczewski, who worked for Dwire, Inc., converting machinery, especially potato pickers, into Jerusalem artichoke harvesters, believed the crop was good. He likened the Jerusalem artichoke's potential profitability to that of the soybean, or to another but smaller jackpot crop of the region, flax. (During World War II it was often possible to purchase a farm with the season's profit from this valuable crop.) According to Skorczewski, "He [Dwire] simply got over his head and . . . the staff was over their heads. They just weren't capable business people and they couldn't stop it once it got going."[22]

Jim Menk, who served as a grower representative then in public relations operations, and who managed the company during bankruptcy proceedings, succinctly offered this assessment of AEFS: It had an incompetent management. He claimed that Dwire made all the decisions yet was a trusting person who didn't have the heart to discharge the incompetent people with whom he had surrounded himself. Menk did not trust the many evangelical types such as "the always-selling Knapper." He saw Hendrickson as unproductive and Kramer as highly influential. He did not believe Dwire's intention was to defraud, offering as proof the fact that Dwire conducted his transactions with checks.[23]

Warren Anderson, a lawyer from Morris, cautioned AEFS in December 1982 about growing bad publicity in the countryside and criticism of AEFS by the Production Credit Association (PCA), a major source of short-term, non-real estate agricultural loans. Anderson was more blunt than most of those interviewed. He had knowledge of the company through his ownership of a one-third share of an artichoke contract (earned by his work for growers) and as a lawyer for the Minnesota Jerusalem Artichoke Association, a successor company to AEFS. Anderson believed that AEFS was truly a grass-roots phenomenon. It was surely more than just another one of those countless scams that proliferated throughout the U.S. farm community during the 1980s. In fact, Anderson conjectured, if it weren't for the petulant enthusiasm of the attorney general's office, AEFS might have had a chance to make it despite its serious flaws. Anderson had cautioned Dwire that AEFS was growing too rapidly, but Dwire didn't listen. According to Anderson "[he] just went nuts, flying everywhere."

While Anderson did not believe that Dwire and Hendrickson started out to cheat anyone, he acknowledged, "They screwed away millions of dollars. . . . It was just a horseshit operation—they got too big too fast." Anderson considered Dwire, who was "brought up in the school of hard knocks," capable of making deals the hard way. He judged Hendrickson to be a naive and ineffective religious individual who embellished people's dreams. Although Hendrickson was "ever ready to give a theoretical answer to everything," he was unable to confront Dwire's excessive spending. Nor was Hendrickson willing to force Dwire to buy him out, since he was bound tightly to the company by the money he was making.[24]

Larry Gauthier, who prepared press releases for AEFS, offered one of the most brutal criticisms of the company, attributing sinister motives to AEFS's directors, consultants, and employees. Gautier judged greed to be their primary incentive. He questioned the large sums of money paid to Dorband, whose research he considered to be not worth the paper it was written on. He believed Skorczewski jacked up prices on converted potato harvesters by as much as several thousand dollars at the very last moment of a sale, using the line "Take it or leave it." He questioned Dwire's transactions with large national and regional growers of Jerusalem artichoke seed stock. Gauthier correctly suspected that numerous companies that served AEFS did not have AEFS's interests in mind. He mentioned, as examples, Kramer's company, Remark (Kramer spelled backward); Bio-Markets of America, owned by Hendrickson and Dwire with Robert Soleta and Pat Derner; and Jerusalem Artichoke Research Center, a company owned by Dwire and Dorband.[25]

Big Shots, Big Deals, and Side Shows

From its beginning, AEFS was a hen house for many money-hungry foxes. However, it was about more than being rich. It was also about being powerful. AEFS permitted its owners, directors, and certain employees and consultants to feel more important than they ever had before.

AEFS meant money, travel, and prestige. It was a chance for company bosses to be big shots—to own big houses, travel to new places, and appear in influential business circles. One of Marshall's barbers recounted how Knapper, who was invariably late for his appointment or missed it altogether, left a note for him when he was two minutes late for Knapper's appointment. The note informed the barber that he, Knapper, was a director at AEFS—an important man indeed, one who didn't have time to wait for a barber.

The big-shot side of AEFS appealed to its owners and managers. Certainly a scientist like Dorband was flattered to make big money for his newly learned opinions on agronomy. L. T. Fan, of Kansas State University, found a use for the research money he was given. Physicist Al Rusk of Southwest State University, a tinker at heart, enjoyed scurrying about, while feeling himself and AEFS to be on the verge of making a breakthrough in the alcohol fuel field. His colleague at the University, chemist Richard Spencer, on sabbatical, accepted AEFS's calling to be its research and scientific director. Spencer let more than one person at the university know he was now working in "the real world."

No one felt as important as AEFS's owners, Hendrickson and Dwire. Hendrickson was flattered by the recognition he received as AEFS's founder. He finally was being paid—and paid well—to think. It didn't hurt Hendrickson's pride that he could now afford to buy a house, pay past bills, make large contributions to his favorite religious causes, and furnish his wife some of the finer things she had been denied. On occasions he even had company airplanes take her on shopping trips.

With his own office in Sioux Falls, Hendrickson took his roles as co-owner, vice president, and head of research seriously. On more than one occasion he even made Dwire and Kramer fly to Sioux Falls to meet with him. From Sioux Falls he attended conferences, contacted people working on alternative energy, issued papers on his views of the company's future, and set forth his dreams of transforming American agriculture.

Hendrickson proudly received laurels as "Mr. Artichoke," and he was invited to share the podium at a few agricultural and alternative energy conferences. He jealously guarded his role as AEFS's "idea man."

AEFS allowed Jim Dwire to stand tall. It made him a somebody in Marshall, where for the first time he cast a really big shadow. He owned a wonderful home in the country, with its own lake. He flashed money around, gave a hundred dollars a week to his church, and even more on special occasions. He had every reason to believe that he, more than any other single individual in the region, accounted for Marshall's economic vitality at that time, even if the city's business community only grudgingly lent him respect and the city's two banks, especially Norwest Bank, whose business had prospered because of him, consistently refused to loan money to AEFS.

Dwire knew AEFS kept Marshall's economy humming. The comings and goings of AEFS employees and prospective growers kept the town's airport busy and, more important, he and AEFS accounted for the purchase of significant property. Dwire purchased the headquarters of failed Marshall Foods, which well into the 1960s was the jewel industry of the town's best-known family. Later he convinced Marshall Foods' former plant manager, Del Lagan, to join him under the name Del Quality Foods, hoping to become a major food processor of Jerusalem artichokes. In April 1983, among the many deals Dwire examined was what would have been a $2 million purchase of the defunct Marshall Foods' main plant.

Numbered among other local business properties Dwire considered buying were the Reese Brothers' alcohol plant in Marshall and Buffalo Ridge State Bank in nearby Ruthton, Minnesota. Dwire actually did buy the large, vacant building that formerly housed the Pamida discount department store. AEFS had become Marshall's fourth largest employer, behind only Southwest State University, Schwan's Sales Enterprise (a food-industry company), and a local branch of Pittsburgh Plate and Glass.

Even if the majority of Marshall's hard-to-please businesspeople persisted in treating him as a renegade of sorts, Dwire knew he was more important than any of them would ever be. He was no small fry. He had his own branch office in Edina, Minneapolis's richest suburb. He had his own consultants, lawyers, accountants, and scientists. He could listen to or ignore them. Once, he ordered AEFS's detective to look into the background of a University of Minnesota crop scientist who was being used by the Minnesota attorney general's office in its investigation of AEFS. At the state capitol, he hobnobbed with those who he thought counted. He hired Governor Rudy Perpich's brother, George, as a lobbyist for AEFS, and he did business with the son of Franklin Delano Roosevelt, Elliot Roosevelt.

Dwire was given reasons to feel self-important. Even though he was a poor speaker, people listened to him when he spoke. Companies sought his business, AEFS turned on his opinions and decisions, and he could hire or fire people at will. At Hendrickson's behest, Dwire hired Pastor Pete's son John as Hendrickson's secretary and offered employment to Pastor Pete's widow, who invested her insurance money in Jerusalem artichokes. He also put a number of his Marshall, regional, and church acquaintances on AEFS's payroll.

Dwire did not hesitate to help his own family and himself. He gave AEFS jobs to his sons, Jim Jr. (known as Moose) and Jeff, as well as his brother-in-law, Jerry Knapper, and his wife's uncle, Don Schleuter. An impulsive buyer, Dwire used the new funds AEFS provided to buy planes, buildings, land, and farms.

The wide-open wheeling and dealing that characterized AEFS made Dwire and Hendrickson and other managers of the new company feel like big shots. No standard operating procedures or guiding policies inhibited them. To a degree, AEFS was for them an experiment in enacting personal wants. Many of the companies that served AEFS belonged to its owners or consultants. Many of AEFS's most significant transactions were carried out with companies owned by AEFS personnel or their friends. This was in measure true of the farms AEFS rented, the planes it flew, the cars it drove, and even the seed and fertilizer it purchased and the financing company it recommended.

This absence of policy showed in its hiring, in the fixing of salaries, and in the assignment of contracts. Paul and Bonnie Laidlaw, Kramer's friends, are extreme examples of how AEFS staffed itself.[26] For them, AEFS was their best and last chance to amount to something. The Laidlaws, who had met at Northwest Bible School in Minneapolis (where Tammy and Jim Bakker met), were both twenty-two when they first met Kramer at the Evangelical Temple in Minneapolis. Paul Laidlaw was working there as a custodian. Paul and Bonnie believed that Kramer, who was leasing the church, was a wronged man of God. Accepting Kramer's explanation of how he had lost his $44 million Challenge ministries to disloyal board members, the Laidlaws took him under their wing. Neither Paul, who worked as a custodian and a sales clerk at Dayton's department store, nor Bonnie, who scrubbed toilets at city hospitals, had good jobs. Yet, they gave Kramer fifty to a hundred dollars a week for his support while they themselves tottered on the brink of bankruptcy.

By chance, one day when the Laidlaws were with Kramer in a restaurant in Glenwood, Minnesota (the former home of Kramer's Challenge ministries), they ran into Jerry Knapper and his wife, whom they knew. Bonnie and Paul introduced Kramer to them and Kramer prayed over and cured Knapper's headache-ridden wife. The two ministers, Kramer and Knapper, took to each other. Knapper, who asked Kramer to preach at his church, spoke of Kramer to Dwire. The Laidlaws lent Kramer twelve dollars to go to Marshall to visit Dwire.

The miracle happened. Dwire instantly took a liking to the quick-witted Christian minister and hired him as a business consultant on the spot. Dwire also lent Kramer money to get home, according to Bonnie Laidlaw. Dwire speculated that Kramer, who had been through the mill of federal courts, would perhaps be able to help them with their emerging problems with the Minnesota attorney general.

Kramer paid back his friends the Laidlaws by introducing them to Dwire, who quickly found work for them as well. Dwire asked Paul to sing gospel hymns at sales meetings in order to increase the religious atmosphere. Soon after, Dwire and Kramer invited Paul and Bonnie to organize their first major convention. They were to be paid $2,000 each and, in addition, they were going to be given ten to twenty thousand pounds of seed. This would give them a 50 percent ownership of one or two contracts. After their work of organizing the convention proved satisfactory, both were retained as AEFS employees. Both were assigned to sales. Paul, soon to be earning $30,000 a year, was first retained to handle special events and later was responsible for development of the fresh food market for the Jerusalem artichoke. Bonnie, who stayed on at AEFS rather than take a teaching job she was offered, received a salary of $20,000 to promote Jerusalem artichokes as food. She wrote a cookbook that was published by the Little Lamb Chokes division of AEFS. It featured countless recipes for Jerusalem artichokes. Among her many recipes was a favorite hotdish called Shipwreck. It called for rice, Jerusalem artichokes, beans, onions, tomato juice, and three strips of bacon.[27]

Initially, AEFS seemed to Paul and Bonnie to be a wonderfully safe and secure haven. Their being there appeared to be the work of God rewarding his faithful. They made a good salary and got partnerships in future crops of Jerusalem artichokes, which could earn them, by their calculations, $170,000. They even made a down payment on a new house in a Twin Cities suburb. With faith, enthusiasm, and youthful energy, they enrolled themselves in the service of AEFS and the Jerusalem artichoke.

In this fantasy world that the Laidlaws joined, only one thing held: the fiction that on the open market Jerusalem artichoke tuber seed was worth $1.20 a pound. This fiction was maintained up to the final hours of the company's existence, when AEFS failed in a bid to sell Jerusalem artichoke tuber seed to Archer-Daniel-Midlands for just five cents a pound.

The fiction of $1.20 a pound was terribly important. It was the promise that brought a river of money into the company. For AEFS it was at one and the same time their pie in the sky and their gold standard. It secured the value of the company's paper transactions; it provided a rational measure to their crazy world of taking advances and draws and then paying them back in seed or notes on future seed. The fiction of $1.20 sustained the illusion that the Jerusalem artichoke had value, made AEFS a world of opportunities, and allowed its people to believe they were about real and important things. As much as anything else, $1.20 a pound made this Christian company run.

6

Killing off the Goose That Laid the Golden Egg

Get out as much as you can when you can because it's not going to last forever.
—An AEFS consultant

In the course of the company's history, Dwire and Hendrickson made their own good AEFS's good. And in doing this they failed to meet the requirement of fiduciary trust. Fiduciary trust insists that owners, directors, and in some instances, consultants engage in "good faith and fair dealing" and that they take "due care" in managing their affairs.[1] As if providing a yardstick by which to measure the actions of Dwire, Hendrickson, and other AEFS associates, fiduciary trust prohibits owners and managers from competing with their own corporation, usurping its opportunities, and having interests that conflict with those of the corporation. Furthermore, fiduciary trust requires that a director or officer have undivided loyalty to his own company and be "influenced in action by no consideration other than the welfare of the company."[2]

Corporate fiduciary obligations fall most strongly on those who, like Dwire and Hendrickson, are both directors and owners. "Directors and owners cannot interfere with the business enjoyed by the corporation and they cannot engage in a competing business to the detriment of the corporation which they represent, nor does the right . . . to engage in enterprises of the same nature entitle [them] to enter into transactions of such a nature as to cripple or injure the company's business, or hinder or defeat it."[3] The law carries with it the reasonable expectation that they not purposely destroy the company they represent.

Fiduciary trust in Minnesota law specifically holds directors liable for losses or harm to the corporation as a result of breaking fiduciary obligations.[4] If, for instance, an officer or agent misappropriates the funds of a corporation for the purchase of real estate and takes title in his or her own name—something both Dwire and Hendrickson did—a constructive trust arises in favor of the corporation, and if a director usurps business opportunities for personal gain or opportunity, any profit becomes subject to claim by the company.[5]

Although neither Dwire nor Hendrickson, a lawyer, understood the niceties of the law pertaining to fiduciary trust, they could not have been oblivious to their responsibilities. As early as October 28, 1982, Hendrickson, in one of his many lengthy letters to Dwire, acknowledged his dissatisfaction with the management of AEFS. He acknowledged that there was no meaningful market for the Jerusalem artichoke as of then and stated that "time is not on our side." Hendrickson further worried about the legality of their practices, acknowledging that he had been "equally neglectful of attending to [AEFS] details" and arguing, "Fair business dealings and practices between the two of us require that there be an open and complete exchange of ideas and information between the two of us in *all* matters, pertaining to the complete operation of AEFS and Bio-Markets of America. It is essential," Hendrickson further exhorted Dwire, that "corporate affairs be in proper order and be properly set up and established, since we are acting as a marketing agent on behalf of sellers (growers) and buyers of the Jerusalem artichoke crop and as such we have a fiduciary responsibility to those parties by virtue of common law principles of our legal systems whenever we handle for a fee other people's money or property. We are charged with handling our affairs in a prudent and business-like manner."[6]

Hendrickson's advice went unheeded by Dwire as well as Hendrickson himself. A lot stood in the way of their taking this advice, primarily their presumption that AEFS's cash was theirs. And the tendency to treat the company's profits and opportunities as their own was given greater impetus by their decision in the fall of 1981 to operate under Subchapter S of the Internal Revenue Code. Subchapter S meant that they were no longer treated as a seller of securities but rather as a partnership that was assessed taxes solely on the basis of profits they took out of the company. Their selfish mismanagement expressed itself in many ways. They regularly ignored their accountants' advice. In several instances they failed to supply their accountants with a record of the transactions they carried out with and for the company. Dwire even neglected to inform their first accountant, Kim Boe, an employee of Dwire, Inc., about significant withdrawals he made. Neither Dwire nor Hendrickson made provision for a clear recording of their increasingly large advances.

In the spring of 1982, they got rid of their first auditing firm, Adrean Helgeson & Co. of Minneapolis, when Helgeson complained strongly about AEFS's accounting and business practices. Among the things Helgeson pointed out in his April 1982 audit was the fact that the owners had taken from the company a million dollars more than it had earned: $945,000 had gone in advances to Dwire; $142,264 had gone to Fred Hendrickson.

In July 1982, they hired the auditing firm of Vekich-Arkema & Company Chartered, whose well-paid-for advice was also ignored. In his grand jury testimony, Michael Vekich testified that his firm's coaxings, pleadings, and warnings about irregular withdrawals and the need to pay back advances went unheeded. Hendrickson and Dwire would not commit themselves to a schedule of repayment, and they even canceled the completion of a financial statement in the spring of 1982. Also, they did not respond to Vekich's critical questioning concerning a transaction in February 1983 in which Dwire, Inc., sold seed to AEFS at 60 cents a pound that it had just purchased at 25 cents a pound.

In the spring of 1983, with AEFS facing a severe cash-flow problem and the attorney general breathing down the company's neck, Vekich-Arkema accountant Tim Ribbens did an emergency audit.[7] On the basis of his work overnight, he penciled a note that declared AEFS to be "inauditable," and he went on to identify a host of business violations.

Ribbens elaborated: The owners mixed company and personal funds, made frivolous use of AEFS money, used corporate money for personal advances and payment of personal credit cards, showed no accountability for funds borrowed, lacked job descriptions, didn't regulate purchases, and failed to keep proper books. As if that weren't enough, Ribbens remarked that he was unable to identify AEFS's practices with a common ownership and even cautioned that the company might be considered a pyramid.

These accusations described a pattern of injudicious management that ran the entire length of the company's history. No sooner did money begin to flow into AEFS coffers than the owners began to treat it as their own. On October 2, 1981, three weeks after its founding, the company's checkbook was already overdrawn. On October 30, 1982, Dwire withdrew $10,000 from AEFS for personal needs. Thereafter, taking company money became a way of life for him. According to state evidence, Dwire personally withdrew more than $106,000 from the period of September 1 to December 31, 1981, while during that period $90,000 went to Dwire, Inc., and $43,000 went to Hendrickson.[8]

From the company's inception to its filing for bankruptcy, Dwire took $1,700,000 in draws, loans, and advances, while Dwire, Inc., took approximately $1,600,000 for services and other uses. Far more modestly, Hendrickson, who began with small withdrawals (which, in effect, were advances on his salary) ended up a year and a half later having taken $770,000 from the company for personal expenses (see table 1).[9]

In the case of Dwire, Inc., only $475,000 of the total borrowed from AEFS was covered by notes, whereas $1,476,000 of Dwire's personal draws and advances were covered by notes. Hendrickson covered $559,000 of his borrowing with notes. Some of these notes were not initially entered in the company's books, however, while other notes were not submitted with a schedule of repayment and were secured, if at all, by the promise of the delivery of future seed. This seed, whose very delivery would work against AEFS's promise to purchase its growers' seed, was credited to Hendrickson at the optimal price of 60 cents a pound.

Dwire and Hendrickson found AEFS a convenient place for a quick loan. Initially Hendrickson nibbled away; he took $500

Table 1.
AEFS, Inc.: Statement of Cash Disbursements by Recipient
(Norwest Bank, Marshall, Minn.), for the Period from Inception to May 23, 1983

	Total	Not supported	Supported by check request only	Supported seed purchases	Supported property, plant, and equipment	Supported service items	Grower advances	Signed notes	Bank transfers and investments	Other amounts
TO INSIDERS:										
James Dwire, Sr.	1,707,100	246,300	1,341,500		9,300			110,000		
Dwire Family:										
James Dwire, Jr.	46,600		39,500			7,100				
Jeff Dwire	40,600		40,600							
Dwire Brothers	36,800		36,800							
Cash (endorsed by Jeff Dwire)	20,000		20,000							
Fred Hendrickson and/or Hendrickson & Associates	680,100	164,600	231,500		24,000	355,400		260,000		
TO POTENTIAL INSIDERS:										
Dwire, Inc.	1,623,300	379,800	813,400		74,700	355,400				
Other Dwire Entities:										
Del Quality Foods	146,200							146,200		
Dwire Enterprises, Inc.	123,000	73,000	50,000							
Bio-Markets of America	50,000		50,000							
Lynd Redi-Mix	41,200		7,500		14,000	19,700				
Faribault Orchard	6,000	6,000								
Southwest Constructors	5,600					5,600				
L.D. Kramer and/or Kramer and Associates and Hillcrest Leasing	338,800	13,500	145,000		10,000	170,300				
TO OTHER PARTIES:										
White Lightning Fuel Co. (seed supplier)	2,503,400			2,503,400						
Other seed suppliers and major growers	2,620,000	546,100	118,000	1,779,100			176,800			
Midwest Aviation	424,300	25,000	35,900		83,300	275,100				
Sol King (distribution system)	125,300					125,300				
Professionals and consultants (other than L. D. Kramer)	1,061,700	95,800	120,300		31,600	814,000				
Disbursements to other debtor bank and investment accounts	6,899,700								6,899,700	
Payroll (including withholdings and payroll taxes)	1,306,700					1,306,700				
Wiese and Cox Trust account	720,600								720,600	
Amounts reviewed but not otherwise summarized above	7,003,200									7,003,200
Amounts less than $5,000 not reviewed	4,186,500									4,186,500
TOTAL	$31,716,700	$1,550,100	$3,050,000	$4,282,500	$251,900	$3,079,200	$176,800	$516,200	$7,620,300	$11,189,700

Source: Touche Ross & Co. audit of AEFS for U.S. bankruptcy court, St. Paul, Minnesota, 1983.

and $600 at a crack to pay for his living costs and past debts. In his 1982 taxes, he reported paying $20,000 in debts.[10] Like Hendrickson, Dwire too used AEFS money to meet personal needs; his appetite, however, was considerably larger. On one occasion alone, in April 1982, he borrowed $600,000 for operating costs for Dwire, Inc.

They became accustomed to taking AEFS money. They used it to buy farms, seeds, and fertilizer. Together they purchased three farms (known as the Corbett Farm, the Cusick Farm, and the Farnham Farm) and shared a research farm in Dwire's name. Along with four other farms owned by Dwire, the three farms they owned jointly—totaling nearly a thousand acres—were leased to AEFS for two hundred dollars an acre, which amounted to more than three times the average rent per farm acre in the region.[11]

The farms provided Dwire and Hendrickson with the seed and the promise of future seed with which they—at least on paper—could pay back the advances they took from AEFS. For instance, on the basis of 165,700 pounds of Jerusalem artichoke seed harvested from twenty-one acres jointly farmed with Dwire, Hendrickson claimed that he had paid AEFS back for approximately $40,000 of $50,000 he had taken in advances prior to December 31, 1981. Future harvests, he added, would cover the remainder of his advances.[12] In addition to the income generated from seeds from these farms and cash received from a range of beneficial governmental programs, such as PIK (Payment-in-Kind) or RAP (Reduced Acreage Program), Dwire and Hendrickson used their farms to sell AEFS research services and to help AEFS secure its insurance acres program, which provided seed to farmers who received bad seed or experienced adverse weather. On the eve of filing for bankruptcy, in May 1983, they counted one year of advanced credits for the lease of their farms against their debts to AEFS.

Hendrickson and Dwire were AEFS's owners, but they weren't its friends. They started themselves at salaries of $75,000 per year in the fall of 1981, but by the fall of 1982 they were rewarding themselves with salaries of $250,000 a year, making themselves among the best paid managers in Minnesota. Ironically, the preceding summer Dwire had rejected a salary of

$250,000 as being too great to pay an outside executive CEO, whom they nevertheless agreed was desperately needed.

Dwire and Hendrickson's partnership increasingly turned on each getting his share, and the company getting what was left over. Replying to this criticism, Hendrickson contended that profits are not odious in business, and since AEFS operated under partnership law (Subchapter S), AEFS's profits were theirs for the taking.[13] Hendrickson further argued that they chose to have their first tax year end in April 1982 rather than in June 1982 for tax reasons: If the tax year ended in June 1982, he and Dwire would have a total income of $5.2 million and profits of $1,200,000, whereas if it ended on April 1, 1982, they would only be taxed on profits of $155,000.

Hendrickson conceded that at the end of the next taxable period, ending on December 31, 1982, he strove to get his equal share, which was no easy matter given Dwire's extensive draws, advances, and simple taking. Believing they had made approximately $500,000 dollars in the tax year ending in December 1982, Hendrickson wrote himself checks worth $210,000 on December 31. In his deposition to the U.S. bankruptcy court in St. Paul, Minnesota, he considered this money "an advance against money I had already earned our first year. So," he explained, "I was taking profits that we had made in the first year."[14] He sent $106,000 of this money to Grow Force Fertilizer, to which Dwire sent a like amount, to be held in escrow for the future purchase of fertilizer.[15] Hendrickson used the remaining $100,000 to purchase the Storden feedlot as a tax shelter and investment.

Hendrickson was spurred on by a desire to keep up with Dwire, and the more he took the greater his appetite grew. On January 17, 1983, he transferred another $100,000 from AEFS to his personal account. Hendrickson considered half the money to be a loan and the other half to be an advance. He explained to the bankruptcy court that he, like Dwire, had taken a $40,000 loan for his share in Bio-Markets of America. He took another $10,000 for an option to buy an alcohol plant at Yankton, South Dakota, and $50,000 in advances against future earnings.

Hendrickson justified his taking by contrasting his smaller and documented withdrawals from AEFS with Dwire's larger and often undocumented withdrawals. Hendrickson also pointed out that Dwire carried out many transactions without his knowledge or permission, and he judged several of these transactions to be illegal. For instance, Hendrickson judged Dwire's purchase of seed at one price and sale of it to AEFS at another price as "absolutely wrong," a kind of insider trading, which might have amounted to embezzlement.[16]

Beyond arguments concerning specific transactions, the question still remains as to how much of AEFS's money was theirs for the taking. Many facts contradict their assumed right to take from AEFS at will. They started AEFS as a security, promising it would develop markets for the Jerusalem artichoke. They, and their agents, promised that AEFS would keep 50 percent of the growers' money in escrow and that they would dedicate a significant proportion of the company's assets to research. (Fifteen percent was the figure that appeared in some AEFS literature.) They always implied that there would be money on hand to pay for seed purchases.

There were four areas in which the two men legitimately could have used the company's money. They could dispense it for operating expenses, which they generously did. They could spend it on research, which they did on a small scale and in a misguided way. They could declare profits for its two owners, which they also did. They could put money in an escrow account, which they did not do at all. Insofar as they took AEFS cash as profits and put nothing in the escrow account, their earnings were not bona fide: They took what wasn't theirs.

Helping Themselves

As would any profit-minded contractor who realized the advantage of owning the companies that service one's company, Dwire owned a bunch of enterprises prepared to exploit AEFS from its inception. These companies included Dwire, Inc., Dwire Enterprises, Lynd Redi-Mix, Dwire Brothers, and Jim Dwire Construction. Also, Dwire owned or was associated with D. and G. Excavating (Dwire and David Gruhot), D & J Enterprises (Dwire and Linda Julian, his secretary at Dwire, Inc.), and yet other local business partnerships.

Dwire, Inc., was ideally positioned to provide labor, construction, field work, and many other services to AEFS at premium prices as the company established itself in new buildings, prepared fields for planting, and sold custom-made harvest machinery to new growers. Often the customized machinery simply amounted to modified old potato diggers. In one instance, a potato digger had lain in a grove so long that a tree that had grown up through it had to be chopped down before the implement could be hauled to Dwire, Inc., for customizing.

In AEFS's eighteen-month existence, Dwire supplied building, contracting, transportation, hauling, leasing, and other services to AEFS. In partnerships with his sons, Jim Jr. and Jeff, Hendrickson, and AEFS consultants Kramer and Dorband, Dwire created more than half a dozen companies whose express purpose was to service AEFS. Displaying how he could subordinate AEFS's interests to his other companies, in one of his earliest transactions as president of AEFS, Dwire leased his property in Lynd, Minnesota, to the company and then borrowed money from AEFS against the lease.

Even though Hendrickson wasn't as vigorous in exploiting AEFS, he also formed companies and started farms with AEFS money. In November 1982, with Dwire and Robert Soleta, a real estate agent knowledgeable about the alcohol fuel field, Hendrickson created Bio-Markets of America, Inc. This company, inspired by Hendrickson, testified to the sincerity of his vision of farm energy. It was based on the dream of "developing a series of decentralized 'world-based' elevator or bio-market yards" for the transformation of agricultural waste into energy. In April 1983 (a month before bankruptcy), he joined Dwire and Kramer in making a first payment of $75,000 for Faribault Orchards, a rural property worth, they estimated, a million dollars on the basis of potential agricultural use and property development.

Dwire and Hendrickson sold seed to AEFS from the outset. Throughout the fall of 1981 and the spring of 1982, there was a great shortage of seed on hand because of the rainy autumn, the absence of AEFS storage facilities, and the boom in seed sales. Always assuming that the open market price was $1.20 a pound, Hendrickson and Dwire sold AEFS both actual seed and seed that they planned on harvesting in the future. This proved a useful device to take cash out of the company. They counted their past, present, or future sales against any draws and advances they took. This proved an ingenious means for them to use company funds to put down payments on personal farms, which they in turn rented back to the company at the handsome rate of $200 an acre. While ostensibly serving the justifiable ends of crop research or of furnishing AEFS with a needed seed bank for growers who had received poor seed or lost seed to adverse weather, it was a means for Hendrickson and Dwire to own several farms.

In his grand jury testimony, Paul Laidlaw claimed that Dwire, Inc., bought seed at 25 cents a pound in Monticello and then sold it again, under the name of Dwire, Inc., to AEFS for 50 or 60 cents a pound.[17] What Laidlaw observed occurred more than once. Such exchanges assured Dwire a hundred percent or more profits as well as allowed him to maintain a monopoly over Jerusalem artichoke seed. In one case, Dwire, Inc., earned $375,000 in credits against Dwire's previous borrowings from AEFS. In the summer of 1982, Dwire, Inc., through the office of L. D. Kramer and Associates, purchased Jerusalem artichoke seed (yet to be harvested) at 25 cents a pound from four farmers in the Big Lake area of Minnesota—Vernon Florell, Ray Devitt, Jim Dechene, and Ray Sundstrom. Then Dwire sold this seed (not yet harvested) at 60 cents a pound to AEFS. Beyond the matter of Dwire making $375,000 worth of credit from AEFS for his own company, other questions about this transaction remain to this day. Who actually paid for the growers' seed? Whose machinery—Dwire's or AEFS's—constituted partial payment to two of four farmers for delivered seed? And how much of the seed was actually harvested and delivered? In another case, Dwire bought seed from another major Minnesota grower, Vince Erickson, at 45 cents a pound, while Kramer and the Laidlaws received credits of 60 cents a pound from future seed they shared through a joint contract with Erickson.

In a lengthy letter to Vekich-Arkema, Dwire explained that Dwire, Inc., had an open purchase order with three seed companies to buy all the seed they harvested.[18] In turn, AEFS—which in this case was Dwire himself—agreed to buy from Dwire, Inc., all his seed at 60 cents a pound, which was the same price AEFS paid its growers. This seed, if the company's history had played itself out, would have annulled completely any need on AEFS's part to purchase its own growers' seed. Dwire once again had found a means to put himself at the head of the line.

Dwire explained this to his suspicious accountants by contending that the prices Dwire, Inc., received were "special transactions involving growers who needed to quickly liquidate their harvest in bulk sale because of a serious cash shortage."[19] Dwire supplemented his argument by contending that Dwire, Inc., itself had a right to make a profit. His clinching argument (which displays an incredible mixture of rationalization and ignorance) was that if AEFS bought the seed directly from non-AEFS growers, "it could be viewed as a breach of good business practices by AEFS, Inc., if not a breach in its contractual obligations."

Dwire rather consistently applied the principle that what was good for Dwire was good for AEFS. In October 1982, he purchased for $432,000 the former Marshall Foods headquarters on the south side of Marshall, and then he had AEFS rent it from him as its own headquarters.[20] When asked in court how this transaction served AEFS's good, Dwire replied that his lawyer, Howard Cox, told him and his father that their earlier purchase of a farm for Dwire, Inc., "was the dumbest thing we ever did, and we should always buy our real estate in our own personal name."[21] When AEFS needed services, Dwire's corporations (accounting for many of the forty accounts he had at Norwest Banks), his family, or his friends met those needs. Dwire had AEFS employ his wife, who had the power to sign AEFS checks, two of his three sons, his uncle, his brother-in-law, and friends and acquaintances. He formed Triple J Aviation with his sons to lease airplanes to AEFS, and five of the nine planes that served AEFS were, at different times, in the names of Triple J or Dwire, Inc. When AEFS needed building or construction work, especially at its main office or its large sales center, Dwire, Inc., predictably did most of the work. Dwire, Inc., which charged AEFS premium prices, reciprocated by borrowing $600,000 in operating loans from AEFS, without offering any assets to secure the loans.

AEFS's research needs were met in the same spirit of self-interest. Research became excuses for the owners to buy farms.

It justified Hendrickson's office in Sioux Falls, where he could pay himself and Dorband high wages while compiling materials on the Jerusalem artichoke, hunting down alternative-energy schemes, and producing sales literature.

Hendrickson and Dwire made themselves middlemen between AEFS and the world. How much money, if any, they gave as perks or were given in kickbacks was never investigated. There is no doubt, however, that they used AEFS funds to pad their own accounts, and that they transformed dubious partnerships and valueless notes on future seed into credit instruments. Hendrickson even considered, in the spring of 1983, forming employees of Bio-Markets and AEFS into a credit union, and Dwire, under the guidance of Kramer, moved AEFS in the direction of becoming a financial agency. In an era characterized by junk bonds, deregulated and desperate savings and loan institutions, high interest rates, and capital-short farmers, one can only wonder where AEFS would have ended if they had ever succeeded in their desire to purchase a rural bank. They examined possible purchases of several banks and spent approximately a year trying to negotiate the purchase of the nearby small regional Buffalo Ridge State Bank in Ruthton, Minnesota.

AEFS became an abiding opportunity for them to transform business into a means to satisfy personal wants, impulses, and dreams. The bankruptcy court's audit leaves no doubt about that. The auditor for their bankruptcy, Touche Ross & Co., estimated that of $26,157,100 AEFS took in, James Dwire and his family received in cash or check $1,851,000; Fred Hendrickson or Hendrickson and Associates received $680,000; and other potential insiders received $2,334,100, for a total of $4,856,300. According to the audit, which covered the period from the inception of the company to May 23, 1983, and listed total payments of $5,000 or more to insiders and potential insiders (see table 1), Dwire himself received $1,707,000; his children, Jim Jr. and Jeff, received $144,000; $1,623,300 went to Dwire, Inc.; Del Quality Foods received $146,200; Dwire Enterprises, $123,000; Bio-Markets of America, $50,000; Lynd Redi-Mix, $41,200; Faribault Orchards, $6,000; and Southwest Constructors, $5,600. Kramer, L. D. Kramer and Associates, or Hillcrest Leasing received $338,800.[22]

Dwire's Right-Hand Man

Kramer became Dwire's right-hand man. He took to Dwire's and Hendrickson's management style like a duck to water. He was proud to serve as AEFS's brain trust. He frequently trumpeted his former success as head of a multimillion dollar nursing home. He told of how he helped AEFS retain Minnesota Governor Rudy Perpich's brother George as a lobbyist and how he also made the governor's neighbor, Robert Vekich—a brother of AEFS accountant Michael Vekich—an AEFS lobbyist.

Kramer had a keen interest in money. As soon as Dwire hired him, he asked for fifty dollars an hour and got it. Dwire put no limit on Kramer's hours, allowing him to bill AEFS for everything and anything he did. Kramer was not shy about accepting his fifty dollars an hour whether he was developing a new program for AEFS, spiritually "warming up" farm audiences, advising Dwire on personnel and finances, or washing Dwire's car, which he did on occasion.

Kramer started billing AEFS in January 1982. By May, he had charged the company more than $125,000 in consulting fees. Averaging more than $20,000 a month, one month he submitted a claim for a staggering 350 hours of work. At the time of bankruptcy in May 1983, in his own name, as Kramer and Associates, or as Hillcrest Leasing, he had taken approximately $340,000 from AEFS.[23]

"Confidence man" and "conniver," as some thought, or simply a sharp businessman, Kramer continually gained influence at AEFS. He repeated the idea that there were three ways to wealth: land, labor, and ideas. He openly admitted not having the first and not believing in the second, and was thus driven to make his fortune doing the third. He knew, as he advised others, that the key to his success at AEFS was to serve Jim Dwire. He did that effectively, so effectively that, according to Paul Laidlaw, Dwire came to depend on Kramer in almost all things. "I believe," testified Laidlaw, "that L. D. intertwined himself around Jim's business. ... He got Jim's business wrapped around him so tight that there was no way that Jim could get rid of him."[24]

On the basis of his own experience at Challenge Homes, Kramer frequently advised Dwire to take care of himself and his family. According to Bonnie Laidlaw, Kramer's advice simply pushed Dwire in the direction he was already leaning. Kramer advised Dwire to get his boys off to a good start in business if he wished to keep their respect. He even urged Dwire to make Jim Jr. president of Dwire, Inc., and make sure Jeff received a good position upon graduation from high school. When Jim Jr., Bonnie Laidlaw testified, questioned something his father suggested he should do, "Jim would say, 'Well, L. D. says it's okay and he's the consultant.' Anything L. D. says was okay, okay, but nobody ever checked."[25]

Kramer became Dwire's gatekeeper. If people wished to see Dwire in their shared Edina suite of offices, they first had to get an appointment with Kramer. Even Hendrickson found it necessary to go through Kramer to talk to Dwire. This aroused Hendrickson's anger and fueled his suspicion.

Kramer made himself indispensable to Dwire. Having gotten himself elected director of Prayer Power in the fall of 1982, Kramer took up the mantle of the deceased Pastor Pete. Knowing business and finance as no one else at AEFS did, Kramer became the company's primary consultant. Being so close to Dwire, Kramer voiced the president's authority on many issues. According to Bonnie Laidlaw's critical view of Kramer, he usually resolved misunderstandings he himself had fomented.[26]

Unlike Hendrickson, Kramer could, and did, think concretely about details. Knowing his way around parts of both the evangelical and the business world, he fit AEFS's needs well. And he fit the company better and better as it moved more and more in the direction of speculation and finance.

Between January and May 1983, Kramer made cash withdrawals from AEFS of approximately $140,000 in addition to his salary and withdrawals of more than $1 million worth of seed. Engaging in the double dipping, at which Dwire and Hendrickson excelled, he created his own company, L. D. Kramer and Associates. (Its figurehead president was Kramer's brother, Wendall, who lived in Florida and never signed a single company check.) He also controlled Dwire Enterprises, headquartered in Edina, whose total income of $123,000 was derived from

AEFS.[27] With $18,000 of AEFS money, Dwire and Kramer purchased Hillcrest Leasing, whose purpose was to lease cars and machinery to AEFS. Shortly thereafter AEFS gave Hillcrest an additional $25,000 to continue its operation. With his friend Paul Hegstrom, Kramer sold to AEFS for $1,000 or $1,200 a piece a dozen or so large-screen televisions. They had bought the televisions for $600 each.

In a far more complex scheme in the spring of 1983, with Dwire's full support, Kramer created a lending fund for growers who were too great a risk to receive a loan from AEFS. Nominally under the presidency of his son Tim and bearing Kramer's spiritual stamp (it was called Challenge Fund), the fund provided Kramer a means to get rid of the company's excess seed at no cost to himself or Dwire. The fund gave seed to growers in exchange for interest on the seed and a two-year partnership on growers' future Jerusalem artichoke crops. Kramer turned Challenge Fund partnerships, and other partnerships, into more than $2 million of financial paper, which, at face value or discounted, could be used—inside or outside AEFS—to raise cash, pay debts, or even make religious contributions.

It was this financial wizardry, best illustrated by his ability to turn useless seed into cash, that made Kramer, especially as the end of AEFS drew near, Dwire's man.

Two's Company, Three's a Crowd

Upon joining AEFS, Kramer perceived almost immediately that he couldn't serve both Hendrickson and Dwire. He chose Dwire, and he defined his relationship with Dwire by a little jingle: "Give Jim the glory, give me the gold."[28]

Dwire knew Kramer liked money. He saw how generously Kramer rewarded himself for his efforts. Yet this did not cause him either to dislike or distrust his consultant. Rather, Dwire prized Kramer for his enthusiasm and intelligence. His quick wit and practical sense made him Hendrickson's opposite.

Dwire respected Hendrickson for his sincerity, and he knew Hendrickson was singularly responsible for the vision that gave birth to AEFS. Nevertheless, he wearied of Hendrickson, who couldn't be reined in and was better at dreaming than doing.

When Dwire was frustrated with Hendrickson, he judged him to be impractical, lazy, and parasitical—simply another painful AEFS personnel problem.

Dwire's answer to "the Hendrickson problem" was to pay him off by giving him a good salary and let him idle away his time in Sioux Falls. At the same time, he increasingly felt justified in acting without consulting him.

Hendrickson was not without his criticisms of Dwire. Sometimes he disguised them in the form of religious exhortation; at other times, he was blunt. He strongly complained that Dwire was taking too much money, that the company wasn't under control, and that he, Hendrickson, wasn't getting the information he should be getting.

Hendrickson often accompanied his criticisms with requests for more money. He didn't hesitate to advise selling their future seed in order to compensate the company for his own past draws, which reached almost $50,000 by December 31, 1981.[29]

The resolutions to their conflicts frequently involved both men taking more from the company. AEFS was the one party that lost all their fights. Bonnie Laidlaw described one face-to-face confrontation between them. Hendrickson accused Dwire of taking money, and he added how dissatisfied his wife Beverly was over the money situation. Dwire settled Hendrickson down by proposing that they both take an equal raise, which they did.[30]

Hendrickson's correspondence with Dwire reveals a consistent pattern of religious exhortation, anger, and then reconciliation brought about by both men taking more money from AEFS. In a July 1982 memo, Hendrickson illustratively wrote, "If I didn't believe [we] were both called by the Lord, I would sell out tomorrow, even possibly today."[31] He started another memo that month with a complaint. He didn't mind Dwire putting his son Jeff on the payroll without talking to him, but to make him an assistant to the president "is a little strong for a teenager."[32] He continued that he wished to keep his title as director for research and development, which allowed "some part of his salary [to be] qualified for Research Investment Tax Credits." He exhorted Dwire to take the responsibility of being a leader of a company that would do $200 million worth of sales, and he concluded his memo by informing Dwire that he and Beverly were planning to meet their accountants, Vekich-Arkema, at Lake Okoboji to get their own estate in order. He suggested that Dwire and his wife should do the same. Yet in August in a three-sentence handwritten memo, Hendrickson asked for $1,500 as "an extra draw for some special things we [he and Beverly] pay for through the end of August." Then he asked for $20,000 for his September "payment on my house." Then, he assured Dwire, "I expect we will see a real positive cash flow about September 1, 1982."[33]

In a lengthy hand-delivered memo of October 28, 1982, Hendrickson reiterated his beliefs that he was being locked out of AEFS and that he could not control Dwire. Also, he confessed that he himself "did not wish to shoulder my one-half of the total responsibility for the functioning of AEFS and Bio-Markets." He proposed that they elect Michael Vekich, Howard Cox, and Kramer as additional board members of AEFS.[34]

In a second memo on October 28, 1982, Hendrickson revealed a further deterioration in their relationship. Appearing to prepare himself for future legal problems, he asked a long set of questions about withdrawals, payments, compensation, and salaries and questioned Dwire's prudence and behavior. He cautioned that "time is not on our side."[35] Less than a month later, Hendrickson voiced fears that his own and Dwire's spending might raise legal questions about a conflict of interest. He proposed that thereafter the relation of Dwire's companies to AEFS should be formalized in the areas of rental property, shop work, and equipment contracts, work or service by Lynd Redi-Mix, all leasing of Dwire's Moony airplane, and all trucking of seed and equipment. Hendrickson conceded that identical regulation should govern his own affairs and, accordingly, that he should formalize the fact that his Sioux Falls office was in his home, that his charges and fees should be consistent, and that the vouchers he submitted should have board approval. Interestingly, Hendrickson also proposed, as if it would be necessary, that no check be written upon corporate funds unless a filed written request defined the nature of the withdrawal and that no request for a loan or advance be approved unless it received board approval and carried with it an appropriate note or receipt.³⁶

Hendrickson's intentions to limit Dwire's abuse of company assets, however, invariably seemed to crumble when he was given the chance to do the same thing he accused Dwire of doing. His virtue never seemed to rise above making sure he got his fair share.

In a November 11 letter, Hendrickson proposed that he and Dwire should guarantee themselves 7 percent each of the total annual sales by designating "profit reserve accounts" for themselves. (If AEFS proved to become the $200 million company he conjectured, his proposal would be worth a nice $14 million a year for them to split.) Additionally, he proposed that each of them receive 1 percent for what Hendrickson called "a seed faith" reserve account. This "tithe of a tithe" would allow them to accomplish what Hendrickson called "seed-faith giving." Also, he suggested, again with his eye on the cash, that they divide the company's cash into five great pools of $500,000 each. One pool he allotted "almost" outright to AEFS itself; two of the four remaining pools—one for his keeping and another for Dwire's—would be corporate reserve against which AEFS could borrow up to one half the amount of their principal. The two remaining pools—again dividing the spoils into one for Hendrickson and one for Dwire—would be personal reserve accounts of $500,000 each; against these they could take advances or loans from AEFS up to half their principal. Dwire and Hendrickson would, of course, get the interest from these accounts; a modest 10 percent of $500,000 would annually yield an income of $50,000 a year.³⁷

This profitable idea amounted to nothing other than taking company money and putting it directly into his and Dwire's private accounts. Hendrickson rationalized these reserve accounts as a means to maintain "a proper credit posture and liquidity." The money in the accounts would be considered an advance and a loan against their profits as stockholders. Leaving open many possibilities, Hendrickson's proposal would allow them not only to borrow up to one half of the amount of principal against these personal accounts but also to use both personal and business reserve accounts to secure joint-venture loans.

Hendrickson's goal had become to stop Dwire from getting everything and to get as much as he could for himself. There was no disguising it; he no longer trusted Dwire. The truth of this deteriorating situation was expressed on the eve of the attorney general's findings, when Kramer was seeking to negotiate a deal to buy Hendrickson out. In a June 30, 1983, memo, Kramer acknowledged that the conflict of the owners was one reason of many why AEFS had failed.[38]

Already in August 1982, Kramer had called for a leadership that promoted self-esteem, squelched gossip, and listened to employees. "We must keep ourselves," he exhorted them, "fresh in the reading of articles, books, and especially the Word of God, spending time in prayer to keep ourselves in a proper spiritual frame of mind." Then, as if exhorting himself as much as Dwire and Hendrickson, Kramer concluded the memo, "The real problem lies in ourselves. That is why it is important we must have faith in ourselves, faith in God and faith in our fellow man, realizing that God has placed us here and it is our privilege to use the full potential that God has given to us, always being on guard of two great M's which have destroyed so many: the big M's of Money and Morals."[39]

All three men exhorted one another to do good, while each one competed to take what he could. Urgency increased the temptation to take what was left. On December 31, 1982, Hendrickson took a cash advance of $210,000 for personal use. Later he took another $178,000, filing notes for $156,000. Kramer took $280,000, of which $166,000 was covered by seed advances and other deposits. Dwire, their leader, took $687,000 for Dwire, Inc., with only $275,000 in notes, and $208,000 for himself, furnishing only $160,000 in notes.[40]

On the evening of May 20, 1983, a Marshall caterer unwittingly served the annually assembled AEFS Christian family of growers its last supper. After the meal, he stood contentedly by, having finally gotten the AEFS account he had so long wished for, until Dwire shockingly announced that AEFS intended to file for bankruptcy. The company formally did so three days later, on May 23, 1983.

7

Folding up the Tent

Of evil grain, no good seed can ever come.
—Anonymous

No sooner was Jim Nichols—farmer, teacher, and state senator from Lincoln County in southwest Minnesota—appointed commissioner of agriculture in January 1983 than he began to push the attorney general's office to broaden its investigation of AEFS. AEFS leaders saw this as a personal vendetta on Nichol's part. They believed that he sought to pay Dwire back for the strong support Dwire had lent Republican Vin Weber, who defeated Nichols in his 1982 bid for the U. S. House of Representatives. (Dwire's support had included a sizable contribution to Weber's campaign and the hosting of a large reception for him.)

Nichols claimed he knew nothing about Dwire's support for Weber, but he acknowledged he had numerous prejudices against Dwire. He believed Dwire had beaten his brother out of his father's business and then had run it into the ground. Fueling Nichols' populist suspicions and antipathies, he had heard about how Dwire played the part of a "high roller" and had taken to carrying a Bible at the same time he began selling Jerusalem artichokes.[1]

Nichols couldn't bring himself to believe that a crop that cost its buyers $1,000 an acre for seed alone (in contrast to corn, that cost $10 or $15 an acre) and for which there was no identified market was going to help the troubled farmers of Minnesota and the Midwest, whose cause Nichols (a self-confessed poor farmer) had vociferously made his own.

According to Nichols, he went to Marshall to see AEFS for himself in the spring of 1983. He and Dwire spent the whole day together ramming around the countryside. Dwire's grandiose attempts to impress the commissioner failed. Dwire's "nobody-tells-me-what-to-do" attitude was roughly identical to Nichols' own. According to grower Ben Steensma, "They were two big bulls in one small pasture."[2]

Nichols returned to the Twin Cities unconvinced. Before spring planting, he announced his doubts about AEFS on radio. Nichols suspected that Dwire and his helpers were "stashing away the money AEFS took in." He strongly urged the Minnesota attorney general to consider bringing criminal charges against them.

The Minnesota attorney general didn't agree. Having restricted its investigation to the validity of AEFS's claims on behalf of the Jerusalem artichoke, the attorney general's office concluded it could not make a case of criminal fraud against AEFS. Nichols himself conceded that AEFS would have had no trouble finding recognized authorities to say that the plant did have potential for the production of alcohol and sugar, and AEFS could prove it had made efforts—feeble as they might have been—to uncover the crop's potential.

Operating in conjunction with several other midwestern attorney generals' offices, the Minnesota attorney general's office accused AEFS of overestimating the promise of the crop and of not disclosing the fact that there were no markets for it. Its essential conclusions were that this was a case of "not such smart consumers doing some bad buying."[3]

The Minnesota attorney general's office reached an agreement with AEFS. Without having to acknowledge wrongdoing on its part, the company would pay the state $40,000 in fines, change its sales practices, and offer its growers a rescission of their contracts. The rescission could amount to an $18 million payback.

In the introduction to its rescission letter to each AEFS grower, the Minnesota attorney general's office explained that the original 451 growers would harvest enough tubers to plant approximately 100,000 acres for the 1983 growing season. They did this at a time when "there [was] no established market for Jerusalem artichokes for production of fructose or butanol"; there were at that time no commercial facilities for producing ethanol; there were "no Jerusalem artichoke tops . . . being processed or sold as animal feed on a commercial basis"; "the total market for Jerusalem artichokes as a human food is . . . satisfied by approximately 1,000 acres"; and "AEFS will not be able to finance the full development of the various markets itself."

The rescission offer got a surprising number of takers. This was due to the advance publicity given the settlement between AEFS and the Minnesota attorney general's office by a February article in *The Farmer*.[4] Approximately a quarter of AEFS growers, nearly six hundred farmers, the great majority of whom were two-year growers rather than the original and more committed three-year growers, quickly accepted the offer.

With only $2 or $2.5 million in cash on hand, AEFS was unable to satisfy approximately $6 million in growers' claims. The company filed for bankruptcy under Chapter 11 on May 23. It claimed that it had $19 million in unpaid debts and, with considerable exaggeration, that it had $11 million in assets. A few months later, when the federal bankruptcy court in St. Paul converted their Chapter 11 bankruptcy to a Chapter 7 bankruptcy, the court custodian claimed that AEFS had even less than a million dollars worth of assets.

The Final Division of the Spoils

The bankruptcy should have come as no surprise to Dwire and Hendrickson. Since the preceding fall, their accountants had repeatedly warned them that they had insufficient cash on hand.

According to accountant Michael Vekich, Hendrickson responded to December 1982 warnings that AEFS was short of cash and that his and Dwire's withdrawals might be considered taxable income by borrowing an additional $250,000 at the end of the year. In February 1983, Vekich warned that the company's $1.7 million in cash on hand wouldn't cover the $3.7 million owed growers.[5] These warnings apparently didn't bother Hendrickson or Dwire or cause them concern about the viability of their company. Throughout the spring of 1983, they continued to take cash out of it.

Their attorneys' warnings also went unheeded. In a lengthy letter in December 1982, AEFS attorney Howard Cox set forth no less than fourteen reasons why AEFS was in disorder: Among other things, he noted, the company didn't have a chain of command. It didn't delegate authority, have plans, or know its costs. He particularly pointed out the division of the company between Dwire and Hendrickson, who initiated a range of "fly-by-night schemes, [which] had the effect of making two companies out of one."[6]

Since the late fall of 1982, Dwire, Hendrickson, and Kramer had already begun to prepare their own lifeboats. As the company's legal problems mounted and their slipshod efforts to transform the Jerusalem artichoke into a viable crop failed, each began to look beyond AEFS. Predictably, Hendrickson, loyal to his vision, turned his attention more and more to alternative energy projects and invested his hopes in Bio-Markets of America. Kramer worked on the development of Challenge Fund as an independent financial agency. Also, he was busy working on a plan to sell off AEFS's rights to independent state operations that would supersede AEFS.[7]

On the very eve of retaining a bankruptcy attorney on May 10, Dwire, Hendrickson, and Kramer took almost everything left in AEFS's coffers, which, by the best calculations of their prosecutors, totaled $686,000. Among their distributions, they gave their attorneys' firm, Wiese and Cox, $260,000, mainly to cover future legal fees; the Vekich accounting firm was given $67,000 to handle the bankruptcy; Hendrickson took $50,000; and Kramer got $74,000. Dwire's eighteen-year-old son, Jeff, who had already earned more than $100,000 working at the company, was paid an additional $12,500 for hauling he had supposedly done for AEFS. In a separate transaction of $85,000, Jeff purchased sales trainer Ron Mann's house in rural Marshall, as well as his plane and tractor. Dwire himself took $224,000 for AEFS bills due to Dwire, Inc., and another $50,000 (a sum equal to Hendrickson's) for Dwire Enterprises.

On May 9, a check for $33,710 was written to Del Quality Foods, another of Dwire's companies. On May 10, Hendrickson and Dwire made a mutually advantageous trade. Dwire gave up his share in three jointly owned farms—the Vermillion farm, the Cusick farm, and the Farnham farm—for Hendrickson's share in the corporate office building. Hendrickson drove off from the final division of the spoils in an AEFS car, $50,000 richer, while Dwire stayed behind and engaged in a mopping-up operation.

On May 11, 1983, attorney Howard Cox reported to accountant Michael Vekich that they had now completed documents essential for terminating AEFS as a Subchapter S company. AEFS would be recapitalized as a corporation and held equally by Dwire and Hendrickson and their families. As part of the transaction, Dwire and Hendrickson transferred their useless shares in Little Lamb Chokes for an equal number of shares in AEFS, which they then claimed as credits against their takings from AEFS. They did the same thing with their shares in Bio-Markets of America.[8]

During the period of May 10 to May 25, Dwire sold AEFS $260,000 "worth" of virtually useless Jerusalem artichoke tubers. He clumsily laundered $100,000 among himself, one of his sons, two banks, and three accounts. He deeded an airplane to his son and farms to his two sons, and he sent his wife off to South Dakota with a $400,000 check to cash. As late as June 28, showing he was not yet chastened by events, Dwire tried to get his hands on the company's 178 100-ounce Engelhard silver bars, worth approximately $30,000, in order to be compensated for what the company owed him for having met AEFS's payroll with Dwire Enterprises money. The only hitch was that Dwire Enterprises' only source of income had been AEFS.

In the closing days of the company, like a drowning man, Dwire grabbed for everything he could reach. In a two-day period from May 9 to May 10, he gathered $795,000 from other regional banks into his Marshall account, and from there, according to McLeod County investigator Jim Newes, disbursed more than $600,000 in checks.[9] In one instance, he used his son, Jim Jr., to peddle a piece of property purchased with AEFS funds.[10] In another instance, he paid off a piece of land by using AEFS money to pay Dwire, Inc., which deeded the land back to him in August 1983. In turn, Dwire deeded the same property to PBX Partnership, a company whose address was that of his son Jim

Jr.'s house. The property was later sold to Donald DeLanghe (see figure 3).[11] In another transaction, illustrating the common, but primitive, money washing of the era, AEFS gave Dwire $100,000 in the name of Dwire, Inc. The $100,000 then was deposited in the Dwire, Inc., account at Buffalo Ridge Bank, out of which three separate checks, totaling approximately $100,000, were issued by Jim Jr. to the Dwire, Inc., account in Marshall. In a month the money had traveled a circle, whose end was never in doubt: Dwire's hands (see figure 4).[12]

Dwire and Hendrickson made the final days of AEFS a review of illegal actions they had learned up to then, as McLeod County district attorney Peter Kasal would charge in subsequent cases against Dwire, Hendrickson, and Kramer. Between May 10 and May 25, they, with Kramer, sold $260,000 worth of seed to AEFS (at the inflated price). They exchanged assets: Hendrickson took full ownership of three farms for surrendering "his share" in the corporate office building. No sooner was the building in his hands than on May 10 Dwire postdated a lease for it to AEFS for twenty-two months ($10,000 a month). He then used the $220,000 earned as credit against past advances he had taken from the company.

In the wake of filing for bankruptcy, Dwire's and Hendrickson's first concern was taking what they could, while protecting themselves against criminal charges. They went so far as to make up bills of lading, notes for seed, notes for money taken, and rent and lease credits to justify what they had borrowed, advanced to themselves, or simply taken. When asked to justify the $50,000 he took on May 9, Hendrickson expressed the attitude that underlay their actions: "There were seventy-seven different ways to justify taking the money."[13]

Long before filing for bankruptcy, Dwire and Hendrickson had made their own interests superior to those of AEFS. They did not treat Chapter 11 as a safe haven for reorganization. Rather, they treated it as a last chance for taking.[14]

As Dwire and Hendrickson dismantled AEFS, they let the company appear to go about its business. Ironically, an intracompany memo dated May 13 announced a "shakedown run" planned to occur at the Reese alcohol plant in Marshall within a week. "Eight tons of Jerusalem artichokes are expected to be liq-

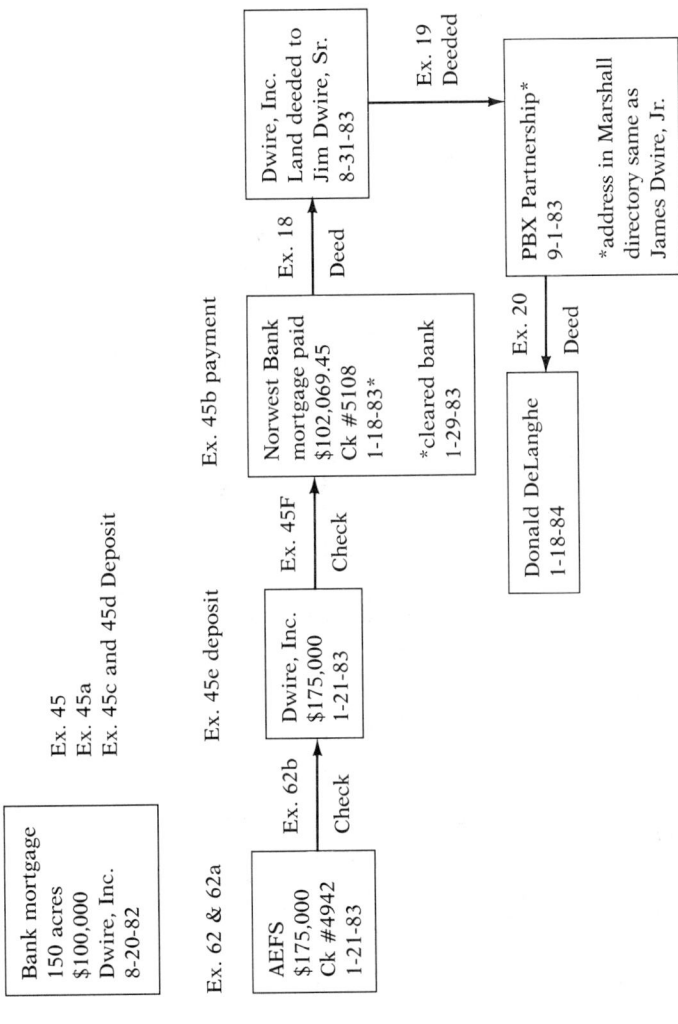

Figure 3. Dwire, Inc./Norwest Bank Mortgage, prepared by Jim Newes for the grand jury investigation. (*Source*: Grand Jury Investigation re: AEFS, exhibit 10, October 15, 1984; resubmitted as state exhibit 13, October 28, 1986.)

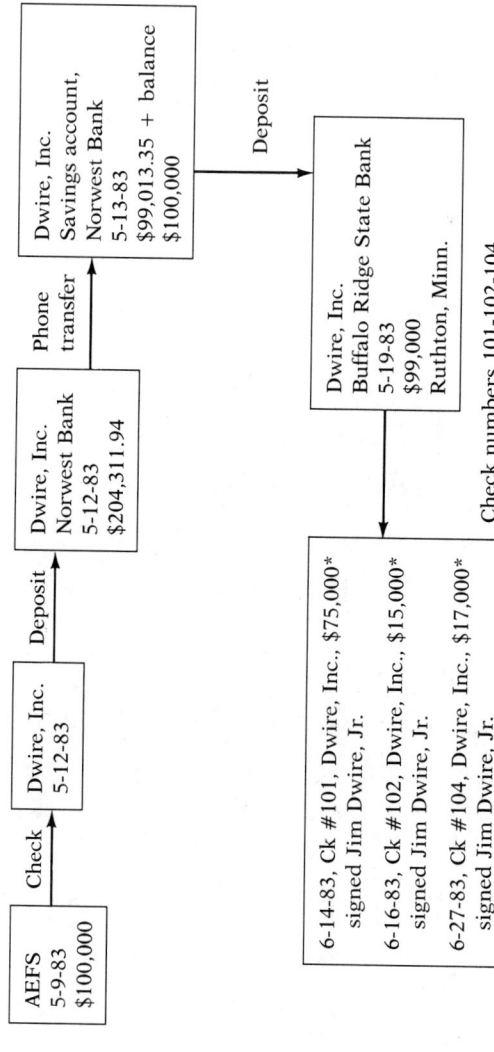

Figure 4. Dwire, Inc., account in May 1983, prepared by Jim Newes for the grand jury investigation. (*Source*: Grand Jury Investigation re: AEFS, submitted as exhibit 18, August 28, 1986.)

uified into 140-160 gallons of choke alcohol next week in the first Jerusalem artichoke shakedown run." The shakedown failed miserably: The dirty and fibrous Jerusalem artichoke tubers eluded processing, blocked driers, and proved resistant to purification.

Dwire and Hendrickson showed no inclination to refund growers their investments or to reorganize the company at their own expense. Among the letters left unanswered was one from a poor farm couple in Starbuck, Minnesota, who wrote to AEFS on May 24, 1983, asking to have their money returned for fear of losing their house and all they had worked for. "We borrowed money on our house to buy seed and . . . to get ahead."[15]

If anyone could have saved AEFS, it was Kramer; who gained greater access to AEFS's assets as Dwire grew more and more dependent upon him. But Kramer, who received approximately $480,000 from AEFS in salary, expenses, seed advances, gifts, and a downpayment on a condominium, increasingly treated AEFS's assets as if they were his own.[16] According to the prosecutor at his trial, he received $150,000 in seed advances and was given $50,000 to buy a house for himself. Kramer disagreed, claiming he was given only $5,000 to make a down payment on a condominium where Dwire, who had received unidentified threats on his life, could safely stay when he was in the Twin Cities.[17]

In the world in which the promise of Jerusalem artichoke tuber seed and the paper it generated had value, Kramer emerged as a wizard-king. Seed, which had been scarce in 1982, began swamping the company by the late spring of 1983 when growers, who had delayed their harvest in the fall because of wet conditions and a shortage of AEFS storage space, began to deliver their crops.

Kramer the wizard had to conjure this abundant seed into spendable cash. His solution was the Challenge Fund. Having operated as a finance agency of AEFS since its inception in March 1983, Kramer's Challenge Fund—AEFS's last big tent show—transformed useless seed into $3 million of financial notes.

The Challenge Fund—owned by Kramer and Dwire and nominally under the presidency of Kramer's son Tim—was truly a lender of last resort. It provided the most uncreditworthy farmers the seed that AEFS had denied them. The fund did so on the condition that the farmers enter a two-year, fifty-fifty partnership on the future seed they produced. Additionally, farmers had to pay two hundred dollars an acre for plantings, with no guarantee that AEFS would ultimately buy their seed.

Verging on bankruptcy, desperate farmers were not interested in examining how leaky the solitary rescue boat on the horizon was. They figured nothing would be lost, since the price of seed and planting was irrelevant to the deal. Jim Nichols summarized their reasoning: If things go well, we can pay them back easily, whereas if things go poorly, "you might as well lose the farm big."[18]

The farmers weren't the only cynical ones. Challenge Fund charged interest payments of 14 percent on the total price of the seed that it had taken for free from AEFS, and it took out a lien against each grower's crop for the following two years.

By the late spring of 1983, thanks to Kramer's financial juggling, Challenge Fund had accumulated thirty notes, ranging in value from $10,000 to the two exceptional notes of Larry Stotts, which were worth $650,000 each. The fund furnished Stotts with enough seed to plant a thousand acres of Jerusalem artichokes. He, in return, wrote his notes against the future sale of his seed, while promising to pay Challenge Fund a hefty 14 percent interest on the notes.

The prosecution later estimated that Challenge Fund's notes—seventeen of which were signed after the rescission order—totaled $2.8 million and involved 1.9 million pounds of AEFS seed.[19] (According to Kramer, the notes were worth $3.2 million.) In either case, Challenge Fund took approximately $3 million worth of AEFS seed without paying a single penny for it or even furnishing AEFS a note for the seed it had taken.

In the spring and summer of 1983, Kramer himself made transactions with five individual farmers similar to those involved in the Challenge Fund. Known in the course of criminal proceedings as the "Five Partnerships," these transactions, crucial to the state's prosecution, involved Kramer loaning five farmers the seed they needed in exchange for five notes for $10,000 apiece. Kramer, in turn, gave a note of $50,000 to AEFS in order to buy its seed. Then, to pay off this note, Kramer presented AEFS with the original five notes from the very five farmers to whom AEFS had declined to loan money in the first place. The consequence of this transaction was that AEFS got a useless note for $50,000, while Kramer, not having spent or risked anything, ended up with a claim to 50 percent of these farmers' future yields. Either Kramer or Dwire (officials from the bankruptcy court were unsure) later used $200,000 credit generated from the sale of the five farmers' seed against draws they made upon AEFS.

In the case of the Five Partnerships and the Challenge Fund, "free" seed became the vehicle for forming a partnership. In exchange for giving desperate farmers a chance to survive in farming one more day, Kramer and Dwire got rid of seed, earned interest, and created financial paper that, however dubious its value, had potential worth in that era of speculation. Kramer contended that prior to filing bankruptcy he had a New York "Jewish" firm willing to offer him as much as $1.5 million for the notes at a discounted rate of approximately 35 percent.[20]

Kramer had even more cards up his sleeve. He and Dwire could potentially transform these Challenge Fund and select partnership agreements into seed credits that they could use against past or future draws of AEFS cash. With no record of their transactions entered in company books, Kramer could gloat that he had made almost the perfect deal: If the seed kept its value until the following harvest, he and Dwire could, if they chose, magnanimously repay AEFS. If the seed lost its value, which could be anticipated, they could repay AEFS at inferior prices, or not at all. Whatever the outcome, wizard Kramer had created paper that conjured yet more paper.

Kramer thrived in this paper world of greed, guile, and illusion. On the very day that AEFS filed for bankruptcy, May 23, 1983, Kramer formed a limited partnership with Tom Stanfield, an Iowa grower, which he assigned to grower and president of Sun Rood Foods Doug Ness and the Norwest Dawson bank.[21] In June, Challenge Fund, continuing "business as normal," entered its second five-hundred-acre partnership with Larry Stotts for $650,000. Stotts agreed to pay $95,000 in annual interest.[22] In August, Kramer sought to use the first Stotts note to solve his growing problems with the law. Under investigation and off

AEFS's payroll since June 30, Kramer offered to turn over to the bankruptcy court the first Stotts note to repay AEFS for the seed Challenge Fund had taken. According to Kramer, the Stotts note squared Challenge Fund's debt with AEFS, even though the value of seed taken was worth more than $1 million even if it was bought at preferred prices.[23]

Upon his attorney's advice, Dwire separated himself from Challenge Fund in August 1983. Operating Challenge Fund through his son, Kramer continued unsuccessfully throughout the spring of 1984 to try to collect on the Challenge Fund notes.[24] More than one Challenge Fund grower was surprised to discover that his note had been assigned as collateral or offered in payment to other parties. Probably none was as surprised as Dean Holland, who discovered that his $19,000 note had been assigned to Kramer's church, the Minnesota District of the Assemblies of God. Kramer generously assigned other notes of dubious value to members of his family, his friends, and companies under his control.[25]

Kramer did not hesitate to make his family part of his dealings. He made his brother, Wendall, the head of L. D. Kramer and Associates, even though Wendall had never seen the company's records or signed a single one of its checks. Confident AEFS was a good opportunity for his youngest son, Tim, a graduate in economics from the University of Minnesota, Kramer persuaded him to quit his job at the Furniture Barn in St. Cloud and go to work for Challenge Fund in Edina, where he was made its nominal head. Kramer's older son, Dale, sat on Challenge Fund's board of directors.

Kramer never conceded that AEFS's failure had anything to do with him. He explained the company's demise as essentially a business failure that could be accounted for by such things as a standing disagreement between the owners, the absence of a clear business plan, the failure to establish a positive cash flow, the tendency to ignore the advice of several "excellent consultants." At other times, Kramer, like Hendrickson, attributed the company's failure to a conspiracy against it of great and antagonistic forces. In the failure he read the machinations of giant companies such as ethanol producer Archer Daniels Midland, state agencies in the service of these companies, and the political ambitions of people who headed these state agencies. As did Hendrickson and Dwire, he saw Jim Nichols as motivated by revenge and Minnesota Attorney General Skip Humphrey (whom he referred to as HHH III) as the pawn of Duane Andreas, the chief executive of Archer Daniels Midland. He also saw McLeod County prosecutor Pete Kasal as a tool of Humphrey.[26]

Kramer also conjectured in more than one interview that AEFS was prosecuted because its leaders were Republicans and Christian fundamentalists. He felt himself especially targeted because he was a father of TV evangelism, which, as he accurately noted, had become fashionably despicable in liberal quarters of the nation.

If given enough time to talk, however, Kramer offered additional reasons for the company's failure. He attributed it to other consultants who never stood trial. The company, he contends, and Hendrickson agrees, was filled with greedy consultants, especially attorneys Cox and Ainsworth, who made more than a "million dollars" from AEFS and used the company to advance their own careers. Their advice, according to Kramer, was always short-term and amounted to telling Dwire and Hendrickson to take all they could.

Kramer did not hestitate to hold Hendrickson and even Dwire responsible for the company's failure. He saw Hendrickson as "a rascal" who could always be bought for a price, a man who, he pointed out, had already failed at selling Jerusalem artichokes in South Dakota, and a lazy man who didn't know how to choose or manage the people under him. Ultimately, Kramer considered Hendrickson incapable of holding up his end of the work and a typical lawyer whose loyalty was measured by how much he was paid.[27]

Dwire, in Kramer's opinion, was a different sort of egotist. He was impulsive, greedy, and to use Kramer's expression, "an opportunist." He wanted everything immediately.[28]

In one conversation, Kramer—in his darkest mood—even postulated that Hendrickson and Dwire had hired him as a fall guy. Given his previous legal problems with the Federal Securities Commission, they may have figured, he hypothesized, that he would prove to be a perfect scapegoat if things went wrong for AEFS.[29]

Going Separate Ways

As Kramer ensnared himself by his own cleverness, Hendrickson was the victim of his own dreams. Lacking a sense of irony and abounding with enthusiasm, he produced an untethered whirl of projects, schemes, and prophecies.

Hendrickson went nowhere without spouting his preachments, and he held tightly to one great associated conceit; namely, that he was "an idea man." This presumption (not uncommon to professors and authors of books) made Hendrickson an ideal prophet for this windy fruit.

But Hendrickson wanted more than a chance to wear the prophet's mantle. As he demonstrated repeatedly, he also wanted earthly things. Near the end of April 1983, he met twice with Kramer to consider what it would cost Dwire to become the sole owner of AEFS. But before the end of the month, Hendrickson quickly climbed back on board. He borrowed from the company $50,000 for a year at 12 percent. He tentatively joined Dwire as a partner in an aborted agreement (no doubt designed by Kramer) between themselves and Larry Stotts, who owned 4,200 acres along the Red River in southwestern Arkansas. This agreement, which failed to pass muster at Stotts's Dallas bank, would have made Stotts an insider and made him and his new partners producers of vast new quantities of seed that would have further diminished AEFS's need for its own growers' seed.[30]

For Hendrickson, who did not hesitate to share the May "division of the spoils," things took a much more serious turn after the bankruptcy. He needed money. He had to pay for his farms and support his family, which was just getting accustomed to a $250,000-a-year salary, owning a decent home, and driving a big car. (Even after the bankruptcy, Hendrickson bought a $14,000 Chrysler New Yorker.) Even more worrisome for Hendrickson, he and Dwire held assets for which they now were legally accountable. They were subject to the investigations of the federal bankruptcy court, the U.S. Postal Service, and the FBI.

Hendrickson increasingly disassociated himself from Dwire throughout the summer. By October, he declared himself willing to cooperate fully with bankruptcy trustee Edward Bergquist in exposing Dwire.[31]

Their deteriorating relationship had already been revealed by two lengthy letters Hendrickson had sent to Dwire a day apart at the end of June. Hendrickson claimed he wrote his first letter June 25 after six hours of praying and meditating. Affirming their initial providential calling, he accounted for their weaknesses by saying they had gotten caught up in the "big money push" of the growers themselves and "the extra business rush" caused by Kramer. While acknowledging a part of the blame, Hendrickson told Dwire that the growers held Dwire uniquely responsible for the company's failure, and that he should resign. Now openly doubting Dwire's faith in the energy farming movement, Hendrickson argued that AEFS should be turned over to the growers and the managers who had a burning desire to serve God. The company requires, Hendrickson sermonized, a "blind trust in God and people like [Canadian alcohol fuel promoter] Harry Noton, Cal Maxwell, Jerry Knapper, and Bob Soleta."

Hendrickson's conclusion to the letter was less sublime. After scoring Dwire for taking loans for the corporate headquarters and the Edina office, Hendrickson claimed he was adamant in his determination to sever his financial relationship with the company and to keep "the three little farms that I have undertaken to acquire." While claiming he would not judge Dwire for his dealings with Kramer, Hendrickson asserted, "Jim, we are going to have to defend the business judgments that 'we' made. We must remain together in defending the way the company was run." Otherwise, he suggested, they would both end up in court for the next several years. Hendrickson ended his letter with a list of demands. "In order to maintain a common front I must be financially secure to meet the minimal financial needs that my family will face in the next twelve months." Specifically, he wanted $100,000 from AEFS owed from past transactions, $50,000 of which was to be used as a credit against money he had borrowed from AEFS in April. He also wanted to keep his Sioux Falls office open for at least another thirty days, $6,000 for payment on his van and AEFS expenses he incurred, and the immediate transfer of the Corbett farm at Corson to his name. Finally, to protect himself against possible future criminal charges, he wanted assurance that it be indicated that the car he took from the company had been earned as a fringe benefit.[32]

In the letter he wrote to Dwire the following day, Hendrickson reiterated his desire to cooperate with the bankruptcy court to avoid being *"faced with the multitude of law suits and difficulties attendant to a regular bankruptcy suit."*[33] Prefacing his letter with a nearly incomprehensible optimism, Hendrickson predicted both he and Dwire would earn their way back into the growers' good graces within six months. They would again head a company that was doing noteworthy research with the support of Larry Tieszen. It would be worth $5 million to $10 million a year. All this, however, would happen only if Dwire accepted his and his lawyer and friend George Qualley's plan for reorganization. True to form, Hendrickson made a final pitch for more money: $5,000 from AEFS for Qualley, and $10,000 more from AEFS attorney Howard Cox so Qualley could pursue AEFS's case against Webb Press for its article in the *Farmer*, which Hendrickson continued to believe had caused the company's bankruptcy. After wishing God's blessing on Jim and his family, Hendrickson signed his letter, "sincerely yours as your partner."[34]

Thereafter, Hendrickson's letters to Dwire, Kramer, and the company's bookkeeper and attorneys became nastier. For the sake of his defense, Hendrickson demanded more details about AEFS's past transactions. In several letters he complained bitterly that AEFS was closing his Sioux Falls office where, he opined, vital research was being organized and from where his Bio-Markets of America was directing the development of alcohol plants in Sherman, Scotland, and Yankton, South Dakota.

In a July 8 letter, Hendrickson futilely tried to take control of AEFS's check issuing and to command the firing of administrator Bob Messersmith, whose faith Hendrickson questioned.[35] In a July 19 letter, he demanded immediate payment from Dwire for $104,600, plus interest, that he, Cox, and Kramer had, under the name of Dwire, Inc., entangled in an escrow account with Grow Force Fertilizer in order to escape taxes in December 1982.[36] In an attachment to this letter, Hendrickson insisted he be bought out by payments of $104,600, plus interest of $5,000; that the three farms he traded Dwire for the company building be transferred to him; and that he get a year's interest on the

"$500,000 or $600,000" owed him. As if this weren't enough, Hendrickson demanded that Dwire step down, the company be reorganized, and Dwire hold and defend Hendrickson as "free from all legal claims, demands, and suits (including criminal suits and attorney fees) arising from Dwire's running of AEFS."[37]

The compensation Hendrickson offered Dwire revealed a momentary madness. He gave Dwire a chance to be the sole owner of AEFS, and—like some sort of great verbal magician, who need only wag his tongue over reality to transform it—he gave Dwire and his companies the right to "enter fully any business activities even in competition with AEFS." Hendrickson then concluded his letter by saying that his wife had been "through enough," and that he would no longer "stand by and be manipulated by Dwire forces and ... the power they have." He summed up by threatening that unless these matters were resolved in a week, he would "commence law suits to recover monies due him, ... go to the Minnesota Attorney General, the U.S. Attorney [General] and IRS or any other federal or state regulatory agency to inform them of his limited involvement ... and [his willingness] to cooperate."[38]

On the same day that Hendrickson wrote that threatening letter to Dwire, he sent a ten-page, single-spaced letter to Jerry Knapper, soliciting his cooperation in the total reorganization of AEFS. Hendrickson proposed that Knapper become president of AEFS, that together they adopt Hendrickson's 132-circle marketing system, that they invite the farmers to take full control of the company ("our exclusion of them has been wrong, wrong, wrong"), and that they let them and their cooperatives market their seed independent of AEFS. "Our total plan will work as it will be simple and," Hendrickson cynically wrote, "[it] will appeal to the individual economic greed factor of each farmer."[39]

By October, Hendrickson was ready to throw Dwire and Kramer to the dogs. In a lengthy, self-justifying letter to Edward Bergquist, bankruptcy trustee, and Daryle Uphoff, attorney for the committee of unsecured creditors, Hendrickson wrote that his main purpose in an upcoming meeting "will be to demonstrate to you that I was not part in any plan or design of either Jim Dwire and/or L. D. Kramer to withdraw large sums of money." Contending that until the Webb article appeared there was ample money on hand—Hendrickson estimated the amount to have been $10 million—he accused Dwire of trying to "cook the books" to disguise his stealing.

Hendrickson further pointed out in his letter that his assignment was research, not the everyday running of the company. He claimed the money he took in the spring of 1983 was only his fair share as co-owner of the company. Testing the limits of Bergquist's and Uphoff's gullibility, Hendrickson argued that his spring withdrawal of $50,000 with a check written at Kramer's suggestion was issued to Hendrickson and Associates, not Fred Hendrickson, and that it had nothing to do with making him $50,000 richer. Then, as if to test their capacity to reason in somersaults, Hendrickson wrote, "Actually the check was taken by me, and any reference to Hendrickson and Associates should be disregarded as this entity was never formed, nor were there any associates.... I am sure this check was written to me to show a general pattern on their part and a participation in their efforts to withdraw large sums from AEFS at a time when they knew the impaired condition of AEFS." Hendrickson concluded his letter: "I want to cooperate in correcting the wrongs that were committed by two gentlemen in running the financial affairs of AEFS ... and I want ... to see that those who have committed wrongs are not allowed to become unjustly enriched and compensated."[40]

Despite such swerves in Hendrickson's reasoning, Berquist and Uphoff were swayed by his cooperativeness, which increased throughout the winter of 1983 and the spring of 1984. Upon that basis they assigned him a small unremovable debt of $10,000, whereas they assigned $250,000 to "the cagy" Kramer and $815,000 to "the recalcitrant" Dwire.[41]

Others Going Their Own Way

The announcement of AEFS's filing for Chapter 11 set people scrambling. The Marshall caterer who served AEFS its "last supper" began a daily ritual of phoning Dwire two or three times. He made one call every night after closing his restaurant at 1:00

A.M. His persistence was rewarded. After fifty or so calls, Dwire paid him.

Most creditors, after being initially shocked by the news of the bankruptcy, secured a lien, or checked their lien, against AEFS's buildings and property. One local Marshall builder did this, having just installed $15,000 worth of carpet in AEFS's main sales office. By dint of his own wits, one local businessman, pretending to be on a service call, gained entrance through the back door of AEFS's main office building in order to repossess his expensive electronic equipment.

The owners of a local office supply store, Bromen Office Supply, were not so lucky or enterprising. They had benefited when AEFS made its large and regular monthly payments but were caught off guard by the bankruptcy and discovered that they couldn't file a lien on the $20,000 worth of supplies that Dwire's executive assistant, Linda Julian, had ordered in April. After initially blaming the attorney general for having hounded the company into bankruptcy, the stationers acknowledged that they had had suspicions about AEFS's solvency when they installed an expensive company security system at its headquarters. (The system required AEFS employees to use a green and white plastic identification card to gain admission to the building.) They ended up buying back some of their own office equipment at AEFS's auction.

AEFS's bankruptcy did not precipitate any other bankruptcies in Marshall. Local merchants had been delighted to do business with the company, and they were particularly pleased that it underwrote Dwire, Inc. Nevertheless, the Marshall business community—home of the awesomely successful private company, Schwan's Sales Enterprises, which grew from one man's local ice cream company to a national and international company that grossed more than a billion dollars in sales a year in the 1990s—kept AEFS at arms' length. The president of Southwest State University, Jon Wefald, had turned down $20,000 to help promote AEFS, and former Marshall school superintendent and state commissioner of education John Feda, following good advice, had turned down the chance to become the company's CEO. Neither of the city's chief lending agencies, Norwest Bank and First American Bank and Trust, had loaned money to AEFS.

Also, the Marshall chamber of commerce had kept its distance. In fact, the Marshall business community so successfully distanced itself from AEFS that to this day Dwire emotionally declares that if he had a chance to do it all over again, he wouldn't have even built "a shit house in Marshall."[42]

Marshall "Main Streeters" saw the bankruptcy as a matter between AEFS and its growers. They themselves didn't have farms and hadn't risked their money. Only a handful of city people got involved with AEFS. Discounting members of the local Evangelical Free Church, bankruptcy records reveal that only one Main Street investor lost his money—$30,000 in all.

Nevertheless, AEFS's bankruptcy got plenty of local attention. It was a juicy subject, worthy of the town's six or seven local coffee klatches. It invited an endless stream of "I told you so" and "I suspected all along," and hypotheses about who corrupted the company abounded. Was it arrogant Dwire, daydreaming Hendrickson or shiny-shoed "television evangelist" L. D. Kramer? Many more "liberal" and secular members of the college community relished the juicy connection between preaching and stealing as well as the close relationship that existed between AEFS and the rapidly growing Evangelical Free Church on the edge of town.

People had fun choosing their own explanation for what had happened, and their speculations were unfettered by evidence. Some, as if they were talking about where Jimmy Hoffa's body was buried, said in hushed tones that Dwire—who did in fact have special money belts made at the local shoemaker's—shipped off tons of money to Switzerland. A distinct minority believed, to the contrary, that he had had his money cemented under the runway of an airport.

A number of good anecdotes churned their way up and down main street. The most popular of them was the telling and retelling how Dwire's brother, Richard, one day after the bankruptcy announcement wore a T-shirt that stated, "I am not Jim!"

As important a local story as the bankruptcy and subsequent prosecutions against Dwire, Hendrickson, and Kramer was, it never focused Marshall's and the region's attention the way a local 1983 murder of two bankers by a father and son had.[43] The story increasingly appeared to be more comic relief than anything when measured against the serious rush of farm bankruptcies, store closures, and weakening businesses that characterized the rest of the decade.

Of course, AEFS's bankruptcy was a serious matter for company employees. With the shortest possible notice, bankruptcy sent a third of the company, sixty-six employees, packing. They included management's executive director Richard Spencer and national sales director Paul Skrien.

AEFS salesmen were at the end of their rope. They no longer had heart for the pitch. It had been hard enough to try to explain away the Webb article and the attorney general's rescission order. Now their task was impossible. The question was no longer whether Jerusalem artichokes could save the family farm and America but whether farmers should simply plough them under, leave them grow for pig and cattle feed, or haul them over to Sioux Falls, where a buyer was paying five cents a pound for them.

With sales dead, AEFS was dead. The employees got a two-week notice and no last check. Some employees left Marshall.

In-house private investigator Ken Nordin stayed on in Marshall as a private investigator. Linda Julian retrained herself to become an emergency medical technician. Pat "Family Farmer" O'Reilly, who never quite had a clearly defined job at AEFS, continued to roam the nearby countryside looking for meaningful employment to support his failing farm. He ran for office as a Democratic party maverick in the 1980s, and it was then, to help his campaign, that he legally took as his middle name "Family Farmer," which he continued to use as recently as the 1992 primary. After losing the primary, he returned to Southwest State University in Marshall to requalify himself as a vocational teacher and, at the same time, actively recruited members for the Lyndon LaRouche National Democratic Policy Committee. He is now back on the farm.

No one was as lucky as the academics. Richard Spencer's university converted the leave he had taken to work at AEFS into a partially paid sabbatical. Larry Tieszen, who did an ample amount of research for AEFS, maintained his employment at Augustana and continued his independent research on the Jerusalem artichoke. Wayne Dorband temporarily continued to teach at Augustana College and also operated his companies in Sioux

Falls and Blue Water Harvester, a company he co-owned with Dwire in Florida. In the spring of 1983, with $10,000 of AEFS money, he formed with Spencer and Dwire what he labeled a "nonprofit" research company on the Jerusalem artichoke, the Jerusalem Artichoke Research Institute (JARI). Managed by Dorband's own Aurora company, JARI was stillborn. Growers were reluctant to respond to his appeal for $500,000 for a research fund; enough was enough. Dorband left Sioux Falls and Augustana behind; at one point he joined Dwire in selling Amway products.

One employee, who allegedly wheeled and dealed in hot computers, is rumored to have ended up in a California penitentiary. Another employee, it is rumored, drove away with a truckload of Jerusalem artichoke tubers to sell to an evangelical church in Chicago.

Many employees had reached the apex of their careers at AEFS. Eight years after the bankruptcy, having been unemployed or having worked at inferior jobs, and with his marriage ending in divorce, company officer Paul Skrien still had not found a job equal in money and power to the one he had held at AEFS. The same was true of Jerry Knapper, who eventually returned to the ministry. As recently as 1992 he was serving a parish in Broken Bow, Oklahoma, and continuing his studies for a master's degree in theology.[44] Other AEFS employees, like Dwire himself, ended up selling Amway products.

Many former AEFS employees, however, found their way to more conventional jobs. Tim Kramer ended up working for a financial agency in Rochester, Minnesota. Jim Menk, who joined the company in its final phase and managed it during bankruptcy, became a bank officer at Norwest Bank in Marshall. Ron Mann, who had trained salespeople, returned to Marshall to start his own car customizing shop.

The most colorful of the AEFS employees, the Laidlaws—Bonnie, the recipe book writer, and Paul, the gospel singer—fought Kramer bitterly over their share of their partnership in a crop. They cooperated fully with all legal investigations against the company, testifying before the multicounty grand jury of AEFS and at both the Hendrickson and Kramer trials, and in the end were very embittered about AEFS and their friend and spiritual leader, Kramer. In the closing months of the company, the Laidlaws had become desperate. Their June 1982 bankruptcy was, Kramer contended, being contested as a purposeful bankruptcy by the Dayton Hudson Corporation. Their only hope was to be found with AEFS.[45] With AEFS temporarily out of seed, Dwire told the Laidlaws that if they wanted seed to plant, they had to sign a limited partnership for $10,000 at 21 percent interest with Kramer. The Laidlaws, not pleased, reluctantly acceded to the partnership on April 9, 1982, signing the note with the names of Paul Laidlaw and his brother Michael, who was a farmer. Dwire responded to their request for additional seed by putting them on the common acres program; that is, Dwire assigned them to twenty acres contracted by grower Vince Erickson of Monticello, Minnesota. Erickson, a longtime grower and believer in the Jerusalem artichoke, succeeded in delivering his Jerusalem artichokes in the fall of 1982 to the main warehouse at Appleton, Minnesota. The Laidlaws accordingly believed that AEFS owed them $171,000 for their share of Erickson's crop, which amounted to a quarter of the 572,000 pounds he harvested, with one quarter going to Kramer (who arguably shared the contract with them). Their claim against AEFS in this fictitious world of seed and paper included yet another ten acres they held with Kramer in the names of Sam Shavers and Paul Laidlaw himself.

In February 1983, with a balloon payment of $30,000 due on their new house in Blaine, and supporting two children, the Laidlaws had to set aside their claim for $171,000 and agree to sign another note to AEFS to get the $30,000 they urgently needed if they were not to lose their house. They offered 50,000 pounds of Jerusalem artichoke seed for collateral for the note. Predictably, the Laidlaws lost their home. Then their marriage fell apart. Of course, they never paid back the $30,000; nor did they, despite legal efforts, receive the $171,000.[46]

In the course of AEFS's failure, the Laidlaws and Kramer became enemies. Kramer bitterly characterized them to defense investigator Vincent Carraher and the author. He said that Bonnie was an excellent student but plagiarized all the recipes in her Jerusalem artichoke cookbook by simply substituting Jerusalem artichokes for other vegetables. Kramer added that she had a bizarre background: her father—whom Bonnie testified to the grand jury she didn't have—belonged to the Chicago Mafia. He was a local racetrack man known as Little Vinny, and she was raised by a black woman minister with whom Bonnie served as an itinerant preacher. Kramer considered Bonnie to be dangerous. She "was dominant, conniving, greedy, and underhanded," capable of being the spy who was leaking information to AEFS rivals and up to killing her husband if he ever cheated on her. Kramer judged Paul, in contrast to Bonnie, to be weak and uncertain.[47]

The Laidlaws, in turn, as their testimony in court showed, did not have a charitable view of Kramer, Dwire, or Hendrickson. Kramer, who for them came to embody evil, lied, fomented discord, and used his considerable intelligence to control others and satisfy his own greed and vanity.

In the end, the Laidlaw's marriage fell apart as they were overtaken by bankruptcy. Bonnie, Kramer said, returned to Chicago, and Paul, Kramer believed, became a street person in the Twin Cities.[48]

Other Friendships

Dwire's old friends, Burt and Gelene Johnson, owners of Sol King Co., ran AEFS's main warehouse at Appleton, Minnesota (the main center of eleven other warehouses in the nation). They turned off the electricity in the warehouse when they were no longer paid. Unrefrigerated, Jerusalem artichokes rotted there by the tons. Dwire had them hauled out and buried on his Lincoln County farm.

Nasty stories of stolen and unaccounted for seed lingered in the wake of the bankruptcy. One local farmer set his whole family and several friends to harvesting, sorting, cleaning, and grading the irregular, mud-covered tubers only to find that AEFS would not take them. In another instance, a neighbor of Dwire's, and one of the first farmers to sign up for the original program, worked diligently to harvest his ten acres of seeds and then delivered them to Texas only to receive no payment.[49] In yet another instance, real estate dealer, financier, and plant developer Thomas Reichert delivered more than 600,000 pounds of Jerusalem artichoke seed tubers of the Columbia variety at seventy-six cents a pound on the very eve of the bankruptcy. Not only was Reichert not paid—which he conjectured was Dwire's punishment for his earlier cooperation with the attorney general's office—but Dwire, he accused, stole 1,600 bags of his artichokes.[50]

A final accounting of AEFS's tuber seed proved impossible because of irregular, missing, inconsistent, and invented bills of lading. Burt and Gelene Johnson's records indicated that, as of May 20, 1983, AEFS had received $24 million of Jerusalem artichokes from two-year growers and $685,000 for Jerusalem artichoke Columbia variety seed; it also had registered the receipt of approximately 27 million pounds of artichokes as well as the shipment of approximately 15 million pounds of tubers to growers. They believed that, on May 23, 1983, the day AEFS filed for bankruptcy, 10 million pounds were held in warehouses and 2 million pounds had been lost to spoilage.[51]

Those Who Believed to the End

Faith in Jerusalem artichokes, especially on the part of original growers, did not vanish with the bankruptcy of AEFS. Many of them agreed with salesman Gregg Bittner, who wrote the attorney general on the eve of AEFS's bankruptcy, that "the Lord has brought this crop to the farmer for a reason."[52] A few even joined one supporter who counseled trust that the Lord would raise up out of AEFS's present leaders "a Moses."[53]

In the aftermath of the bankruptcy, however, even the three-year growers of Hendrickson's home state, South Dakota—who on April Fools' Day, 1983, had carried out a protest against an investigation of AEFS by the Minnesota attorney general's office—quickly ran out of faith in AEFS's management. They showed a mixture of indifference and anger at Hendrickson's prophetic claim that God was responding to their renewed prayers with "a new burst of energy." None responded positively to his summer 1983 announcement of the formation of a "Covenant Christian Farmers, Inc.," which he designed to be "a tax-deductible seed-faith fund." Even its head, Kenneth Barker (who defined himself as a former director of AEFS sales), acknowledged that most growers considered the new Christian farmers association as "nothing more than an AEFS play [sic] to save its own hide."[54]

Nevertheless, self-interest pushed the three-year growers in the direction of wanting reorganization, not bankruptcy. Having husbanded their crop through the wet fall of 1982, they were now on the verge of delivering and being paid for the seed in which they had invested their labor, money, and hope.

Many believers revealed their ambivalence. Dan Fisher from Blue Ball, Pennsylvania, wrote Hendrickson and Dwire on behalf of his new association, one of the dozen or so that sprang up during the spring and summer of 1983: "We, as Pennsylvania Artichoke Growers Association, formed to protect our own interests and to let you fellows know we are rallying behind you." Fisher wrote that it would be best somehow to keep AEFS alive rather than start a new company, yet he suggested that perhaps Knapper should be made president, AEFS should be sold to Knapper, and a new company should be formed that would do away with attorneys and many middlemen. The company, Fisher further advised, should settle down for the long struggle to develop the crop in the hostile world of attorneys general.[55]

In February 1984, Hendrickson replied to Fisher in mystical terms. He wrote that he rejoiced in Fisher's calling to be a "modern day Joseph" and announced that he, Hendrickson, "was trusting God that his mercy is giving me a 'second chance' to be a leader in 'establishing' this crop not only in America, but throughout the world." Hendrickson explained that "it was Satan who stopped the Jerusalem artichoke because of the good it would do in the hands of the soil people of this great country," and after promoting one of his new schemes, Hendrickson prophesied, "We will get our financial reward before long."[56]

Other growers, like Andy Van Zee of Platte, South Dakota, who had sold hundreds of thousands of dollars worth of Jerusalem artichokes, took a less mystical view of things. He started his own company to sell Jerusalem artichokes. He, like a handful of others in the nation, adopted and modified AEFS's contract to what he thought to be his own advantage and started, under the name of Uncle Andy's, Inc., to buy from growers and to sell what he called Uncle Andy's Sunchokes. Lyle Kilthau of White Lightning in Wapato, Washington, who, according to the bankruptcy audit, received more than $2.5 million from AEFS, continued to sell Jerusalem artichokes under the name of A.N.W. Seed Corp. with a contract identical to AEFS's, until the state of Washington issued a cease-and-desist order against A.N.W. in 1983 for false representation of the product and started an action against it in January 1985.[57]

Even prior to the bankruptcy announcement, reacting to the Minnesota attorney general's findings, three-year growers sought an alternative path to AEFS. In June 1983, the Minnesota Artichoke Growers Association (MAGA) was formed in order to make sure Minnesota growers were represented at the July bankruptcy hearing.[58]

South Dakota farmers formed their own South Dakota Jerusalem Artichoke Growers Association in April 1983. In conjunction with the Wisconsin and Mid-States Jerusalem Artichokes Growers Association, the South Dakota Jerusalem Artichoke Growers Association passed a host of resolutions at a June 1 meeting. They called for the return of investments to the growers, the appointment of new management, and the transformation of AEFS into a public company, though they strangely drew short of passing a resolution that would have made the personal and corporate assets of Dwire, Hendrickson, and Kramer available for debt settlement. The group also decided to hold a national growers convention in Sioux Falls in August, and they designated Pat "Family Farmer" O'Reilly as interim organizer for the potential formation of a national organization.[59] The group continued to survey the revelations of misconduct that came forth during bankruptcy proceedings as well as to examine critically alternative groups such as the New Covenant Christian Farmers group associated with Hendrickson, whose character and explanations lacked integrity, according to president Robert Engbricht.[60]

In July 1983, 165 growers from Minnesota, South Dakota, Colorado, Texas, and other states formed the National Alternative Crops Growers Cooperative to market Jerusalem artichokes. Under the leadership of Ben Steensma and originally headquartered in vice president Cal Maxwell's hometown, Montevideo, Minnesota, the National Alternative Crops Growers Cooperative strove to develop the long-term promise of the Jerusalem artichoke for fuel, food, and feed.[61] It specifically sought to develop immediate markets for the Jerusalem artichoke as a nutritional animal feed and a source of chips for bedding, pelletized and liquid fuel, flour, and molasses for livestock feed. Their efforts failed. After their August 1983 convention, their membership peaked at 185 of the 2,800 Jerusalem artichoke growers they had contacted. Farmers would not pay a hundred dollars to join.

As if history were repeating itself, in October 1983, South Dakota's department of commerce, division of securities, summoned the cooperative to a hearing on possible legal infractions.[62] Approximately a year later, the National Alternative Crop Growers Cooperative died an unnoticed death. Tired of personally financing what he eventually had to concede was a losing endeavor, Steensma drove north to Felton, Minnesota, where the cooperative had relocated itself. He picked up the cooperative's remaining files and took them home. To this day he keeps them (along with the near complete files of Ford's Chemurgic Council, which continued in the 1950s as the National Farm Chemurgic Council) as a keepsake of his days with the Jerusalem artichoke.[63]

The Last Ball

No magic prince ever came to court the "Cinderella of crops." Not Campbell Soup, or Archer-Daniels-Midland, or General Mills, or Land O' Lakes, or Quaker Oats—not one of the prospective suitors identified by Hendrickson's friend and head of market development Pat Derner appeared a courtin'. (Derner said AEFS made a great mistake when it didn't simply give the Jerusalem artichokes to Archer-Daniels-Midland for free, for if nothing else, ADM's acceptance would have shown the crop's legitimacy.[64])

The only company to call for Jerusalem artichokes was Agricultural Growth Industries, Inc., a company formed by Hendrickson himself. It offered twenty-five dollars a ton for Jerusalem artichoke tops—if they were in the 15 to 20 percent moisture range—which was only slightly more than 1 percent of the standard $1.20 a pound for which AEFS had sold its tubers. The price of the savior crop was less than a fourth the price of a ton of alfalfa, and not half the price of hay.

None of the new state and other associations, including the short-lived and small companies such as the Artichoke Farmer of America Market Development Corporation of Cedar Falls, Iowa, could alter the market. They were, so to speak, small potatoes, with memberships of fewer than two hundred growers. Even the more thoughtful promoters of the artichoke gathered around the new and short-lived journal, *The Artichoke Connection*, published out of State College, Pennsylvania, were helpless. In November they called a major national conference in Topeka, Kansas, to discuss all aspects of the crop, as well as to form a national society. It marked the end rather than a beginning for the Jerusalem artichoke.

In August 1993, according to the Minnesota attorney general's files, a sole stockbroker on the Isle of Man in Great Britain still offered stocks in AEFS as an investment opportunity. On September 13, 1983, Judge Kressel converted AEFS's Chapter 11 bankruptcy into a Chapter 7 bankruptcy. The romance was over. The great economic high wire had been lowered, the great drum roll had fallen still, the three rings were empty, and except for a handful of stragglers, the crowd was gone. It now fell to a few court-appointed managers to supervise the dismantling of the AEFS tent and what had been, for a short season, "the greatest crop show on earth."

The last company get-together had occurred approximately a month before Bergquist signaled AEFS's end. Kim Boe and his new friend, Lola Johnson, held a potluck on August 6, 1983, at their place in Cottonwood. Their invitations—found in company files—offered free beer and a place to stay to fellow employees, "if for some reason you are not able to drive home."

8

The County Attorney and His Investigator

They used God and apple pie, but in all the wrong ways.
—Jim Newes

Liquidation

Bankruptcy judge Robert Kressel converted AEFS's bankruptcy from a Chapter 11 to a Chapter 7 bankruptcy on September 13, 1983. There would be no more plantings or harvests for AEFS. Kressel based his order to convert the bankruptcy to Chapter 7 on the fact that the company's owners took $4.5 million from the company and disbursed almost $600,000 on the eve of its declaration of bankruptcy. Also, Kressel could find little reason to be hopeful about AEFS's future.[1] With less than $500,000 in cash, he asserted, the company was in no position to pay $6.4 million in rescission claims against it. AEFS had lost $170,000 in June, and almost $100,000 in July, and it had no income at all from July 4 to August 4. Since filing bankruptcy, the company had failed to collect a single dollar in accounts receivable, which totaled $3.5 million according to the Touche Ross & Co. audit.[2] (AEFS contended that it was owed $8 million; in addition to money owed by Dwire, Hendrickson, and Kramer, it was owed $3.5 million for delivered seed, $2 million in advances to outside growers, and $250,000 in advances to employees.)

The Touche Ross & Co. audit supported Kressel's pessimistic judgment about AEFS's future. It indicated almost $3 million in draws from AEFS supported by checks alone; another $7 million not supported at all; $1.5 million in unsupported payments by principals and potential insiders; and a host of unexplored preferential payments to Dwire, Hendrickson, and Kramer equaling almost $5 million. The auditor's report, which ignored all transactions of $5,000 or less, drew Kressel's attention to myriad suspicious transactions, which would have taken a small but costly army of investigators, lawyers, and accountants to explore. One West Coast seed supplier, White Lightning, sold AEFS $2.5 million worth of seed, while a host of other parties, including AEFS's law firm and its accounting firm, may have received "a potential preferential payment of an antecedent debt."[3] And no one—not even Dwire himself by his own acknowledgment—knew, or even knew how to calculate, how many pounds of Jerusalem artichoke seed AEFS owned or how many pounds were owed to it.[4]

In his judgment, Kressel noted that Dwire had failed to cooperate with the bankruptcy examiner and that, during the court's examination of him, he had repeatedly invoked the Fifth Amendment, exercising his privilege against self-incrimination in light of an ongoing U.S. postal inspection into AEFS. Also, Kressel pointed out that AEFS was without a market plan for 1984; the only market that remained for the crop was seed stock, and that market was largely saturated by the owners of AEFS who, against their growers' own interests, had planted 1,200 acres of Jerusalem artichokes on land they owned or rented.

Kressel made attorney Edward Bergquist bankruptcy trustee of the estate of AEFS for the court. It was Bergquist's responsibility to liquidate AEFS fairly, promptly, and as inexpensively as he could. The efficiency with which Bergquist carried out his responsibility made him seem cold and passionless to AEFS's creditors such as Tom Reichert, who lost hundreds of thousands of dollars of seed to AEFS. The largest creditors and suppliers of seed were lumped together with all the unsecured creditors (those who didn't have liens or mortgages on AEFS property).

One specific calculus shaped Bergquist's calculations. First, he had to weigh the value of an object against costs of its recovery. (Bergquist himself worked initially for $120 an hour, and then for $130 an hour; the attorneys he appointed for the creditors and debtors worked for similar amounts. Touche Ross & Co. charged the bankruptcy court $100,000 for AEFS's first audit.) Aside from easily recoverable bank accounts, which were found in such distant places as Chugwater and Lingle, Wyoming, there was the matter of machinery, small facilities, and seed scattered over half a dozen states whose titles and locations might be in question.[5]

Bergquist did not shoulder this matter alone. He appointed James Levy of the St. Paul firm Oppenheimer, Wolff, and Foster to defend AEFS. Once the company entered a Chapter 7 bankruptcy, he assigned Daryle Uphoff, who previously represented the committee of unsecured creditors when AEFS was under Chapter 11, to pursue all AEFS recoverable assets for the company's creditors. Uphoff's responsibility to locate all AEFS assets extended not only to assets in the company's name but also to all assets that were illegally transferred to owners, managers, their families, other companies, and creditors. An Illinois farm boy by background, Uphoff pursued these assets with a special vigor, kindled by his observation that AEFS had committed one of the most flagrant abuses of the provisions of Chapter 11 he had seen in his many years of working on bankruptcy cases. In his opinion, AEFS leaders not only had exploited the provision of safe haven provided by Chapter 11 by taking all they could on the eve of the filing but had continued not to play by the rules after filing for bankruptcy.[6]

Uphoff even began to research the possibility of bringing what would have been a highly complex action against AEFS's attorneys, Wiese and Cox, for what arguably could have been their failure to meet fiduciary obligations as counsel to a company selling securities. He brought a successful action against Continental Insurance Company, whose policy guaranteed AEFS up to $100,000 of loss by theft.[7]

Proceeding as representative of the Chapter 7 trustee, Uphoff filed plaintiff interrogatories against Dwire, Hendrickson, and Kramer to discover their assets and holdings in other companies and the property they bought and improved with AEFS funds. Starting in early 1984, Uphoff filed a succession of liens against Dwire's property in Lyon, Lincoln, and Murray counties in Minnesota and properties in South Dakota. He even filed a lien against Dwire's house, for which AEFS had made payments against a mortgage that extended to 1999. He garnished $130,000 in funds held in a Colorado bank for Pegsons, a new contracting firm owned, as the name indicated, by Dwire's wife Peg and their two oldest sons. He also took or considered taking other property in Dwire's and his wife's and children's names, as well as property that Dwire held with other people or had recently passed on to others, such as the property with which he had paid local attorney James Anderson for fees owed.

In the end, Uphoff was convinced that the three defendants, Dwire, Hendrickson, and Kramer, got away with very little. He lent no credence to rumors—the type of rumors commonly associated with suspicious bankruptcies—that Dwire had sent great sums to Swiss banks and buried fortunes under an airport runway. "Their sort," Uphoff contended, "didn't prepare for bankruptcy." They were not brilliant at laundering money. In Uphoff's opinion, like so many who went broke in the late 1970s and early 1980s, they had tried to get rich—"to leverage themselves up," to use Uphoff's phrase—by putting small sums down on all sorts of things but binding themselves to long-term high-interest payments.[8]

Uphoff was less certain he had gotten everything in the case of AEFS scientific consultant Wayne Dorband and in the case of Lyle Kilthau of A.N.W. Seed Corp., which owed AEFS $85,000 because it violated its agreement to sell seed directly to AEFS rather than to growers. Kilthau's company, White Lightning, allegedly received $1.6 million from AEFS in 1982 as a down payment for seed AEFS intended to buy. AEFS claimed that White Lightning either seized or let spoil the 3.5 million pounds of the seed when AEFS failed to make its June 1983 payment of $169,000.[9]

Like Uphoff, Bergquist too contradicted AEFS creditors' predictable belief that the principals got away with significant sums of money after declaring bankruptcy. He contended that they had bought too much and had paid too dearly for it. Bergquist was certain he got what was left in their bank accounts. He located approximately $250,000 in banks in Marshall, nearby Cottonwood, Sioux Falls, and the Twin Cities. He reclaimed insurance premiums, got payments from the PIK programs, and confiscated tax returns. Wiese and Cox surrendered

$78,000 in "unused" attorney fees to Bergquist, who also took possession of AEFS airplanes and fertilizer worth another $215,000.[10]

An auction of AEFS's goods and some goods from Dwire, Inc., and Dwire's family was held in the fall of 1983 in the parking lot of AEFS's main corporate building. It netted another $350,000. Wearing a bullet-proof vest, Dwire himself attended the auction. He mingled freely with friends and former AEFS growers, commenting on the rows of goods that once defined his and AEFS's fortunes. He even had a friend purchase a thing or two of his back.

Buyers, remarking on the good condition of most things on the auction block, were pleased with the goods they bought. Some treated these goods as if they somehow embodied the person and powers of their former owners. Months after the auction, one of the local auction buyers confided to the author that she was nervous when she drove Dwire's elaborately converted van. She feared a misaimed reprisal by an angry artichoke grower.

In addition to money earned from the auction, Bergquist picked up $225,000 in interest from banks, brought in $50,000 from Dwire's estate, and settled an insurance claim for $35,000. Bergquist also held in dispute against the attorney general's office the $635,000 that AEFS, under directives from the attorney general, had put in escrow for the upcoming rescission. Bergquist was far more intent on liquidating the $2 million he had recaptured than trapping wrongdoers. First, he paid those who are always paid first: $100,000 was given to the accountants of Touche Ross & Co.; $90,000 went to Daryle Uphoff; $10,000 went to James Levy, lawyer for AEFS; $28,000 went to Bergquist himself. In the end, he was forced by a court ruling to surrender the rescission fund of $500,000, in addition to $135,000 in interest to the state of Minnesota. After paying yet other expenses incurred in settling the bankruptcy, Bergquist had $1 million to distribute to creditors.[11]

Approximately $220,000 went to the company's few secured creditors, among which numbered banks and a handful of companies such as General Motors, Chrysler, and Cessna. Next, payments were made to those owed during the period between

AEFS's filing for Chapter 11 and its liquidation. Then employees received compensation up to $2,000 for wages earned up to ninety days prior to filing for bankruptcy. Finally, last to be paid were the unsecured creditors, among whose ranks numbered thousands of growers and a handful of seed sellers. The two largest were Thomas Reichert, who claimed $600,000, and Vince Erickson, who claimed $95,000. The ensemble of AEFS's unsecured creditors submitted preposterously high claims totaling $75 million; in the end they divided $450,000, which amounted to six-tenths of a penny on the dollar. The standard $12,000 contract in itself was now worth $72.[12]

AEFS's bankruptcy case was finally closed September 15, 1989. As part of the final settlement with bankruptcy court, Dwire had agreed to a nondischargeable debt of $815,000; Kramer, a nondischargeable debt of $250,000; and Hendrickson, a nondischargeable debt of $50,000. Kramer and Dwire couldn't, and didn't, pay their debts. Dwire, who on the eve of AEFS's bankruptcy owned several companies and farms, remarked "I haven't paid them anything yet. I don't have any money. I'm busted."[13] Hendrickson settled his debt for $10,000 in April of that year.[14] More difficult judgments lay ahead for each of them.

When It Rains, It Pours

In the wake of declaring bankruptcy, Dwire, Hendrickson, and Kramer, not really believing the worst, continued to scramble for money. They even boldly entered claims in bankruptcy court against AEFS for unpaid wages and seed deliveries.

Dwire, who was not easily humbled by the law, tried to hide money, covering his tracks as best he could. He generated past credit claims against AEFS for seed and leases, while at the same time offering notes to AEFS to cover his past takings. In fact, in company papers there was in his name an unsigned note, dated June 1, 1983, for approximately $1.3 million (due in one year at 12 percent interest), which equaled approximately the sum he had taken from AEFS by check request alone. There was a similar note for $370,000 prepared for Hendrickson.[15]

Dwire's scramblings were in vain. He lost his wonderful house, his 1981 Plymouth Reliant was repossessed, and his children and wife lost the property that AEFS money had purchased. He also sought to sign up for unemployment, which Bergquist opposed on the ground that "among other things that claimant fraudulently took property of debtor for his own benefit."[16]

Throughout 1983 Kramer continued to try to wheel and deal: In one case he offered a Cadillac for debts owed. He tried to vend his Challenge Fund notes and the special partnership notes, which McLeod County investigator Jim Newes labeled "L. D.'s Confederate money." He assigned some of his notes to friends and family before eventually offering them to the bankruptcy court itself to display cooperation and satisfy his debt. With a certain spiteful relish Kramer assigned the Laidlaws' note he held to the Bible college from which they had graduated. In August 1983, he pledged, upon the receipt of funds in the following year, a gift of $20,000 to the Reverend Herman Rhode of the Minnesota District Council of the Assemblies of God for various charities.[17] With bad publicity denying him access to church and pulpit, Kramer reverted to his pre-AEFS hand-to-mouth style of living, which didn't exclude being well dressed and living in motels. At one point he took up residence as an aide at a St. Paul inner-city religious mission to black youth. In 1987, Kramer reported a gross income of $3,000 to the IRS.[18]

Hendrickson, who had tithed during the good days of AEFS, fared no better than Dwire or Kramer in the aftermath of the company's bankruptcy. He scrounged around for money to keep himself and his family afloat. Serving as a lawyer for farmers facing foreclosure harvested him some good character references but did little to get him the cash he needed. Aware of possible criminal charges, he, like Dwire, scrambled to find justifying "offsets" against his "draws," "advances," and other takings and borrowings. In January 1984, he even entered a bankruptcy court claim against AEFS for $135,000 for unpaid seed and small expenses and $8,000 in unpaid wages.[19]

Later that spring Hendrickson took off his economic mask. In an April 1984 financial report to the bankruptcy court, Hendrickson demonstrated that his assets were only paper assets.

They were composed of unrecoverable "wages" and loans owed him, business receivables from Dwire, stocks of no worth, and farms that he bought at inflated prices with high interest and with small down payments. Aside from a car, household furniture, and personal effects, Hendrickson was flat broke.[20] In 1986, Hendrickson continued to be pursued by the IRS for back taxes of $2,500, which, like his other public debts, he eventually paid. On February 20, 1986, Hendrickson wrote to Uphoff that his family was suffering, that he was without resources, and that the liquidation of three research farms and the feedlot tax shelter resulted in only $8,500 total.[21]

As if to prove true the old saw that "When it rains, it pours," in the spring of 1984 McLeod County attorney Peter Kasal summoned a county grand jury to investigate AEFS and its officers and managers. Initially they dismissed this investigation by the "small-time county attorney" as small potatoes, especially when they compared it to ongoing investigations by the FBI, the Minnesota attorney general's office, U.S. postal inspectors, and the federal bankruptcy court.

Underestimating Kasal proved to be a serious mistake, however. Kasal had been pursuing AEFS's owners since the company's bankruptcy had cost several of his friends and acquaintances money. Like one of those unshakable detectives from the world of fiction, Kasal was incredibly tenacious in pursuit. The IRS and the FBI finally did not pick up the case, federal postal inspectors dropped it, and the Minnesota attorney general's office and other state attorney generals' offices did not press a criminal case against AEFS's owners, but Kasal did.

At least on the surface, it made little sense that a county attorney from a rural county sixty miles from the Twin Cities should pursue a criminal case against Hendrickson, Kramer, and Dwire when no one else did. Not altogether irrationally, the three men suspected that Kasal was the agent of someone else. They postulated that he was a pawn of Hubert Humphrey III, who, in turn, was an agent of Dwayne Andreas of the corporate agricultural giant Archer-Daniels-Midland.

Although this theory significantly overestimated the importance of AEFS and the personnel and monetary resources at Kasal's disposal and ignored the refusal of Humphrey's own officer to press criminal charges against AEFS, it nevertheless fit the paranoia of Hendrickson, Dwire, and Kramer, a paranoia that was both common and widespread in the American countryside at the time. The theory was wonderfully grandiose and it had a degree of plausability. There was certainly a long-standing connection between the Humphrey family and Dwayne Andreas, "king of corn" and chief executive of Archer-Daniels-Midland. When Hubert H. Humphrey was vice president, he frequently took Andreas with him on trips throughout the world. Andreas did not fail to reciprocate by donating generously to Humphrey's campaign, managing Humphrey's blind trust, and even asking Humphrey to be the godfather of one of his children.[22]

This theory flattered Hendrickson, Dwire, and Kramer by making them and their growers the object of immense machinations of a major international corporation and the government. Like their midwestern predecessor, prophet Fred Johnson, who blamed his failure with Jerusalem artichokes in Nebraska in the 1930s on large sugar companies, Dwire, Hendrickson, and Kramer blamed great powers to excuse their own small wrongdoings.

The defendants also invoked another great American conspiracy theory, one that has long been popular in the Midwest, to explain why they were prosecuted. Kasal, they noted, was a Catholic, so was his investigator, Jim Newes, and so was Judge Richard L. Kelly, who presided over the trials of Kramer and Hendrickson.

This theory particularly attracted Kramer, an evangelical minister. He conjectured that Kelly had special reason to be against him since, Kramer claimed, under his tutelage an Assembly of God congregation had grown at the expense of the local Catholic Church Kelly attended in Springfield, Minnesota. Also, Kramer knew how Kasal had successfully convicted another minister of the Assembly of God church in 1980, just a year after becoming McLeod County Attorney.[23]

But something far simpler than international conspiracies explained Kasal's actions: He was the kind of man who got hold of something and didn't easily let it go. He remarked in one interview, "I hate undone projects."[24] When the AEFS investigation bogged down, as it often did, Kasal was fond of exhorting Newes with a line from a Clint Eastwood film: "We must endeavor to persevere."[25]

Kasal, born in 1947, was brought up on a farm in the vicinity of Glencoe, Minnesota.[26] He was brought up a mile east of Stewart, Minnesota, on one of those small and taxing farms where the time-consuming raising of animals—cows, pigs, and chickens—had not been given up for the far easier life of grain farming. Kasal, whose family first settled in New Prague, Minnesota, belonged to a number of successful Czech Catholic farming families of southern Minnesota that couldn't separate survival as a family from success on the land. Outsiders, not understanding such a strong attachment to land and family, say Kasal belonged to a clan rather than a family.

Kasal felt he owed his family doubly. Aside from the normal debt of a son to his family, he believed he was indebted to his family for his education. After high school, where he was a good student, ran track, wrestled, and played linebacker on the football team, he earned a chemistry and math degree from St. Cloud State University. He did graduate work in chemistry at Kansas State University and eventually earned a law degree in 1975 from William Mitchell School of Law in St. Paul.

Kasal's mother made sure the family followed the teachings of the church. Kasal's oldest brother, Francis Kasal, his senior by ten and a half years, went off to seminary when he was thirteen. She named her next son James. Then she named Peter's twin brother Paul, making the twins sound like churches in Rome. Kasal's father, a hard-drinking and restless man, was never happy on the farm. He was happier in town than working on the land. In fact, when Peter was very young, his father spent a lot of time in Glencoe, where he served for several years as a McLeod County commissioner. The father left a lot of the farming to Kasal's mother and siblings, and of all the siblings, none was as hardworking and trustworthy as Peter. "Leave it to Pete," was a standing family formula.

After practicing law in the Twin Cities for several years, Kasal, country boy that he was, grew sick of city traffic and hubbub. The first outstate job to come his way was an assistant district attorneyship in Glencoe. He took the job and he fit it well. He knew the lay of the land. He was married, went to church, and didn't put on airs. He drove a small car, a Chevette, and dressed neatly but was not a clotheshorse.

As county attorney, Kasal established a particular interest in prosecuting perpetrators of fraud and white-collar criminals. This interest fit a need of McLeod County's, which found itself responding to increasing numbers of welfare frauds and scams that, so to speak, overflowed the Twin Cities into the surrounding countryside. Also, fraud and white-collar crimes challenged Kasal's skills as an attorney.

Kasal said that murders are easy to try; the evidence is there or it is not there. White collar crimes are an entirely different matter. They demand a lot more skill to investigate and to prosecute. Kasal vividly asserted: "A white collar crime is a million documents, which is a room full of pony shit, and the trick is to find the pony therein."[27]

Revealing the prejudice of the country boy, Kasal judged white-collar criminals to be city slickers. The city slicker, in his opinion, takes advantage of rural peoples' natural tendencies to be open and accept people at their word. Explaining his particular animus against Kramer, Kasal judged the religious con man the worst kind of slicker. Kasal remarked that it is easy to cheat a person who gets down on his knees with you.

More selfish reasons also motivated Kasal. Success against AEFS in what could prove to be an important case would demonstrate his concern for the plight of Minnesota's beleaguered farmers and help prepare his campaign for U.S. Congress against incumbent Vin Weber, a young Republican whose star had risen high during Reagan's presidency.

A New Investigator

In the late spring of 1984, on the eve of filing his grand jury request for subpoena power against AEFS, Kasal found himself without an investigator. With one investigator sick and the other seeking alternative employment, Kasal hired Jim Newes, an acquaintance of his twin brother, to be his investigator.

Newes, whom Kasal called "a great detail man" was ideal. Like Kasal, Newes was interested in white-collar crimes. He didn't find them at all boring. "Right out of the blocks," Newes said, "everyone knows who the crook is. The question is, can you put the evidence together?"[28]

Investigating white-collar crimes fit Newes's background as a former postal inspector, a position he took after graduating with a degree in economics from St. Thomas College in St. Paul in 1971.[29] After leaving the corp of U.S. federal postal inspectors, Newes ran several chain stores. First, he ran a Woolworth store in Omaha, Nebraska, in the vicinity of his wife's conservative German Catholic farm family, and next he ran the Gibson store in Marshall, Minnesota, which, oddly enough, a few years later became AEFS's main office and sales building. Just before joining Kasal, Newes, who had bought a small retail store in Cannon Falls, Minnesota, helped his wife with her bridal store. It was a pleasure for him to be back on the trail of criminals after several years in the more sedate retail business.

Newes is a small man who dresses modestly. He has bountiful energy, judges quickly, and is quick-witted, sharp-tongued, ribald, and like Kasal, tenacious in pursuit. He took personally the assignment Kasal gave him. He considered Kasal not just a boss but a friend who happened to be—hands down—the best prosecutor in the state.

Sharing none of the era's mystique about speculation and big business, which so moved the defendants, Newes got—and still gets—pleasure out of bringing the big guys down. This fits his background in the working classes of St. Paul. His father worked at the post office, and he himself started to work at an early age as a caddy at Hillcrest Golf Club. Although he was a hockey fan, he didn't have time to play any sports during high school. His sense that people shouldn't cheat others and his working-class resentment against the rich combined to form a moral sense that he expressed once as, "What I don't get in money, I get in 'get even.'"[30]

Newes and Kasal made good partners. They were both Catholics. They were both cunning and energetic, and filled, as young men commonly are, with a sense of righteousness. Early on in their investigation, when they were contending for records they needed, Kasal instructed Newes, "Fuck 'em! Subpoena 'em!"[31]

Newes, like Kasal, never hesitated in judging AEFS a scam from top to bottom. He conceived the whole AEFS affair to be about greed, "kids at the jelly bean scramble."[32] He assumed that Dwire, Hendrickson, and Kramer were crooks. He didn't stop to speculate about the actual potential of the Jerusalem artichoke as a crop, the degree to which the farmers themselves knowingly undertook the risk of growing the plant, and the considerable number of growers who continued to believe in the crop and the company even after the rescission.

Newes was better at assembling evidence than his predecessors at McLeod County, investigators Dick Moisand and Linda Shamla. The latter, he said, chased rumors, relying primarily on hearsay and oral interviews. Newes took a different tack. Good postal inspector that he was, Newes followed the money. He subpoenaed all the bank, company, and personal financial records he could. Without clear permission, he boldly went to the building in Blaine, Minnesota, where AEFS's records were temporarily housed for the aborted postal investigation and took all the records he felt might prove useful. He took them by the box full.

In his matchbook, ten-by-twelve office in the court house, with records piled and strewn everywhere, he followed the money in and out of the company and in and out of other accounts held by Dwire, Hendrickson, and Kramer. Once it dawned on Newes that the very act of taking money from AEFS was wrong, the case seemed to him to be a "turkey shoot."[33]

Newes found Kramer's transactions to be the most difficult to reconstruct. It was easy to show that Kramer operated as far more than a consultant, that AEFS money frequently ended up in the hands of companies that he and Dwire mutually controlled, and that AEFS funds were used for his personal interests. Reconstructing the Challenge Fund and the Five Partnerships, however, was a different matter. According to Newes—Kramer disagrees—he literally used the threat of a crowbar to open the Challenge Fund to investigation. Newes went with a police officer to Kramer's Edina office, which was stacked with office machinery, computer equipment, and a pile of briefcases. When Kramer told Newes he had no key for the files in his fine walnut desk, the police officer suggested "What about a crowbar?" This jogged Kramer's memory, and he instantly produced a key out of one of the many briefcases. In the files found in that desk—Kramer's Challenge Fund notes to AEFS—Newes believed he had found at one fell swoop conclusive evidence that Kramer's Challenge Fund had not yet paid or left a note for the seed it had taken from AEFS.[34]

Newes took Kramer to be a worthy opponent. He did not, however, hold the same opinion of Hendrickson, whom he judged to be ineffective, lazy, and as self-deluded as he was crooked. Neither did Newes have any sympathy for Dwire. He judged Dwire to be "intensely greedy," "stupidly bullish," "too dumb to ever make a company succeed," and "cut out to be a bulldozer driver."[35] Dwire, considered Newes, was only "a crook in embryo" when he met Kramer.[36] Newes believed that Kramer moved Dwire a long way down the road of corruption—how far Newes measured by Dwire's willingness to corrupt his own sons and wife and risk landing them in jail. He detected Kramer's influence in Dwire's opening an office with him in Edina and allowing him to run Dwire Enterprises. In the end, Newes stated, "Dwire couldn't go to the bathroom without holding Kramer's hand. . . . If things went on long enough," Newes believed, "L. D. would have taken J. D."[37]

Newes believed that Kramer added color, or "snazz," to the crooked troika. If any one of the three got away with money, he believed, it was Kramer. While Dwire laundered money by moving it in obvious circles, Kramer conjured three million dollars out of "shit seed." If Kramer, "the original back-dater," had lived a hundred years ago, Newes conjectured, "he would have went [sic] from town to town selling snake oil."[38]

Newes claimed that Kramer taunted him on more than one occasion. "You are just a hole-in-the-wall operation,"[39] he said once, and then later, "The SEC looked into me for two years. What makes you think you can do anything?"[40] On yet another occasion, when Newes asked Kramer how he got $3 million worth of seed for one $625,000 note from Stotts, Kramer replied, "I got a real good deal."[41]

Unwittingly, Kramer also taunted Newes when he drove big cars and wore fancy suits and shoes and diamond rings on his fingers by making a display of precisely the kind of stuff that Newes didn't have and didn't like.

At least on a couple of occasions, almost with pride, Newes declared that he had studied at "the L. D. Kramer school of advanced crookedness." The AEFS case was a once in a lifetime investigative jigsaw puzzle for Newes. He relished putting it together piece by piece even though he had to work under considerable pressure to provide evidence for the newly empaneled five-county (Lyon, McLeod, Redwood, Renville, and Sibley) grand jury called for October 1984. The essence of his work was displayed on eighteen charts made up by he and his wife, a former postal inspector herself, on the eve of seeking indictments from the multicounty grand jury.

Before the Grand Jury

The work of Kasal and Newes paid off. At the end of October, the multicounty grand jury brought indictments against all three men. They were indicted for the diversion of corporate assets, theft, and theft by swindle. Dwire and Hendrickson were charged with additional theft counts. "Dwire was indicted on 21 counts: 17 of diverting a total of more than one million dollars in corporate assets, one count of theft of more than $650,000 and three counts of theft by swindle of $3.35 million." Hendrickson, co-owner and manager, was charged with only "three counts, two of diversion of corporate assets of more than $260,000 and one of theft by swindle of more than $365,000," while consultant Kramer "was indicted on nine counts of diverting corporate assets of more than $243,000, one count of theft of more than $650,000 and three counts of theft by swindle of more than $2.68 million."[42]

With these indictments in hand, Kasal and Newes were confident they would convict the three men. Their confidence, however, was crushed when they discovered that that very spring the state legislature had de facto repealed the criminal statutes defining the diversion of corporate assets by failing to include them in its redrafting of the pertinent sections of the statutes. In Kasal's opinion, the legislature transformed a hard case into an extremely difficult case. It was now necessary to prove the more difficult charges of theft, theft by swindle, and conspiracy to commit theft by swindle.

Showing theft necessitated proving that indicted owners Dwire and Hendrickson stole from "their own" company and that Kramer, a consultant, stole from the company while working under the direction of its owners and managers. Proving theft by swindle and conspiracy to commit theft by swindle demanded more than simply proving theft. Swindle connotes a type of thievery. Like embezzlement and confidence games, it belongs to the family of larceny. In addition to being theft by guile, swindle requires, according to Minnesota statutes, the use of "a deliberate artifice or scheme."

Proving theft by swindle and conspiracy to commit theft by swindle required that Kasal prove that AEFS, if not functioning in its entirety as an artifice to cheat people, at least did so in many of its significant activities, and that it served as an artifice to steal money or seed. Additionally, these charges required proof that the growers had unwittingly been ensnared into this artifice. Kasal and Newes had to return to the empaneled grand jury to secure additional counts of theft and theft by swindle against Dwire, Hendrickson, and Kramer.

Kasal was not without evidence to prove swindle. Many growers and company officials, including the head of sales, Jerry Knapper, vouched that AEFS promised that the company would dedicate a significant portion of growers' money to research and market development and, more important, that it would establish an escrow account in which 50 percent of each sale would be set aside in order to purchase seed tubers from growers.

Kasal also argued during the second hearing of the multicounty grand jury in December 1984 that the company had promised to help its growers in the future. Kasal offered this example: "If I am running . . . a car dealership and I tell you to give me a thousand dollars and I'll get you a car, [and] you give me a thousand dollars . . . and later on I don't deliver the car to you, and I say, well, it's a profit and I took it . . . then that's obviously a swindle because I induced you to give me the money on a false promise."[43]

Kasal once again convinced the multicounty grand jury. It added to Dwire's and Hendrickson's indictments one count of conspiracy to commit swindle, in addition to two more counts of diversion of corporate property.

In Court

The pretrial defense was led by Dwire's counsel, John Lundquist, who forewarned Kasal and Newes that "when this is over we will have given you a lesson in the law."[44]

The defense argued unsuccessfully that Kasal had abused his subpoena power by compelling people to come to motel rooms for interrogation, by summoning records of contributions to Vin Weber's campaign, by characterizing defendants according to their religious beliefs, and by suggesting wrongdoing without defining the specific characteristics of the act. The defense successfully objected, however, that the illegal presence of Kasal's paraprofessional, investigator Linda Shamla, had tainted the grand jury indictments. In February 1986 the court of appeals dismissed the grand jury's indictments.

Fearing that the three-year statute of limitations on white-collar crimes would soon prohibit a new set of indictments, Kasal responded in advance of the expiration date of the earlier indictments by issuing a new set of complaints in January 1986. He accomplished this by the unusual move of getting himself deputized as assistant county attorney in Lyon County by the county attorney, David Peterson.

The defense moved to dismiss the new complaints. It argued among other things that the prosecution could not legally issue these complaints without first having withdrawn the original grand jury indictments, for it amounted to being charged twice with the same alleged crimes. In February 1987, in a two-to-one vote, the Minnesota Supreme Court, reversing a lower court, agreed with Kasal. While the Supreme Court considered Kasal's belief in the applicability to this case of the three-year statute of limitation to be in error, it found his concern reasonable and it saw no violation of the law in his action. At the same time, it found no worth to the defendant's claim that being charged twice for the same crime is equivalent to being tried twice for the same crime.[45]

Kasal was now ready to go to court, but Dwire and Lundquist were not. On November 13, 1987, a week before he was to go to trial, Dwire, out of money, pleaded guilty to the charge of theft by swindle. The two other charges made in Lyon County—theft and conspiracy to commit swindle—were set aside. Dwire was sentenced to 180 days in jail with work release, which he would serve in El Paso, Colorado, starting in January 1988. Also, he would pay a $5,000 fine, in addition to a surcharge of $500, and was put under probation for a term not to exceed five years. At the time of his sentencing, Dwire acknowledged that the growers had not been paid for their seed or gotten the seed they paid for. Also, he admitted that he had taken money from the company prior to and after the rescission, knowing that AEFS owed creditors money.

Dwire had been humbled, but he had not lost his sense of humor. He is reported to have said, "My attorney told me at the end of my legal battles I would be broke, but free. My attorney was half right."[46]

Kasal and Newes were pleased with Dwire's plea, which had the effect of cutting the legs out from under Hendrickson and Kramer. Hendrickson should have expected Dwire to pursue his own interests, since Hendrickson had done the same since AEFS filed for bankruptcy. But Kramer said he felt betrayed by Dwire. He had remained loyal to Dwire, and Dwire, he claimed, hadn't even bothered to consult him before entering his plea.[47]

The Wizard of Oz

Compared to pretrial proceedings, trying and convicting Hendrickson and Kramer proved a relatively easy affair. Each case, both of which were tried in Mankato, took three weeks, with a four-day break between them.

Hendrickson's court-appointed lawyer, John Scholl of Worthington, picked away at the elements of the specific actions that comprised the charges of conspiracy to commit swindle and theft by swindle. He asked: What was actually promised and agreed to? With whom, when, and where? What was taken (money or seed), when, where, and from whom? What really occurred, when, how, and between which parties? What, if any, role did Hendrickson play or not play in any specific action? These questions challenged the defining elements of Kasal's case. But in the end Scholl was left without a saving story to tell. Hendrickson's self-interested actions could not be explained away. Only one narrative appeared consistent: Hendrickson, co-owner of AEFS, had served himself at the expense of others.

Kasal's charges had the effect of legally forking Hendrickson: Either the tuber seed AEFS sold was of no value, which meant swindle, or it had value, which meant theft. If the tuber seed was of no value, AEFS's promise was a part of the artifice by which it took other people's money. If the seed had value (a stand the defense was almost compelled to take, given all that AEFS had said), Hendrickson had stolen it. There seemed no way around Kasal's fork.

Nevertheless, Scholl tried to offer Hendrickson a defense. The company had grown rapidly. The attorney general's judgment and the unfavorable press associated with it had damaged the company. Hendrickson's takings, conceded to be approximately $800,000, were not disguised, as were Dwire's, and amounted to less than 3 percent of the company's earning. Hardly the takings of a swindler, Scholl contended.

Scholl attacked Kasal's case along other fronts. For instance, one of the key witnesses for the defense—Kasal's friend Charles Dale, who testified to the existence of the escrow account—had never met, or even heard of, Hendrickson. Two other prosecution witnesses, Les Van Dyke and Ben Steensma, were told of this account only after having signed up (hard to swindle someone after the fact), and they both made at least some money from AEFS.

In the end, Scholl had no story to overcome the prosecution's story. As he noted in his closing statement, American courts, unlike Scottish courts, did not permit the finding case unproved; one was either innocent or guilty. Scholl conceded that his client "had pocketed enough to appear criminally guilty . . . and so for the jury he was. It is hard to tell a convincing story to a jury," Scholl added, "when the owner had drawn so much money from the company. . . . The affair turned on greed."[48]

Scholl faced an additional burden in the case. He had to try to control Hendrickson. Hendrickson came to the case "with a mountain of stuff." This included pad upon legal pad, tape after cassette tape, a host of documents, and a maze of theories and conjectures he and some lawyer friends had assembled. Scholl remarked that Hendrickson "came ready to try the case himself, while at the same time adhering to the proposition that he didn't know what was going on." Mirroring the ambivalent role he had played at AEFS itself, Hendrickson, according to Scholl, "wanted it both ways. . . . He wanted to distance himself from the defense and yet take an active role in it."[49]

Under extensive cross-examination, Hendrickson appeared at best to be confused and ignorant; at worst he appeared to be evasive and even mendacious. His exaggerated conspiracy theories about what brought AEFS down played into Kasal's hands. After Kasal noted that Hendrickson blamed the Minnesota attorney general, the federal bankruptcy court, Webb Press, Archer-Daniels-Midland, Cargill, and Norwest Bank for AEFS's failure, he asked Hendrickson, "Is there anybody else I've missed that you would like to blame?" Hendrickson replied, "Yes." "Who?" Kasal asked. "You," Hendrickson replied. "Thank you. I'm in good company," Kasal concluded.[50]

Kasal's closing statement was predictable: By himself and in conjunction with Dwire and Kramer, Hendrickson took money from AEFS that was owed to the growers and creditors. He turned company money, which legally belonged to growers and creditors, into farms, a home, and vacations for himself. In one instance, he donated $21,000 to his church. This handsome sum, Kasal sarcastically explained, was an act of generous tithing on Hendrickson's part; he gave 10 percent of $210,000 he had taken from AEFS. Just after deciding to have AEFS file bankruptcy, Hendrickson, mindless of growers' and creditors' interests, took $50,000 and a company car for himself and split $5,000 cash in the company safe with Dwire. Hendrickson further revealed his deviousness by putting only his wife's name on the house he bought with company money and keeping three sets of notes for the same withdrawals.

Kasal accused Hendrickson of making promises about the Jerusalem artichoke that he knew were false and of claiming that the company was sound when he knew it wasn't. He also promised, or at least was present when others promised, that there was an escrow account, which he knew was false.

Kasal concluded his final statement by identifying Hendrickson with the Wizard of Oz. Behind "the flashing lights and great booming voice . . . is a little man with a big microphone and switches and dials. You see enormous profits. You see cash all over the place. You are told about plants.... [But] when you pull the curtain back ... you see two very greedy men [who have] two concerns ... to take as much money as [they] can out of the company while it lasts ... [and] before it ends to cover up as much as [they] can with phony credits and leases and whatever you want."[51]

The jury agreed: Hendrickson was the "Wizard of Oz." It found him guilty of theft by swindle and conspiracy to commit theft by swindle.

Getting the Goods on a Television Evangelist

Calvin Johnson, a young public defender from Mankato, defended Kramer. He took the case seriously. He overspent his budget and gave his time freely to the case. He opened his office to Kramer, who worked there day and night with exemplary energy and intelligence, helping prepare his own case.

Johnson found Kramer charming. He liked Paul Glorvigen, the detective assigned to him. More significantly, accepting the first premises of his client and AEFS, Johnson believed in the Jerusalem artichoke as a crop of promise and in the national need for entrepreneurship in crop development. He also believed that Kramer was on trial partly because he was a Christian fundamentalist. He took exception to the way Kasal pronounced "television evangelist," stressing the last syllable with a hiss as if he were naming a type of moral monster.[52]

Johnson found himself at war with Judge Kelly right from the start when the judge insisted on trying Kramer before Hendrickson. It made no sense to Johnson to try the consultant before trying a co-owner and officer of the company. The judge cited Johnson for contempt when Johnson refused his order to start the trial on the grounds that he needed more time to prepare himself for this complex case. Johnson had complaints about the judge's handling of the trial, especially when, just before closing arguments, the judge, in chambers (Johnson and Kramer claimed), explicitly accepted Kasal's position that Kramer had aided and abetted Dwire and Hendrickson in the swindle.

Johnson's defense of Kramer resembled Scholl's defense of Hendrickson. Against the first charge of theft by swindle he argued that some state witnesses were not themselves swindled of money in 1983, during the period in which the state claimed they were cheated. Other state witnesses, such as the Laidlaws and Stotts, never invested a single penny in AEFS and thus could not have lost anything to it, while other state witnesses never entered into a relationship with Kramer.

Johnson fortified his defense by arguing that Kramer as a consultant could not conspire to swindle. He lacked powers to establish the escrow account, to tell growers that they would be paid for what they harvested, to deliver seed, to assure that the company set aside funds for research, and so on. Making his most important point, Johnson argued in his opening statement that Kramer couldn't have swindled AEFS itself, for he himself bought seed from it like any other grower.

Johnson's defense against the second charge of theft focused on defending Kramer's role in Challenge Fund. Johnson argued that in establishing the fund Kramer was seeking only to dispose of AEFS's rotting, spoiling, and shrinking tuber seeds; that he attempted to transform them into commercial paper (with the full knowledge of the company); and that he intended to repay AEFS as could be "proved" by receipts found in his possession. Furthermore, Johnson argued that Kramer was not the sole or majority owner of Challenge Fund. He only owned shares in it, as his two sons did, and only his son Tim signed its agreements.

As Johnson confessed in his opening statement, his defense was long, complicated, and tedious. Johnson's basic argument was that Kramer, who had worked hard and faithfully for AEFS, should not be punished for the wrongdoing of management.

Kasal's prosecution was relatively simple. Kramer played a paramount role in looting AEFS. He was not just a consultant among consultants. He had control over Dwire and Dwire Enterprises, and he wheedled money out of AEFS in many ways. There were his exorbitant monthly salary claims, reaching 340 and 350 hours a month, at $50 an hour. He put AEFS money and seed directly into L. D. Kramer and Associates, Hillcrest Enterprises, five special partnerships, and—the queen of Kramer's creations—the Challenge Fund. Kramer tried to hide some of his power by naming one of his companies Remark (Kramer spelled backward) and by the equally clumsy device of making his brother Wendall, who visited Minnesota only once during AEFS's existence, the head of Kramer and Associates. Additionally, his youngest son, Tim, headed Challenge Fund, while his older son, Dale, sat on its board. Finally, Kramer assigned $3 million of Challenge Fund notes to family members, secretaries, his own companies, and his church.

Kasal, in his concluding statement, asked the jury how they could trust a man who apparently kept a double set of books and notes, laundered money, tried to pay Paul Laidlaw to keep his mouth shut, siphoned off money from one company to another, and gave testimony in contradiction to an array of other people. For Kasal, Kramer was no consultant but a thief who stole by guile. The nub of Kasal's story was that Kramer used religion to barker farmers into AEFS's tent and then stole from them heartily right along with Dwire and Hendrickson.

The jury found Kramer guilty of theft and theft by swindle. Four jurors, including the jury foreman, who were interviewed by the author a little more than a year after the trial, offered different reasons for their judgment. One fellow was concerned that there were no AEFS notes from Kramer in AEFS's records. Others, with less precision, remarked variously, "Nobody was tending the store"; "They were in it to make a fast buck"; and "All wanted their dollar—and they got greedy." While one juror reported that another juror had held out against finding him guilty because he was a minister, she herself said that Kramer reminded her of Billy Sunday and he "looked like a city slicker." "That guy," another juror said, "just wasn't on the up and up."

"They Ain't Coming Back"

The trials and convictions of Dwire, Hendrickson, and Kramer had terrible consequences for them. They each experienced shame, prison, loss of community, and poverty. Men of fifty, their last bid to be somebody on the stage of history had failed miserably—and in all likelihood they weren't coming back.

Conversely, Kasal and Newes, men of forty, had won. Indeed, the case was a high point of their early careers. They had shown Kramer, Hendrickson, and Dwire—and Dwire's hot shot lawyer, Lundquist—what they were made of. At the same time, they had shown the big legal guns in the Twin Cities that they, the "Davids" of outstate law enforcement, did what their urban counterparts could not do: They got "the artichoke crooks."

To this day Newes is proud of their victory. He loves to describe how Kasal cut all three defendants to shreds when they took the stand. His eyes light up when he tells how Dwire, angered by Kasal's treatment of him on the stand during the Hendrickson case, loudly kicked the door with his cowboy boots as he exited from the courtroom after Kasal had "savaged him" on the stand for having broken his promise to cooperate with the state. Kramer, he recalled, remarked of Dwire's loud exit, "I guess he ain't coming back." "Nope, he ain't coming back," Newes responded. "He might not stop until he gets back to Colorado."[53]

Newes continued to harbor strong feelings about the defendants and those who represented them, as one incident reveals. In the wake of the trial, defense investigator Glorvigen, under Johnson's instructions, stopped off at the McLeod County court house "to get the goods" on Kasal. While there, Glorvigen gloatingly reported to Newes that the convictions of Hendrickson and Kramer would be reversed in light of Kasal's recent trouble with the law. (As reported in the *Hutchinson Leader*, Kasal was one of thirteen regional defendants named "in a civil suit filed by the Federal Deposit Insurance Company [FDIC] in an attempt to recoup nearly $1.5 million dollars in defaulted loans." With the failure of Gibbon Bank [involving criminal actions of its bankers], the FDIC called in the bank's loans, including those of Kasal. He had taken them out during 1984 and 1985 to help his brother Francis, who defaulted on seven loans totaling $240,000. While Kasal had made payment on three of the loans, he defaulted on the original amount of four loans totaling $90,000.[54])

Newes steadily boiled as he listened to Glorvigen inferring criminal behavior on Kasal's part. A few days later Newes, still angry, retrieved a newspaper article that had amused him several weeks before. He sent the article to Johnson. It described a worker who went through a large city's sewage to estimate condom use. Newes scribbled on the article that Johnson would make a good candidate for the job. Johnson, who continues to practice law and serve as public defender in Mankato, didn't bother to respond.[55]

Kasal did overcome the matter of the Gibbon Bank. Later he underwent a divorce initiated by his wife, which was painful for the Catholic and family-oriented man. He remarried in February 1992 and continues his private practice in Hutchinson.

Disappointed by Kasal's departure and not infatuated with the new McLeod county attorney, nor pleased with his salary, Newes started an earnest search of help-wanted ads. In 1990 he landed a job as an investigator for the Minnesota Supreme Court running background checks on attorneys seeking to be certified to practice law in Minnesota.

The AEFS case remains an unforgettable episode for Newes and Kasal. For them the case was about right and wrong, and it marked the high time of their young manhood, as it was the nadir of the mature manhood of Dwire, Hendrickson, and Kramer.

9

The Lost Covenant

A crook doesn't fall out of the sky.
—A folk saying

As the times swept Hendrickson, Dwire, and Kramer on to the stage of history, so the times discarded them. Of the three, Hendrickson alone remains loyal to the vision, while continuing to assert his innocence and issuing a stream of legal appeals. His wife and son have left him, and poverty has driven him to return to live with his parents.

After bouncing around in Colorado and out west for a while, Dwire eventually reestablished his household in southern California where he again works in construction. After a period of separation, he has been reunited with his wife and children.

Kramer has ended up as he started: he is alone, and he spends a lot of time on the road. He lives on the margins of the world of small churches, preaching revivals from time to time, consulting with churches, and selling religious publications. On a regular basis he returns from Texas to Minnesota to meet with his parole officer. He frequently visits his elderly parents and his two successful sons. In the spring of 1991, after a fifteen-year separation, his wife divorced him.

Dwire regrets the consequences of AEFS for its investors and creditors. Kramer wishes things would have worked out otherwise. Hendrickson, on occasion, acknowledges greed on his part and regrets certain decisions he made.

All three, however, excuse themselves for AEFS's failure. There was "hyper-growth," bad press, and the rescission order, without which, they believe, in Dwire's words, "The company would have been a viable business entity yet today."[1] None of them anguished over the plight of their growers, whom they judged to be speculators, desperate farmers, or secure farmers who risked only modest parts of their wealth. All their growers, they believe, knew the crop was a gamble.

Their religious faith allowed them to weather the bad times that followed the collapse of AEFS. It provided them with a standing source of forgiveness and hope. It shielded them from acknowledging ingrained character flaws (which all humans have) that caused them to yield to the temptations AEFS offered in abundance. It also weakened the doubt that helps immunize humans against self-deception.

Press On

In his many interviews with the author, Kramer, aggressive in his own defense, never acknowledged any personal wrongdoing, although he did not deny that he added big-tent enthusiasm and paper-cunning to AEFS.[2] He willingly pleaded ignorance about the crop's real potential and conceded he was not without suspicions about AEFS's scientist, Wayne Dorband, and others. He openly acknowledged that he often mediated between Dwire and Hendrickson, and he characterized Dwire as "a rascal" with ties to criminals.

Yet Kramer found none of this as implicating him in wrongdoing. In and out of court, he consistently argued that he never intentionally took anything from anyone. He did not, and does not, believe that he received excessive compensation for his work, that his companies operated illegally, or that farmers were billed for seed they didn't receive. He even denied taking seed for Challenge Fund, since Dwire, owner of AEFS, was a co-owner of Challenge Fund.

In conversation with the author, Kramer, nonrepentant, repeatedly pointed out that he was only one adviser of several. He frequently remarked that representatives of the bankruptcy court refused to accept his Challenge Fund notes for AEFS's creditors. He also asked why he, only an adviser, was convicted of two felonies while the officers and owners, were only convicted of a single felony each. Contending that the prosecution was politically motivated, he argued on several occasions that his case proved the truth of the old proverb: "Little thieves are hanged, while great ones escape." Also, Kramer depicts his plight as a price that he, an evangelical Christian, paid for facing a Catholic prosecutor, a Catholic judge, and a jury chosen (he fervently contends) to eliminate fellow evangelical Christians.[3]

Although Kramer's conversations were free of self-righteous pieties, they revealed an ample dose of paranoia. He was concerned about the taking over of America by outsiders, including "the Jews," and believes that he was the victim of a massive vendetta carried out against him and other evangelists to get at Pat Robertson so that Bush could win the Republican nomination.

Kramer fought his conviction. For lack of sufficient evidence, the charge of simple theft was reversed by a higher court in June 1989, leaving him guilty only of the count of theft by swindle. He was placed on a ten-year probation and was expected to serve one year in the Lyon county jail and pay a fine of $5,000 and legal costs of $5,000 over the next five years. Only part of his term was stayed in light of his previous pleading of nolo contendere in federal court in Texas.[4]

Since serving his sentence in 1989, Kramer has been on the road again. While he reports quarterly to his parole officer in Marshall, he has been in Texas more than anywhere else. He has an answering service in the Twin Cities and travels throughout the Midwest. He lives in modestly priced motel rooms and drives borrowed cars (the last one a big, old, four-door Lincoln whose trunk was filled with religious materials). Off and on Kramer spends a lot of time caring for his sick parents in Texas. He has had no steady income.

When AEFS and Challenge Fund collapsed, Kramer went to the Twin Cities and did volunteer work at the African-American youth foster home of the Reverend Walter Battle in St. Paul.[5] He received free room and board for his work. He devoted a significant amount of time to helping write a book whose purpose was to raise money for North Central Bible College of Minnesota.

Starting in 1990, Kramer sold religious educational material for a small religious press called Christian Communication, Inc., based in Wichita, Kansas. Among its publications are Hart Armstrong's multivolume *Complete Commentary on the Book of Revelations* (1992). In the fall of 1991, he worked successfully and received praise for his work as a consultant to resolve a serious split in an Assembly of God church in Irving, Texas. In November 1991, Kramer presented a "Challenge Seminar" at Daniel's Park Church of God in Cedar Rapids, Iowa. Kramer is described in an advance poster as "Mr. Challenge" as well as "a writer, lecturer, pastor, evangelist, businessman, and philanthropist."[6] The announced message of his seminar states: "Anyone can come out of the hot oven of trial and triumph victoriously through Jesus Christ." "L. D. Kramer," the poster notes, "inspires people to believe in God . . . like few can."

Kramer ends his days as he began them, working as an evangelical entrepreneur. The American dream has eluded him. He has no home of his own. He, who once headed a multichain nursing home, faces old age without health insurance or a place to call his own.

Yet the road has not broken Kramer. There is some truth in what his older son Dale wrote to him: "Over the years I have observed the intense battles you have endured and I admire your stamina and strength. Your track record proves you are no ordinary man. The average man would have succumbed to the pressure many years ago, but you withstood the assault. I have always known," Dale continued, "that my father carried a very significant commission by God for the building and the restoration of his kingdom. Even though you have experienced a set back [*sic*] recently, I still know in my heart that God, in his mercy, desires to fulfill the original commission he placed on your life many years ago."[7]

Dale was correct. Kramer was not the kind of man who surrendered easily. Scattered throughout the papers he used to prepare for his trial were multiple copies of a poem called "Press On." Its opening lines read "When your faith in your fellow man and good friends let you down / Press on. / When the world is closing in upon you, and your ability to reason is gone / Press on." Kramer's faith in self, God, nation, and life was, and is, all about pressing on.

Amway and Wild Rice

Dwire held the begrudging respect of many Marshall business leaders by not breaking under misfortune and by paying his bills. Shortly after AEFS's bankruptcy, Dwire—who unsuccessfully applied for unemployment—found a new career as an Amway salesman, which he pursued enthusiastically. He paid off the Lyon County Co-op with Amway merchandise and offered other creditors goods and dealerships to cover past debts.

On the eve of Dwire's sentencing, having pled guilty to theft by swindle, more than twenty of his acquaintances wrote to the court requesting leniency for him.[8] New friends at Amway testified too, often revealing more about themselves than Dwire. They praised him for his enthusiasm, energy, devotedness, optimism, and knowledge of sales. A Southwest State University official, himself an Amway salesman and known as a super booster, claimed that Dwire's business was a "multi-level network marketing business" and praised Dwire for "his business," which "is accountability."[9]

Old friends from the contracting business also testified for Dwire, claiming that he worked hard, kept his word, was a good family man, and had suffered enough. One prominent local contractor who vouched for Dwire's character noted that Dwire "could have stuck him" for approximately $70,000 in bills but didn't.[10]

Dwire's attorney and fellow church member James Anderson was convinced that Dwire never set out to defraud anyone. His accountant and Anderson's brother, Duane, said Dwire was almost like Job. He lost all, his wife was diagnosed as having cancer, and yet through it all "he never questioned his faith or said why me?"[11]

Friends from his church did not fail Dwire either. They wrote of how well he bore the hardship of bankruptcy and trial. They stated that he was a devoted and good family man. Richard Spencer, a member of Dwire's church, a believer in Amway, and former head of AEFS research, judged Dwire to be a committed father and husband who didn't drink or gamble. He judged Dwire to be "sober and straight forward [sic], honest and trustworthy . . . a man of his word . . . [and] courage."[12] Dan Blowers, who sold insurance to AEFS and who has a theology degree, remembered affectionately undertaking "a study of [the book of] Revelation with [Jim] and his family." He also revealed how Jim had "to sell his house for peanuts."[13] Dwire's brother-in-law, Jerry Knapper, who headed AEFS sales, argued that the real James was not the haughty man he appeared to be but that haughtiness was a cover for a deeply painful childhood. He argued that Dwire's concern for the survival of the family farm had always been authentic. Above everything else, Dwire was human.[14]

Another testimonial came from a man named, appropriately, George Farmer. Having gotten to know Dwire in Amway, Farmer believed he had fully given his life to Jesus Christ. As a fellow member with Dwire of what Farmer described as "a mutual forgiveness group," a group more than likely seeking God's restorative grace for its members, Farmer continued to believe "that something good could [still] come out of the great effort that was put into the artichokes."[15]

How much, if at all, these presentencing character testimonials influenced the judge is unknown. In any case, for theft by swindle the judge sentenced Dwire to one year and one day of jail and five years of probation. His sentence was stayed and he was required to spend six months in the county jail with work release, which he served by arrangement with local authorities in El Paso, Colorado, beginning January 1, 1988. He also paid a $5,000 fine.[16]

Some town critics still believe that Dwire made off with a bundle. Others disagree. Included among the latter is a barber who, having once seen Dwire flash hundred dollar bills, remembers how Dwire offered to pay him for his haircut with Amway goods. Evidence against the proposition that Dwire stashed away money are the facts that he now drives bulldozers and heavy machinery in California and that one of the last times he was seen in Marshall, as reported by former acquaintances, he drove a run-down camper and tried to sell wild rice.

The Prophet Abides

Two weeks after AEFS filed bankruptcy, Hendrickson, ever buoyant, proposed that the growers form a new Christian association of Jerusalem artichoke growers, Covenant Christian Farmers, Inc. He wrote,

> My heart is heavy for what has happened to AEFS, Inc., and the financial effect it had on three- and two-year growers, recision growers and employees of AEFS. Even though I am discouraged in many ways, I feel that through the reorganization of AEFS, that which was started by God as a movement of the soil people of America will climax by being a "success story" rather than a "failure story" and that in all our trials and testing God will get the glory for work we have all begun. I know that many of you are growing the Jerusalem artichoke because you felt the Lord's leading. I believe and still believe that God called Jim Dwire and Fred Hendrickson to establish the Jerusalem artichoke among the soil people of America. My purpose in this letter is . . . to call God's people to arms. I am confident in my heart that God will still have His way with his people. Obviously, all of us to some measure failed God and strayed from seeking Him and looking at the spiritual aspects of the Jerusalem artichoke program.[17]

A kind of buoyant Job, whose belief in God and America contains the irrepressible promise of progress, Hendrickson reiterated in this letter his belief that he was a prophet of national restoration and that his prophecy would be crowned with both gold and glory. Guided by prayers, some of which were originally given to him by Pastor Pete, Hendrickson saw the founding of the Covenant Christian Farmers as providential. He proposed that his new organization would have a board of twelve members, the number of Christ's apostles. Even though he was sharply rebuked by former allies, such as the Reverend Robert Engbrecht, president of the South Dakota Jerusalem Artichoke Growers Association, Hendrickson still did not doubt the religious nature of his calling. Instead, he responded to criticism by founding a National Jerusalem Artichoke Growers Market Association. His theme was that 1983 could still be the year, to use his phrase, of *the birth of the rebirth* of the energy farming industry.[18]

Misfortune proved Hendrickson's insubmergible buoyancy. He met his woes by forming alone, and in association with others, a succession of companies that embodied his vision of a renovated AEFS. Each company he created was made in the image of the one preceding it. Each bore the stamp of his "prophetic" reading of the Bible and his grandiose vision of American agriculture, and each was shaped by his sales pitch for Jerusalem artichokes. Each of his companies promised to restore the family farm and America as a Christian nation.

In Hendrickson's forming of all these companies was his vision of himself as a leader of a new order of life on the American prairie. His utopian vision belongs to a long tradition of midwestern prophets. He peopled his utopia with small, self-sufficient yeoman farmers and autonomous economic farm cooperatives, empty of giant corporations, big government, large cities, native people, and other marginal people. Hendrickson's vision reflects the open western South Dakota from whence he came and where he returned.

His first post-AEFS company, which existed on paper rather than in fact, was Penta*Tech.[19] Sketched out in August 1983, it was named after the five-sided sugar molecule supposedly found in the Jerusalem artichoke. Based on "truths" he gleaned from reading farm materials from the 1930s and the Chemurgic Council, Penta*Tech affirmed that 1) the land was the basis of all wealth; 2) agriculture was the key to American success in the world (he often cited author and Iowa farmer Carl Wilkin's concept of "soil wealth economics"); and 3) the Jerusalem artichoke would be the foundation crop for "emerging Energy Farming Industry." The farming energy system itself, Penta*Tech proposed, would "develop over the next seven years the planting of 35 to 50 million acres of traditional food and feed crop land into new alternative crops" such as sweet sorghum, sudan, costal Bermuda grass, and of course, above all else, the Jerusalem artichoke. Additionally, harking back to Hendrickson's first pre-AEFS visions, it would integrate approximately 150 million acres to develop vast rural-based, decentralized value-adding plants.[20]

In November 1983, Hendrickson launched Agriculture Growth Industries. Echoing AEFS, it was based on the fuel-alcohol vision: It sought five hundred growers to enter into an extended contract for twenty acres of their land for research and development of the Jerusalem artichoke.[21]

In January 1984, as if it were his intention to prove the adage that old dogs can't do new tricks, Hendrickson organized "The First Annual Jerusalem Artichoke Seminar."[22] Somehow Hendrickson still thought he could draw a crowd of former AEFS growers to hear Dorband and Tieszen, alcohol buff Gene Johansing from the West Coast, and farm advocate Charles Walter, Jr. Hendrickson's plans included soliciting sponsorships from AEFS's former law and accounting firms and seeking sponsorship funds from such individuals as Thomas Reichert and Tom Lukens, who both had numerous reasons to never want to hear from him or about Jerusalem artichokes again.

In the spring of 1984, Hendrickson joined Jerry Fish, the owner of a firm called SILOPRESS in Sioux City, Iowa. Hendrickson used his newly conceived Eco-Ag, an affiliate of SILOPRESS, to push his views.[23] Explicitly harking back to Henry Ford's Dearborn conferences and the founding of the Chemurgic Council, his new company would be, Hendrickson claimed, a covenant company. It would be a kind of commercial ark, which among other things would affirm the Judeo-Christian character of American agriculture; declare land the basis of wealth; develop the Jerusalem artichoke; and renovate America through the creation of energy farms.

In 1986, Hendrickson proposed the formation of the "Spirit of America Society."[24] The society gathered all his past dreams and visions into one great pitch. He explained it as "a dynamic new network of people who see the economic and moral or spiritual problems facing rural America, and Under [sic] Divine Providence are dedicated to solving the problems for themselves and many others. That has always been the 'Spirit of America' and that is why the society takes this name." The society would have four parts: a cooperative assurance corporation, a federal credit union (which would provide a credit card and a line of credit), a farm and family justice center, and a soil wealth institute, which would be based on a fifty-acre "Eco-Intensive Farming System."

Increasingly, Hendrickson was captivated by magical biblical numbers, prophecies, revelations, apocalypses, and great quadrants. He was especially bewitched by the power of the number seven in the Old Testament. Accordingly, Hendrickson specifically proposed that those who joined the Spirit of America's Project 49er (seven times seven) Program would join the Concept 21 (seven times three) Seven Year Plan, which would include, the following seven steps: 1) becoming a "Pioneer club member" in the society; 2) drawing up a Seven Year Farm Plan; 3) creating a fifty-acre eco-intensive homestead; 4) legally separating the homestead from the member's "regular farm or simply starts over again"; 5) concentrating on growing two of the seven basic food groups; 6) participating in the credit union and assurance program; and 7) enrolling in a major network of like-minded farmers.[25]

In a tape he dictated to Jerry Fish, Hendrickson prophesied that God exposed his people to seven years of famine to open their hearts. Hendrickson saw a new age for the American farmer amidst a world famine. The world would end soon, or—for some unexplained reason—within thirty-seven years.[26] On a separate sheet of paper, written in pencil on July 17, 1986 (believing himself to be a prophet, Hendrickson dated everything he wrote), he declared that "America is the 'Ark' of the New Covenant." This was true for seven reasons. Two of those seven reasons were that Noah, Moses, and America are three arcs and that God chose America to fulfill his commission six thousand years ago.[27]

Believing himself providentially called to carry out such great plans, it is not surprising that Hendrickson explained his failures in terms of conspiracies. Each failure expanded the network of conspirators Hendrickson imagined were allied against him. Assembled among the conspirators were bankers who wouldn't lend him money, journalists who wrote unfavorably about AEFS, and extension agents who cautioned farmers against planting Jerusalem artichokes. The core of the conspiracy was comprised of farm chemical and seed companies, the whole petroleum industry, major multinational grain dealers, and these industries' puppet-clients in government. Hendrickson grandiosely concluded that the same forces that had attacked the Jerusalem artichoke, AEFS, and himself in the 1930s had warred against Henry Ford and his Chemurgic Council; the

Rockefellers and the petroleum industry, in Hendrickson's long-held opinion, never could—and still cannot—tolerate the search for renewable energy.

Hendrickson was vulnerable to such a conspiratorial view of the world. There wasn't a bit of irony in him, and the idea that he could deceive himself never crossed his mind. His sense of self-importance made it easier for him to postulate being attacked by world enemies rather than being duped by himself.

The idea that there was a world conspiracy aimed equally against him and rural America established a moral bond between himself and the troubled farmers whom he served energetically from 1984 to 1988. Indeed, in his active imagination it joined him to all those distressed farmers who spoke both the older populist language against monopolies and cartels and the newer Lyndon LaRouche-inspired language of the international conspiracies carried out by the Rockefellers and the Trilateral Commission.

Hendrickson's sense of community with troubled farmers did little to convince the world he was innocent. Few accepted his notion that he was being persecuted by Skip Humphrey, or "H.H.H. III and his scheme team."[28] He won little sympathy with his argument that recent attempts to criminally prosecute financier John DeLorean and former Labor Secretary Raymond Donovan demonstrated the work of an over-zealous U.S. attorney general.[29]

Try as he might, Hendrickson failed to reverse the conviction that marked him as a criminal and stripped him of his attorney's license. While he succeeded on appeal in defeating the first of the two counts against him—conspiracy to commit theft by swindle—he could not convince a higher court to set aside his conviction of theft by swindle. Hendrickson argued that Kasal, on the eve of his trial, had ingeniously switched the substance of the second count against him from theft by swindle of money to theft by swindle of seed. Kramer and Dwire, he argued, had stolen seed; he had not. He further claimed that he had no knowledge of the Challenge Fund, nor was he party to the Stotts notes, which were the two ways they took seed from the company. (One assumption that underlay Hendrickson's rather complex argument was that in finding him guilty not of the first count, the jury cleared him of having been guilty of taking money.) In April 1989, the Minnesota Court of Appeals sustained the lower court's finding. In July 1989, the Minnesota Supreme Court refused to listen to his case. In February 1990, the United States Federal Court in South Dakota refused his habeas corpus motion against Lyon County, where Judge Richard L. Kelly had sentenced him to serve six months in prison starting in February 1990. Since then Hendrickson has initiated additional appeals; most recently, in January 1992, he optimistically sent forward four new appeals. They failed in April 1992.[30]

Hendrickson spared no effort to save himself from disbarment in South Dakota. He encouraged approximately thirty friends and clients to write the South Dakota Supreme Court on his behalf.[31] A considerable number of the writers were farmers from South Dakota and Minnesota, many of whom he had served pro bono during the preceding few years. They wrote the South Dakota Supreme Court describing Hendrickson's work in glowing terms. These letters were nearly unanimous on the point that Hendrickson was a unique lawyer who truly cared about the plight of economically troubled farmers. They echoed the praise of a farmer from Woodstock, Minnesota, who described Hendrickson as "the man who has helped make it possible to harvest another crop. . . . He has helped my family and I and many other friends and neighbors through the farm crisis. He . . . charged only what many could afford, which was often nothing."[32]

Others from different walks of life also praised Hendrickson. A South Dakota banker signed his name "Duane Loots" and parenthetically noted that his name was "pronounced Loats."[33] A lawyer from Ortonville, Minnesota, Ronald Frauenshuh, suggested Hendrickson's "honest intent has always been an asset to the farmer during a very tough economic time."[34] A colorful letter was also sent by Dana Jennings, Hendrickson's friend from SILOPRESS. In addition to a short biographical piece on Hendrickson, Jennings has also written a dozen books on the American West under such titles as *Days of Steam and Glory, Greatest Steam Show on Earth*, and *Black Hills Gold Slick Trick*. Jennings argued—and he was not alone—that Hendrickson was betrayed by "AEFS associates, who loudly professed Christianity while robbing the organization." Hendrickson, he concluded in his letter, "was the victim of Bible-thumping thieves who deliberately contrived to make Fred look guilty while they robbed."[35]

Hendrickson boldly argued against disbarment before the South Dakota Supreme Court. He "offered no excuses for his actions and showed no remorse," according to Justice Robert Morgan. " 'Instead,' said Morgan, who prepared the written decision, 'with a pyramid of Jerusalem artichokes stacked as props at his side, he spent much of his oral argument extolling the virtues of the Jerusalem artichoke and expanding his vision of solar greenhouse heat by artesian wells as a means to revitalize the South Dakota farm economy." The court was not swayed, believing that he used "the same sort of pitch that he used to separate his investors from their money." It denied Hendrickson's request to be able to continue to assist farmers, concluding, "that's not the kind of assistance farmers need."[36] He was disbarred in May 1989.

Hendrickson struck back with an open letter to the press. He claimed that "only judicial incompetence or negligence on the part of the South Dakota Supreme Court" could account for its ruling. Hendrickson promised that one day he would prove the connection between Humphrey and Kasal, "the master at deception, deceit, and other prosecutor tricks," and "sometime Hendrickson will be able to 'piece' together the Cargill/ADM-Humphrey/Nichols 'scheme' to 'bury' AEFS and the J/a [Jerusalem artichoke] and everyone who promoted this marvelous crop." Hendrickson vowed he would fight on. "[It] is important to me personally, and even more important to my wife and children, who have supported me for the seven years I have had to fight the McLeod County Prosecutor, that I not give up. I pray that I can clear my name while my father (age 92) and my mother (age 85) are still living."[37]

The AEFS affair not only destroyed Hendrickson's public image but it engulfed his private life as well. The price of defending himself and his Jerusalem artichoke dream left him broke. In 1988, Hendrickson lived in a rented house and drove a leased car, a 1984 Datsun. He owed the IRS $20,000 in back taxes, and he owed another $20,000 to a local hospital for medical treatment of his son. Hendrickson fared even worse in 1989, the year of his disbarment. His wife had an operation for cancer in January. Hendrickson himself started to serve a six-month jail term in Sioux Falls on work release. His sentence also included a $20,000 fine, a $10,000 county reimbursement fee, and ten years probation. His sentence was drawn up in light of a presentencing report that found him, on the one hand, devoid of remorse and denying any culpability, and on the other, a person without a past criminal record, not a user of drugs or alcohol, who had remained stable amidst the most difficult circumstances.[38]

Hendrickson, however, was not yet through. In a 1990 published loose-leaf described as "Appendix A to his New Wealth Institute," he defended himself with a collection of positive testimonials against the South Dakota Supreme Court's disbarment. He included positive articles on the Jerusalem artichoke, citing Ralph Waldo Emerson along the way: "A weed is a plant whose virtues are not yet discovered." He identified himself consciously with 1930 Jerusalem artichoke advocate Fred Johnson, the goals of the Chemurgic Council, and, as if that were not enough, the Populist farm platform of 1892. Hendrickson, indeed, seemed irrepressible.

In 1990, things took yet a further turn for the worse for this buoyant American Job: he lost his family. Disbarment assured him a place in the ranks of the unemployed. His wife returned to college in Iowa to prepare to resume her career as a teacher. He wandered from place to place, friend to friend, trying to find a niche in the world he had once tried to save. He had no phone of his own; he was flat broke, without even money for gas. By his own admission, he was at the bottom of the barrel.

In the fall of 1990, I interviewed Hendrickson in the company of his son. At the time, Hendrickson worked ten hours a day on the line in a Del Monte food processing factory in Faribault, Minnesota. Before the interview began his son angrily blurted out, "AEFS—Shit! You have no idea how difficult it was to live with AEFS." Then, in an aside to his father, he told him—in some words or other—to be easy on me, for "he might even have a family." Hendrickson told me that he now identified with the urban underclass. He wondered out loud if he were to be its leader. He thought so. Assuming history repeats itself, he suggested the workers would rise up in 1992, as they did in 1892. He seemed confident that this great revolution would free him from the canning factory and his newfound industrial class from oppression.[39]

By the spring of 1991, Hendrickson had returned home to live with, and help care for, his elderly parents in Rapid City, South Dakota. Disbarred, without family, publicly judged a criminal, he was left the boy dreamer he had always been.

Hendrickson began the last interview I had with him in the spring of 1991 with an announcement that he too, like me, intended to write a book. While claiming he wanted my advice as a writer, he quickly set out to solicit my agreement with the thesis of his proposed book. In his nervous, rapid style he mixed words of polite self-deprecation with scattered speculation. He said that in reading the Old Testament he had come across what he took to be textual proof that, at the time of the Garden of Eden, America was joined to the Old World. Consequently, no migration was necessary from Old World to New World. And "logically," God's covenant with the people of America was equal to that with the other tribes of Israel. (Kramer, who a year or so earlier had been summoned 150 miles to a meeting with Hendrickson to hear the same ideas, dismissed them as nothing other than a paraphrasing of a popular idea of radio preacher Reverend Hart Armstrong.)[40]

Despite my reluctance to hear any more about numbers, eons, and revelations (at one point I even pointed out that I preferred biblical parables to biblical prophecy), Hendrickson pushed on. He sought to affirm that America's restoration depends on a revitalization of a covenantal interpretation of its history. Before we parted, Hendrickson insisted I borrow a copy of what he took to be an important book, Peter Marshall and David Manuel's *The Light and the Glory: Did God Have a Plan for America?* Predictably, this book, published in 1977 during the time when Hendrickson fused his views of energy farming and America's covenantal history, affirmed that God does have a plan for America. Together we left the restaurant (hardly a stone's throw from AEFS's old company headquarters). In a small car Hendrickson drove north from Marshall "on business."[41]

Conclusion: The Planets Went Astray

As the planets were in order for the creation of American Energy Farming Systems in the early 1980s, so they were out of order for AEFS by the middle 1980s. Kramer was correct when he commented on the meteoric rise and fall of AEFS: "Timing is everything."

In the early 1980s, when Hendrickson and Dwire gave birth to AEFS, the times favored their work. The cost of oil soared, the Arabs were feared, and the presumption was that the nation desperately needed new sources of energy. Earlier hopes of an alcohol industry, lost in the 1950s and 1960s to low fuel prices, were again heard beyond the quarters of experimental stations. The demand for alternative crops mounted throughout the late 1970s and early 1980s as farmers, caught between depressed crop prices, overproduction, declining land values, and the high cost of borrowing money, looked for ways to save their farms.

Although Reagan promptly repealed Carter's legislation offering tax breaks, subsidies, and special programs for energy conservation and alternative energy sources, he gave a considerable boost to free enterprise, religious fundamentalism, and patriotism, all essential elements of AEFS's philosophy. Speculation was respiritualized and made essential to the nation's health. Catching the spirit of the era, more than a few companies pledged their "corporate essence" to the restoration of the American way. AEFS was one of them.

AEFS failed its mission almost as quickly as it had discovered it. With its failure, the Jerusalem artichoke lost its claim to the fields of the nation's farmers. Having failed in her night at the ball, the Cinderella plant was again reduced to the status of an outcast weed. It became what it had been all along for the vast majority of the nation's farmers: a pernicious weed whose charms appealed only to the odd pig farmer or enticed the occasional gourmet cook who finds the sly, tastefully nutty charms of the water chestnut in its irregular tubers.

In the aftermath of the Jerusalem artichoke circus, Jerusalem artichokes were again systematically eradicated from farmers' fields. Alternative-energy and new-crop people were placed on the margins of national discourse and swept into the corners of the national scientific academies. Only a handful of unfunded, and thus disarmed, scientists and agronomists still dared to mention the commercial promise of the Jerusalem artichoke. Very few entrepreneurs or speculators were any longer betting on its promise. No government or private funds declared its study a worthy matter.

The market had eliminated a substantial percentage of the farmers of the 1980s who had bet, or who would have been most likely to bet, on the Jerusalem artichoke. As usual, help for the farmers of the midwestern states came not essentially in the form of new crops but from government programs, which, among other things, allowed many farmers to renegotiate their loans. In Minnesota, government aid took the form of legislation requiring binding negotiations between farmers and their creditors and, harking back to the farm crisis of the 1930s, led to moratoriums on farm payments. Cultural sensibilities increasingly interpreted distressed farmers as victims worthy of a nation's full compassion.

As farmers took up the halo of victim, so correspondingly AEFS was depicted as a victimizer. There was less and less understanding for the company, which had set up tents and gaming tables that gave desperate farmers one last chance to roll the dice for their survival. Most partisans of the farmers forgot how well-cautioned farmers had been about the Jerusalem artichoke by state extension agencies and the farm press. They also conveniently overlooked the simple proposition that farmers, more than anyone, should have known how risky new crop development is; they entirely ignored the fact that as a general policy

AEFS encouraged farmers to make only a "limited purchase"—ten acres for $12,000—and cautioned farmers between the lines of its great promises that things might not work out. They chose not to apply a "buyer beware" responsibility to the farmers who bought Jerusalem artichokes.

In the climate of the late 1980s, it became increasingly easy for a part of the public to reduce the whole AEFS affair to three swindlers taking advantage of a lot of innocent farmers. There was a whole literature—Sinclair Lewis's *Elmer Gantry* foremost among it—that supported (in truth, even created) the interpretation that this was another case of farmers being taken advantage of by slick traveling preachers. Many interpreters of the circus took great pleasure in pretending to be shocked, dismayed, and—to use a fashionable word—outraged to discover evidence for their long-held view that fundamentalist ministers are crooks.

When judging the Jerusalem artichoke circus, however, there is a tendency to overlook how much good old boosterism, the founding and abiding philosophy of American and midwestern commercial and civic philosophy, supported AEFS—formed the imaginations and enthusiasms of its owners, consultants, salesmen, and buyers. Indeed, many would argue, the bigger the problems, the more desperate the needs, the worse the times, the greater the optimism of the responding boosterism.

Also, many people now forget how, during the period that AEFS was formed, new gambling casinos of all sorts were being set up across the nation. Greed, which corrupted Dwire, Hendrickson, Kramer, and others associated with AEFS, was fashionable. States started lotteries, the rhetoric of free enterprise was shrill, and high interest rates allured and addicted many to gambling—called speculation and aggressive investment in more polite circles. Junk bonds found their way into the most established portfolios. The official national background message suggested that taking a risk and making a buck were pleasing to God and nation.

In the course of the 1980s, reasons for a sympathetic reconstruction of "the Great Jerusalem Artichoke Circus" diminished, while grounds for moral accusation increased. By 1990, the national pageant of high speculation and greed was over—at least for the time being. As Dwire, Hendrickson, and Kramer were being tried and judged, much of what made the Reagan presidency successful was being severely judged in legislative committees, in court, and by public opinion. Again, it became fashionable to sneer at unregulated capitalism, aggrandizing individualism, pious patriotism, and evangelical Christianity. They had shed their magic skins and were vulnerable to moral accusation.

Events corroborated disenchantment. Government officials were brought by droves into courts for influence peddling. The stock market took a great tumble on Black Monday, October 16, 1987. Prestigious Wall Street firms jettisoned their young energetic brokers, the quintessential Yuppies, who were the new priests of an old game. Great speculators fell, none so flamboyantly as Donald Trump, who, like a Jerusalem artichoke grower himself, was driven to stake everything on one last roll of the dice. Frothing with irony, the fall itself took the form of his building an immensely luxurious gambling casino in New Jersey called the Taj Mahal. He was just one of countless speculative Icaruses to have fallen out of a sky that once was the limit.

Judgment was at hand in the late 1980s. The nation judged Wall Street to be greedy. In 1990, the court severely judged Michael Milken, king of the junk bond, while throughout the nation courts continued to prosecute those who had speculated in bonds and real estate. The farm credit system was severely examined. The savings and loan industry's failures and corruption damaged the whole nation's budget as government bailouts reached hundreds of millions of dollars in the Bush years. The 1991 revelations of the world banking scandal associated with Bank of Credit and Commerce International (BCCI)—by date of origin a contemporary of AEFS—may dwarf all others in offering insight into a decade of unregulated greed and corruption.

Even the nation's most public believers of the 1980s, the powerful television evangelists—"the children of L. D. Kramer"—fell on bad times at decade's end. Money, sex, and pride undid them. Adultery undid Jimmy Swaggart. Oral Roberts, it seemed, had blasphemed God when he sought to coerce his followers (who included Hendrickson) by declaring that if they did not give enough money, God would call him home. Charges of conniving and skullduggery injured Jerry Falwell as he purportedly tried to clean up the world of Jim and Tammy Bakker's Praise the Lord ministry.

None fell as far as Jim and Tammy Bakker. Their careers as preachers ascended and descended across the northern skies not without parallel to those of Kramer and other aspiring Assemblies of God stars, whose ministries reached from storefronts and tents to big churches and televangelism programs. Jim and Tammy went from being itinerant preachers to heading a successful television ministry and directing an immense Christian fun land—and from there to a gaudy world characterized by opulent wardrobes, an air-conditioned dog house, animal weddings, homosexuality, adultery, and irregular financial practices. It was the latter that did Jim in and led to the unwarrantedly severe initial sentence of forty years in prison. As Kramer remarked more than once to me, the 1990s were no longer a good time to be "a TV evangelist."

Across the nation, judgments followed failures. The mandate of heaven appeared to be changing. Even Reagan, the most popular president, increasingly fell under judgment as his second term drew to a close. (The national debt had grown immensely on his watch; he made public plans to lay a wreath at a German cemetery that held the remains of SS troops; and he, who claimed to be beyond blackmail, was discovered—despite his denials to the contrary—to have traded weapons and money with Iran for the return of hostages.) One final, indicting revelation came just after the Reagan presidency ended: It was discovered that his wife, Nancy, who regularly gave him advice on national affairs, had done so on more than one occasion upon the advice of her California astrologer.

At decade's end the stars and planets (a metaphor for time, circumstances, and ideas) were surely out of order for Jerusalem artichoke boosters and the alternative crop and energy movements. National sensibility now dictated against a sympathetic hearing for AEFS and its founders. Their defense fell on deaf ears. No audience was willing to listen to their claims that they were responding to the energy crisis and that new crop development, as their growers knew all along, is risky business. They were judged guilty of greed and theft by swindle.

The Jerusalem artichoke, thanks to them, became the laughingstock of alternative crops, the symbol of all the folly associated with new-crop experimentation. It now truly became the bastard cousin of the sunflower and the dark flower of all the plants that were successfully fashioned into crops in the nation's farmlands. Its tangled, irregular tubers no longer held mystery; it no longer carried the reverenced promise of a wonder crop, "the new soybean." Only a handful of holdouts from AEFS, a few new-crop scientists, a few committed farmers, and a West Coast specialty food supplier who used Sun Chokes believed in the Jerusalem artichoke. Mocked, this saving plant, promoted as the redeemer of the nation, was cast out of the nation's fields.

The Jerusalem artichoke was seen in retrospect as a pipe dream of the desperate, and AEFS merely an artifice, a large and complex scheme, to defraud farmers of their money. Few now heard the concept of Christian entrepreneurs and a Christian company without hearing overtones of naivete or scam. Times had changed.

However, to explain is not to forgive. The company founders and others associated with AEFS deserve to be judged for what they did and what they failed to do, for the vast discrepancy between what they promised and what they delivered. At nearly every turn ignorance and greed marred what the company did. Not having an understanding of crop development or knowledge of how to organize a new industry, they concentrated their energies on sales, for sales made money, and it was money that interested them most all along. No sooner did the money begin to flow into AEFS coffers than they began to take it for themselves. They used religion to win wide trust and approval, while behind the scenes they bilked the company's money, sapping its strength and undercutting its promise to its growers. They did not sacrifice themselves to the company but rather sacrificed the company to themselves.

His funds exhausted, Dwire acknowledged his guilt in a plea-bargain agreement. In separate trials, juries found Hendrickson and Kramer guilty. Nevertheless, all three believe they were scapegoats, and they argue, as Fred Johnson did in the 1930s regarding his efforts to establish a commercial market for the Jerusalem artichoke, that they were the victims of antagonistic world corporations. They contend their original intentions had merit and, not without a partial claim to truth, they excused much of what they did by blaming the rapidity of the company's growth and the hysteria that surrounded its early success. But, whatever the worth of their arguments, they could not convincingly prove that they were loyal servants to the plant and the company. Their efforts did not appear sincere to their jurors. And by decade's end, it was easy to judge them as being no better or worse than all the corrupt speculators and greedy evangelical Christians who surfaced during the 1980s.

Whatever one makes of Hendrickson, Dwire, Kramer, and others at AEFS, they appear to have served causes larger than themselves. Perhaps the Midwest has a disproportionate array of dreamers, boosters, salespeople, evangelists, and others to help make it what it claims to be. In any case, history (to speak metaphorically) drafted them to sell a redeeming American crop, and conscripted business people, farmers, salesmen, and so many others to make the AEFS affair what it was.

Possibly, though around a different crop and at a different time, AEFS may be resurrected. As long as there are desperate farmers, there will be gambling on new plants. As long as there are large sums of money to be made from hitting the jackpot of establishing a new crop, speculators and con artists, disguised as entrepreneurs, patriots, and preachers, will appear to exploit the risky, important, and speculative business of new-crop development. As long as America conceives of itself as a Christian Republic, the people of the Midwest will cast their most basic economic needs in religious and moral language. Finally, as long as necessity, fortune, greed, myth, and folly shape human experience, the buying and selling of any new potential crop has the possibility of giving rise to circuses and get-rich-quick schemes. It appears "the gods of history" (whoever they are) may gloat as much about folly's victory as reason's triumph.

The memory of how much difference a new crop can make, as exemplified by the soybean, continues to tantalize the farmers of the Midwest who, over the long haul, have tended to outproduce the markets and depress the prices of every crop (including the soybean) with which they have cast their fortunes. A recent crop of promise like canola (a new strain of rape seed that has already become the third largest oil seed in the world) presently stirs the northwest corner of the corn belt. Even the Jerusalem artichoke itself may still hold promise, especially in light of another energy crisis and the inevitable corresponding searches for renewable energy. Indeed, two Jerusalem artichoke growers from the heydays of AEFS, Doug and Alton Mjolness, were featured on the pages of the once adversarial *Farmer* in February 1991. They announced, "We've grown them since 1982 and found our markets," but declined to identify those markets.[1]

Favoring the reduplication of circumstances that gave rise to the Jerusalem artichoke circus, fossil fuels are nonrenewable and a damage to the environment, and the United States' strongest economic resource, arguably, still remains its rich and fertile lands. Also, belief in the family farm and faith in God's deliverance will not quickly perish. With just a little imagination, down the road can be espied an advancing column of believers, entrepreneurs, and preachers. In the lead can be seen Fred Hendrickson, James Dwire, and L. D. Kramer. They can again be heard preaching the promise of a new saving plant.

A plant, however, is never easily transformed into a crop. Even the exceptionable success of the soybean in making this transformation from plant to crop in the Midwest rested on more than thirty years of research, agronomic experimentation, and exceedingly large new needs for oils (especially margarines) and protein feeds after the Second World War. Furthermore, scientists never know all the science they need to know; industrial processes are more easily wanted than established; the fields of American farmers are not easily opened to costly experiments; and markets do not automatically embrace new crops or stand by them in perpetuity.

As long as new crops both require cash for their development and offer cash as a reward for their successful development, there will necessarily be speculators associated with them. Consequently, if the Jerusalem artichoke (or another Cinderella plant) beckons again, odds are that barkers, midways, and tents will once more arise on the prairie. From time to time, the stars insist on a circus.

Chronology

1981

October 2. AEFS is incorporated.
October 30. Co-owner James Dwire makes a $10,000 withdrawal from AEFS.
December. Minnesota attorney general's office begins its investigation of AEFS.
December 21. Consultant the Reverend Lowell D. Kramer receives his first paycheck.

1982

April. Dwire borrows $600,000 from AEFS for Dwire, Inc.
April 30. AEFS accountant Adrean Helgeson warns the company about shortfall and irregular practices.
June 10. First National Growers Convention is held in Marshall.
September. McLeod County begins its investigation.

1983

February 19. A widely circulated critical article printed in *The Farmer* and *The North Dakota* reveals that AEFS is "being investigated by 12 states and the federal government."
February. AEFS concludes an agreement with the Minnesota attorney general's office, agreeing to pay a $25,000 civil penalty and to offer refunds to its growers. Also, it pays a fine to the Iowa attorney general's office.

March. Accountant Tim Ribbens declares that the company is no longer accountable.

March 24. First limited partnership is formed with Larry Stotts.

May 9. $400,000 is passed out to AEFS insiders.

May 20. Dwire announces that AEFS is to file for bankruptcy.

May 23. AEFS files for bankruptcy.

June. U.S. bankruptcy court proceedings reveal that Dwire and Fred Hendrickson paid themselves salaries of $250,000 per year, in addition to receiving $1.3 million in loans and advances.

June 9. Second limited partnership is formed with Stotts.

June 30. Kramer goes off AEFS payroll.

September 13. AEFS is declared bankrupt. A $10 million suit is filed in U.S. bankruptcy court against owners Dwire and Hendrickson and consultant Kramer.

1984

May. McLeod County grand jury probe into AEFS prompts the convening of a multicounty grand jury.

October. Kramer's office in Edina is searched by McLeod County investigator Jim Newes.

October-November. Dwire, Hendrickson, and Kramer are indicted by a multicounty jury for diversion of corporate assets. Dwire is indicted on twenty-one counts; Kramer nine counts; Hendrickson, fifty-three counts.

December 12-13. Dwire, Hendrickson, and Kramer are additionally charged by a second multicounty grand jury with conspiracy to swindle and diversion of corporate assets.

1986

January-February. Fear of suppression of multicounty grand jury charges by a higher court leads McLeod County prosecutor Peter Kasal to make similar complaints against Dwire, Hendrickson, and Kramer in Lyon County.

February 18. The Minnesota Supreme Court dismisses earlier multicounty indictments against the three men.

April-May. Kramer and Hendrickson are appointed public attorneys.

September. In U.S. bankruptcy court an out-of-court settlement is reached. Creditors receive much less than 1 percent of their investments. As part of a final settlement, Dwire agrees to an $815,000 nondischargeable debt; Kramer, a $250,000 nondischargeable debt; and Hendrickson, who cooperated with the court, a $10,000 nondischargeable debt.

September-October. Mankato Judge Richard L. Kelly dismisses Lyon County charges against the three men, but upon appeal in July 1987 his ruling is reversed by the Minnesota Supreme Court, leaving the charges stand.

1987

November 14. Dwire pleads guilty to theft by swindle; in December he is sentenced to a year in jail, five years probation, and a $5,000 fine.

1988

February-March. Hendrickson is tried in Mankato and convicted of theft by swindle and conspiracy to commit theft by swindle. Upon appeal first conviction is overturned.

March. For the second conviction, Hendrickson serves six months in jail, is fined $20,000, and given ten years' probation. Kramer is tried and convicted of theft and theft by swindle; the conviction of theft is reversed by a higher court in June 1989. For theft by swindle Kramer is sentenced to a year in jail, a $5,000 fine, and ten years' probation.

May. Hendrickson's license to practice law in South Dakota is suspended; the following year he is disbarred by the South Dakota Supreme Court. Hendrickson continues to appeal his conviction. His most recent appeal was made in January 1992 and was unsuccessfully argued in court in April 1992.

AEFS Organizational Structure

Board of Directors

James Dwire, Chief Executive Officer, President
Fred Hendrickson, Secretary, Vice President, Director of
  Development

Board of Administration

Richard Spencer, Director of Research
The Reverend Jerry Knapper, Public Relations Officer
Kim Boe, Accounting Director
Bob Messersmith, Director of Human Resources
Paul Skrien, Director of Sales and Marketing
Gary Gould, Director of Facilities and Purchasing

Advisory Board Members

Howard Cox, Attorney
Michael Vekich, Certified Public Accountant
The Reverend Lowell Dale Kramer, Business Consultant
Wayne Dorband, Agronomics Consultant
Eric Johnson, Public Relations Consultant
Robert Soleta, Energy Farming Consultant
Roger Seratt, Alcohol Fuel Consultant
Wendell Peden, Veterinarian Consultant
L. T. Fan, Chemical Engineering Consultant
Larry Tieszen, Consultant

Paul Hegstrom, Marketing Presentation Video
Roy Wemeier, Banking Consultant
William L. Ginnodo, Personal Consultant
Larry Gauthier, Free-lance Writing Consultant
Robert Vekich, International Marketing
James Lukaszewski, Media Relations Training
George Perpich, Government Interfacing

Notes

Foreword

1. A complicated man, Butz had thought of becoming a minister before he earned his Ph.D. in agricultural economics, but he also had a weakness for barnyard humor; he was driven from office after telling one obscene joke too many about "the coloreds."

2. Butz eliminated production controls and price supports; farmers responded by putting 50 million acres of marginal lands back into production. Domestic food prices also soared during his tenure—by nearly 50 percent in the first three years—but this was never, so far as Butz was concerned, a problem. His outspoken contempt for women and racial minorities extended also to the poor generally, to consumers, to environmentalists, and with a special vehemence, to small farmers. Asked about the millions of farmers who had been destroyed by an experiment in the 1950s with free-market farm economics—he was assistant secretary of agriculture then—he said, with shades of Marie Antionette, "There are some people who just weren't cut out to be farmers. It's not all that cold blooded to suggest that they seek other employment." He felt differently, though, about the big grain merchants. When he got wind of a big crop failure in the Soviet Union in 1972, he did not make the news public but conveyed the information privately to the grain companies, which were then able to buy commodities futures on highly favorable terms. The huge grain sale to the Soviets that was subsequently negotiated in secret included additional subsidies to the grain companies and generous loan subsidies to the Soviets. He tried the same thing again in 1976, but by then the public outcry was so loud that he was forced to cancel the deal.

3. Earl Butz had predicted in 1971—the outcome seemed entirely desirable to him—that there would be a million fewer farmers by 1981. He was right.

4. Between 1910 and 1990, the farm share of the U.S. agricultural dollar fell from 41 cents to 9 cents; in constant dollars, farm income fell during the same period. This was not, as is so often claimed, a result of labor efficiencies in agriculture but rather a result of a shift in the agricultural economy from production to manufacturing. The average return on investment to U.S. food processing companies is about 50 percent higher than the average return to manufacturers as a whole. We do not have, as farm advocates like to say, a cheap food policy; we

have a cheap commodities policy. This helps to explain why we have in this country both failing farmers and a significant incidence of malnutrition among the poor.

5. *Alternative Agriculture* (Washington, D.C.: *National Academy Press*, 1989).

6. Earl Butz, "Our Greatest Risk," *The World & I* (December 1992): 251. There could hardly be a more direct expression of the paradigm of farming as the enemy of nature, the paradigm that has been at the heart of the development of modern industrial farming.

7. Quoted in Cary Fowler and Pat Mooney, *Shattering: Food, Politics, and the Loss of Genetic Diversity* (Tucson: University of Arizona Press, 1990), 83.

8. This account based on Dee Brown, *Bury My Heart at Wounded Knee* (New York: Holt, Rinehart & Winston, 1970).

9. See Margaret Visser, *Much Depends on Dinner* (New York: Collier Books, 1988), chapter 1.

10. For a general account of the transition from subsistence agriculture to industrial agriculture, see Wayne C. Rohrer and Louis H. Douglas, *The Agrarian Transition in America* (Indianapolis: Bobbs-Merrill, 1969).

11. John Fraser Hart, *The Land That Feeds Us* (New York: Norton, 1991), 372.

12. Ibid., 374.

Preface

1. David Pimentel et al., "Perennial Grains: An Ecology of New Crops," *Interdisciplinary Science Reviews* 2, no. 1 (1986): 42.

2. Gary Ritchie, ed., *New Agricultural Crops* (Boulder, Colo.: Westview Press, 1979), 4.

3. Ibid.

4. Useful introductions to the relation of plants and cultures and societies are Edgar Anderson, *Plants, Man and Culture* (Berkeley: University of California Press, 1967), especially sections on weeds, 16–30, 136–50, and the sunflower, 186–206; Charles Heiser, *Seed to Civilization* (Cambridge, Mass.: Harvard University Press, 1990); and Henry Hobhouse, *Seeds of Change: Five Plants that Transformed Mankind* (New York: Harper & Row, 1987).

5. N. W. Simmonds, *Evolution of Crop Plants* (New York: Longman, 1976), 36–38.

6. Erich Hoyt, "Wild Relatives: In Wilderness Lies a Genetic Bank Account We Have Been Drawing on for Generations," *Wilderness Summer* 53, no. 189 (1990): 48.

7. Noel Vietmeyer, "Guayule, Domestic Rubber Rediscovered," in Ritchie, *New Agricultural Crops*, 169.

8. Ibid., 170.

9. James Brown, president of Jojoba Growers and Processors, was kind enough to send me an advance copy in manuscript of his keynote address to the eighth international conference on jojoba and its uses, held in Asunción, Paraguay, June 17–22, 1990.

10. Ibid.

11. Noel Vietmeyer, telephone interview with author, May 15, 1990.

Introduction: A Beckoning Plant

1. R. N. Salaman's argument is found in "Why 'Jerusalem' Artichoke?" *Journal of the Royal Horticultural Society* 65 (1940): 338–48, 376–83.

2. L. Wyse and Lori Wifahrt, "Today's Weed: Jerusalem Artichoke," *Weeds Today* 13, no. 1 (Spring 1982): 14.

3. N. W. Simmonds, *Evolution of Crop Plants* (New York: Longman, 1976), 37.

4. The genesis of the French name *topinambour* is intriguing: "In 1613 native Indians of the Tapinambous tribe from Brazil were brought to France and excited considerable interest. Apparently some street hawker appropriated their name for the rather newly introduced tubers in order to increase their sales." Ibid.

5. According to James Duke's unpublished draft of a scholarly paper, "Helianthus Tuberosus," July 1987.

6. Ibid., 2.

7. Ibid., 3–4.

8. The Jerusalem artichoke has an "average tuber yield of 16,000–20,000 kg/ha when grown under ordinary farm conditions." Ibid., 4.

9. This biographical material was primarily taken from Dorothy Weyer Creigh's "The Great American Dream," in *Tales from the Prairie*, vol. 3 (1976; reprinted as *The American Artichoke: The Weed that Whips OPEC* [Ephrata, Wash.: Washington Gasohol Commission, 1981], 1–8.

10. Ibid.

11. Fred Johnson's first publication on the Jerusalem artichoke was "Storage Roots of the Jerusalem Artichoke," *Journal of Agricultural Research* 43, no. 4 (1931): 337–52.

12. Creigh, "The Great American Dream," 2.

13. Fred Johnson's ideas are found in "An American Weed Worth a Million Dollars," which was the title of his address to the Dearborn Conference of Agriculture, Industry, and Science, 1935, published in the *Proceedings of the Dearborn Conference of Agriculture, Industry, and Science* (New York: Chemical Foundation Inc., 1935), 171–81; reprinted in Creigh, *The American Artichoke*, 9–18.

14. Cited in Creigh, "The Great American Dream," 2.

15. Ralph Hixon optimistically contended that "[although] there are no commercial plants producing alcohol from artichokes, the problems in this industry are not complicated." *Proceedings of the Dearborn Conference*, 178.

16. Cited in William Hale, "Organic Chemistry Points the Way," *Proceedings of the Dearborn Conference*, 126.

17. Ibid., 127.

18. Cited in William Hale, *Prosperity Beckons: Dawn of the Alcohol Era*, rev. ed. (Minneapolis: Rutan, 1979), 100.

19. Ibid., 133.

20. Ibid., 133, 138.

21. Hale finished with a poem: "The farmers' waste shall give us power / To stem the tides and save the hour. / Oh, blessed be the industry / That strives and builds for chemurgy." Ibid., 156.

22. Johnson, "An American Weed Worth a Million Dollars," 180.

23. Prominent industrialists in attendance at the first Dearborn conference were Henry and Edsel Ford, Alvan Macaulay, Charles W. Nash, Robert C. Gra-

ham, and Roy D. Chapin. The first chair of the meeting was Francis Garvan, president of the American Chemical Society. This society was born out of the national economic needs occasioned by the First World War. For a description of the first Dearborn conference, see *Proceedings of the Dearborn Conference.*

24. For example, see ibid., 227.

25. Ibid. "The Declarations of Dependence upon the Soil" is found in the *Proceedings*, 30–35.

26. Ibid., 33.

27. Ibid., 35.

28. Much of what was most valuable at the Dearborn conferences found a place in the continuing work of the National Farm Chemurgic Council and that of its successors, the Council for Agricultural and Chemurgic Research and the Chemurgic Council, which held conferences and published papers up to 1970. Fred Hendrickson and AEFS supporters later identified the Chemurgic Council as part of their inheritance.

29. William Beaver, "The U.S. Failure to Develop Synthetic Fuels in the 1920s," *The Historian* 53, no. 2 (Winter 1991): 241–53.

30. Johnson joined the Chemurgic Council committee on the Jerusalem artichoke. The committee, headed by Dr. John Buchanan from Iowa State University, was made up of three university professors, including Buchanan and Hixon; a government official specializing in polarimetry; a director of the American Potash Institute; the president of the House of Gurneys, a company that for decades had a wide range of interests in unusual plants for the northern gardener; and Johnson himself, whose title was president of the United Artichoke Company, Hastings, Nebraska. Ibid., 171–80.

31. Joseph Amato, *When Father and Son Conspire: A Minnesota Farm Murder* (Ames: Iowa State University Press, 1988), 23–24.

32. For the soybean and its development as a crop, see William Lockeretz, "Agricultural Diversification by Crop Introduction," *Food Policy* 13, no. 1 (May 1988): 154–66; also useful are B. E. Caldwell, ed., *Soybeans: Improvement, Production, and Uses* (Madison, Wis.: American Society of Agronomy, 1973), and Leo Windisch, *The Soybean Pioneers, Trailblazers, Crusaders, Missionaries* (Galva, Ill.: self-published, 1981).

33. Lockeretz, "Agricultural Diversification," 163.

34. Ibid., 155.

1. A Country Prophet

1. Fred Hendrickson, letter to author, January 31, 1992, sent along with an earlier letter January 15, 1992, in reply to a preceding draft of this chapter.

2. "A Day with Fred," by his friend, Dana Jennings (September 1982, 20 pages including pictures), part of the Hendrickson files in my possession, which contain several boxes of personal letters, company prospectuses, AEFS materials and correspondence, diverse legal material, and alternative energy, sales, and religious materials Hendrickson gave me to use.

3. Fred Hendrickson, interview with author, June 19, 1990. Also Hendrickson, letter, January 31, 1992.

4. Ibid.

5. Jennings, "A Day with Fred," 8.

6. Hendrickson, interview, June 19, 1990.

Notes 213

7. A college classmate of Hendrickson's, interview with author, April 29, 1990.

8. A second college classmate of Hendrickson's, interview with author, March 1990.

9. Hendrickson, interview, June 19, 1990.

10. Hendrickson, letter, January 31, 1992.

11. Jennings, "A Day with Fred," 40.

12. Resume, letter on AEFS stationery, January 1982, found in company papers in author's possession.

13. A Rapid City business associate of Hendrickson's, telephone interview with author, April 11, 1990.

14. A second Rapid City business associate of Hendrickson's, telephone interview with author, April 11, 1990.

15. A third Rapid City business associate of Hendrickson's, telephone interview with author, April 30, 1990.

16. Ibid.

17. Lance Crombie, interviewed by B. Woods, "Energy and Self-sufficiency Now!" *Mother Earth News* 55 (January 1979): 16–18.

18. Prospectus for Energy Age Marketing and Management Corporation, Rapid City, South Dakota, n.d.

19. Jim Ruen, "The Jerusalem Artichoke: A Promising New Alcohol Fuel Crop," *North Dakota Farmer*, October 4, 1980.

20. Fred Hendrickson, "Special Report: The Jerusalem . . . Energy Farming's Answer to OPEC," composed of multiple documents and articles on Energy Age Marketing and Management Corporation stationery, April 1981.

21. Hendrickson, interview, June 19, 1990.

22. Hendrickson, letter, January 31, 1992.

23. Jennings, "A Day with Fred," 13.

24. James Dwire, telephone interview with author, September 15, 1991.

25. Jennings, "A Day with Fred," 14.

26. Fred Hendrickson, interview with author, July 12, 1990.

27. Dwire, interview.

28. The article Hendrickson marked up and converted for sales was by Robert Garfield, "Amway Isn't Just Another Soap Company," *Argus Leader* (Sioux Falls, S.D.), December 13, 1981. In annotations written on his copy, he compared Dwire and himself to Amway's founders Richard DeVos and Jay Van Andel. Further revealing the underpinnings of his thought, he had copied on the back of his promotional piece a newspaper article praising alcohol fuel and describing Ford and the Chemurgic Council's opposition to Rockefeller and Standard Oil by Hal Bernstein, "The Fuel Wars," *Omaha World Herald*, August 22, 1979.

29. Jennings, "A Day with Fred," 15–16.

30. Fred Hendrickson, letter to Rose Mary Peterson, September 1982.

31. Memo to James Dwire, July 7, 1982.

32. Fred Hendrickson, letter to James Dwire, March 15, 1982.

33. Fred Hendrickson, memo to James Dwire and the Christian Growers Association, January 11, 1982.

34. Jerry Knapper, introduction to Fred Hendrickson's speech, "What's New at AEFS?" National Growers Convention, June 18, 1982.

35. Fred Hendrickson, "What's New at AEFS?" National Growers Convention, June 18, 1982.

36. Ibid.

2. A Bulldozing Businessman

1. James Dwire, lengthy telephone interview with author, September 15, 1991.
2. Fred Hendrickson, letters to James Dwire, August, 18, 1981; September 3, 1981; and September 19, 1981.
3. Jerry Knapper, telephone interview with author, September 21, 1991.
4. Presentence investigation report on James Dwire done by state officer Andrew Doom for sentencing of James Dwire by Judge Richard L. Kelly, December 11, 1987.
5. Richard Dwire, lengthy telephone interview with author, September 22, 1991.
6. Ibid.
7. An employee of Dwire's, interview with author, July 17, 1990.
8. A business acquaintance of James Dwire's, interview with author, summer 1990.
9. Richard Dwire, interview.
10. Ibid.
11. An employee of Dwire's, interview with author, August 16, 1991.
12. A business acquaintance of Dwire's, interview with author, June 2, 1990.
13. Richard Dwire, interview.
14. Ibid.
15. A business partner of Dwire's, interview with author, February 29, 1990.
16. Lyon County final accounting and inventory and appraisal in the matter of Allen Dwire, June 26, 1981; also of interest is the inventory and appraisal of Allen Dwire's estate, August 21, 1973, file in Lyon County.
17. A longtime fellow contractor of James Dwire's, interview with author, November 9, 1991.
18. The inventory and appraisal of Allen Dwire's estate, August 21, 1973, shows James owed Allen's estate an additional $12,000 in notes and accrued interest.
19. An employee of Dwire's, interview with author, July 17, 1990.
20. A creditor and acquaintance of James Dwire's, interview with author, November 7, 1991.
21. A business associate of Dwire's, interview with author, May 29, 1991.
22. An employee of Dwire's, interview with author, July 17, 1990.
23. A second employee of Dwire's, interview with author, July 16, 1990.
24. A third employee of Dwire's, interview with author, July 17, 1990.
25. Another employee of Dwire's, interview with author, July 16, 1990.
26. A business associate of Dwire's, interview with author, summer 1990.
27. A third employee of Dwire's, interview with author, July 17, 1990.
28. An employee of Dwire's, interview with author, July 17, 1990.
29. Richard Dwire, interview.
30. A third employee of Dwire's, July 17, 1990.
31. The 1979 financial statement drawn up by Dwire as a basis for borrowing was found in company papers accumulated during McLeod County's investigation of AEFS.

17. AEFS's one-page Three Year Jerusalem Artichoke Crop Growing Agreement, in Hendrickson's papers.
18. Richard Spencer, *Freedom News*, September 1982.
19. AEFS's *Communicator* was a single-sheet, bimonthly publication that ran from December 15, 1982, to June 1, 1983.
20. Jerry Knapper, transcript of sales videotape, prefaced by Cal Maxwell, 1982, in Kramer files.
21. Jerry Knapper et al., a weekly update tape for all AEFS salespeople, 1982, in author's collection of company materials.
22. Jerry Knapper, testimony in matter of State of Minnesota, Counties of Lyon, McLeod, Redwood, Renville, and Sibley, in matter of the Grand Jury Investigation re: AEFS, October 1984, vol. 3, 556.
23. Ron Mann, interview with author, January 23, 1991.
24. Ibid.
25. Ibid.
26. Wayne Paige, interview with investigator Gregg LeCuyer of the Minnesota attorney general's office, September 21, 1982.
27. Sales Representatives Commission, "Schedule of Selling Expenses," examiner's report by Touche Ross & Co. to bankruptcy court, September 2, 1983, Schedule A-1, part of bankruptcy file in federal bankruptcy court, St. Paul, Minnesota.
28. Greg Bittner, letter to Minnesota attorney general's office, May 9, 1983.
29. According to Bittner, ultimately $36,000 of his commission went unpaid, interview with Vincent Carraher, June 5, 1984, Kramer's files.
30. In one of AEFS's contracts, salespeople were offered 5 percent of the gross sale for the first ten acres, 6 percent for the second ten acres, 8 percent for the third ten acres, and 10 percent for the fourth through the tenth ten-acre sale. A thousand-dollar bonus was given for the tenth sale. A significant number of alterations were made concerning growers' sales in the October 27, 1982, AEFS Administrative Board Plan, company records and Kramer's files.
31. Fred Hendrickson, deposition for Edward Bergquist, Trustee of the Estate of AEFS, Inc., United States District Court, *District of Minnesota v. James Dwire, et al.*, June 14, 1984, 136–41. The bankruptcy audit by Touche Ross & Co. estimated that Van Zee received $528,000, 16.
32. AEFS, *Freedom News*, spring 1983.
33. Ben Steensma, interview with author, January 5, 1991.
34. Ibid., and interview with author, February 12, 1991.
35. The $850,000 owed to the group known as the Van Dyke Brothers rested on a claim that they were owed $149,627 for seed delivered from September 1982 to May 1983; $270,965 for seed delivered in April and May 1983; yet another $307,609 for deliveries of seed in May and June 1983; and a debt for fifty-four unharvested acres. Les Van Dyke made an additional claim of $14,000 for cleaning of seed for AEFS customers. (Steensma claimed he lost an additional $20,000 in salaries alone, as he tried to support a successor Jerusalem artichoke association for a year after AEFS's bankruptcy.) Hendrickson, without denying the extent of Van Dyke's and Steensma's involvement with AEFS, argued that they were paid $137,000 in commissions for advance sales. Fred Hendrickson, letter to Doug Thompson, John Scholl, and others, April 26, 1988, and Fred Hendrickson, telephone interview with author, September 7, 1991. (Steensma claimed he never received any part of either sum.) Additionally, they received

$120,000, plus a $100,000 credit on the alcohol plant for a CD that AEFS pledged to a South Dakota bank on a loan they were getting to buy an alcohol plant. (This profile was based on a summary and analysis of an AEFS Jerusalem Artichoke Growers Questionnaire distributed in the spring and summer of 1982.) Hendrickson remarked bitterly, "[This is] hardly a case of being swindled out of their initial seed money or their delivered Jerusalem artichoke seed in May and June 1983."

36. AEFS Jerusalem Artichoke Growers Questionnaire, distributed to growers in spring and summer 1982.

37. Hubert Bietz, letter on AEFS stationery, n.d.

38. Thomas Sanger, letter to Jerry Knapper, March 1, 1983.

39. This is based on an analysis of two company documents. There were smaller concentrations in Texas, 40; Kansas, 38; Wyoming, 25; Arkansas, 24; Michigan, 23; Colorado, 19; Pennsylvania, 15; Ohio and Louisiana, 14; Tennessee, 13; Washington, 12; and Oklahoma, 10. There were six or fewer growers in Oregon, New Mexico, California, New York, Maryland, North Carolina, Nevada, Georgia, and three Canadian provinces. "Analysis of AEFS Growers Creditor Listing: J/A Growers—Ranked by no. Growers per state, 1982" and "Circle System Report Forms of Two and Three Year Growers," which lists them by state, address, and number of acres.

40. Minnesota's 174 three-year growers purchased an average of 13 acres; of these 174 growers, 27 bought 7 or fewer acres; 27 bought 15 or more; 17 bought 25 or more; and only 4 bought more than 40 acres. In addition, an examination of 258 two-year Minnesota growers showed an average purchase of 12 acres. This suggests, as AEFS officials contended, that the company did not encourage rampant speculation in the ranks of the growers. About 13 acres was the average unit purchased by 55 South Dakota three-year growers, 14.5 acres by 13 three-year Missouri growers, and 15 acres by Oklahoma's 4 three-year growers. Additional insight into AEFS growers is provided by analysis of an AEFS questionnaire that was sent out in the spring and summer of 1982. The results were based on 80 growers: 24 from South Dakota, 19 from Nebraska, 12 from North Dakota, 7 from Minnesota, 6 from Texas, 5 from Wyoming, 2 from Iowa, 2 from Missouri, and 1 each from Wisconsin and Colorado. Although sent to solicit grower evaluation of the company's media strategy, the questionnaire does make clear that the average grower had 14.2 acres of the average 880 he farmed in Jerusalem artichokes. The average farmer owned 460 acres of land, although 20 percent owned no land whatsoever but rented, on the average, 420 acres, while 25 percent rented no land. These farmers had an average of 100 acres in corn (with a range from 0 to 650 acres). Of the 80 growers who acknowledged they had livestock, 46 were predominantly raisers of cattle (51 percent) and hogs (20 percent). More significantly, proving that growers were transformed into salesmen by AEFS, of the 54 who responded, 67 percent intended to market their own crop, while 26 percent gave no answer, with less than 7 percent certain they would not market their own crop. Of those 54 growers who intended to market their crop, 6 intended to contact 1 to 5 prospective farmers, 22 intended to contact 6 to 15 farmers, 9 intended to contact 16 to 30, 8 intended to contact 31 to 100, and 3 enthusiastically planned to contact more than 100 farmers. Ibid.

41. Comparative data derived from using agricultural yields indicated in John Paxton, ed., *The Statesman's Year-Book, 1981–1982*, 118th ed. (New York: St. Martin's Press, 1981), xiii-xviii.

42. Pat Derner, phone interview with author, January 20, 1992.

43. Fred Hendrickson, preliminary draft of "Marketing Bulletin of the Marketing Techniques Involving Total Acreage to be Developed into Jerusalem Artichokes in [the] Next Three to Five Years and Urgency of the Sale[s] Technique and Approaches, September 5, 1982, in company papers.

4. A Perfect Consultant

1. A Glenwood business acquaintance of Kramer's, interview with author, June 4, 1990.

2. Randy Frame, "Assemblies of God Celebrating 75 Years," *Christianity Today*, September 22, 1989, 45.

3. Frances FitzGerald, "Reflections: Jim and Tammy," *The New Yorker*, April 23, 1990, 70.

4. A useful introduction to televangelism is Jeffrey Hadden and Anson Shupe, *Televangelism: Power and Politics on God's Frontier* (New York: Henry Holt and Company, 1988).

5. Challenge Chapel's high steeple and four doric columns in the front and three windows on each side made Kramer's chapel far more elaborate than the typical midwestern roadside chapels that dot the highways. Aside from serving the conventional purpose of providing a place for travelers to stop and meditate, Challenge Chapel displayed Kramer's spiritual guides, which formed the spine of his Challenge of Truth radio and television ministries. In the chapel a visitor could push one of four buttons, activating a hymn and a spiritual message by Kramer on one of life's four phases. During religious holidays, sacred music would be broadcast from the steeples of the chapel, and a picture of the chapel was used to sign on and sign off his Challenge of Truth telecasts.

6. "Nursing Homes Growth Exceeds Kramer Dream," *Pope County Tribune*, December 19, 1968.

7. Some of his pamphlets were titled "The Challenge of Being a Christian," "The Challenge of Submission," "A Challenge to New Converts," "A Challenge to Shut-Ins," "The Challenge to the Sorrowing," "The Challenge of the Home."

8. "Galilean Service to Have Pioneer Motif," *Pope County Tribune*, July 28, 1968.

9. "Kramer Receives Honorary Degree," *Pope County Tribune*, June 6, 1974.

10. A Glenwood acquaintance of Kramer's, telephone interview with author, June 4, 1990.

11. A former secretary who is now a social worker, interview with author, June 6, 1974.

12. A relative of one of Kramer's fellow directors, interview with author, June 4, 1990.

13. A Glenwood resident, two telephone interviews with author, May 1990.

14. A Glenwood business acquaintance of Kramer's who worked closely with a director who was against Challenge Home's move to Dallas, interview with author, June 4, 1990.

15. Complaint of *Securities and Exchange Commission v. Challenge Ministries, Inc., Challenges Homes, Lowell D. Kramer, Jesse A. Toav, E. Veon Scott, et al.*, filed Dallas, Texas, January 23, 1976.

16. A former colleague of deceased attorney Norvell Callaghan, interview with author, June 4, 1990.

17. In a lengthy interview in May 1992 and a lengthy phone interview on August 20, 1992, Kramer offered corrections of an earlier draft of this paper, explaining among other things how interest limits in Texas hindered Challenge Home's borrowing power. On this point, see also *SEC v. Challenge Ministries*, 6–7.

18. SEC hearings summarized by Sam Newland, "Magnetic Preacher," *Minneapolis Tribune*, June 6, 1976, and "The Donation that Didn't Materialize," *Minneapolis Tribune*, June 7, 1976. Kramer takes great exception to the veracity and spirit of these articles.

19. Newlund, "Magnetic Preacher," 1A, 10A.

20. Kramer, telephone interview, August 1992.

21. Complaint, *SEC v. Challenge Ministries*, 6–9. In "Magnetic Preacher," Newlund additionally describes Challenge Homes' economic problems in Minnesota and South Dakota. In a separate case, two officials of the Challenge Homes of the Dakotas were charged with embezzlement of patient funds, 10A.

22. *SEC v. Challenge Ministries*, 8.

23. *News from Securities Division*, State of Minnesota, Commerce Department, May 1976, 2. Possible instances of other irregular business practices on Kramer's part were uncovered by the SEC. In his testimony to the SEC, Challenge accountant Charles Doughtery, a stern opponent of Kramer, testified that Kramer made personal use of $185,000 of Challenge funds. In 1973, Kramer borrowed money from the bank for the express purpose of buying a mobile home for Challenge's use, but part of the money was "used to pay damages Mr. Kramer incurred in a lawsuit involving a 'pyramid sales' lawsuit." In the same year, Doughtery further testified, Kramer, without reporting the transactions, took two Challenge CDs worth $40,000 for collateral for a loan to Assured Funds. When the CDs came due, Kramer kept $20,000 surplus for Assured Funds. In a transaction similar to those he later carried out at AEFS, Kramer, according to Doughtery, made a loan of $25,800 to Motor Homes in Louisiana in exchange for a $28,000 note. In turn, Kramer gave the note to the Glenwood State Bank in exchange for a $28,000 CD payable to Challenge Homes. The CD secured the loan. When Motor Homes defaulted, the bank took all but $1,483, which Kramer pocketed for himself. Ibid., 10A, 11A.

24. *News from Securities Division*, 3.

25. Kramer in "Challenge Home Settlement: Bondholders Get 100 cents on Dollar," *Pope County Tribune*, December 8, 1978.

26. Kramer's resume, used for AEFS's first annual convention program, found in company papers.

5. What Made the Company Run

1. L. D. Kramer, memo to Richard Dwire, August 31, 1982.

2. Fred Hendrickson, letter to Richard Dwire, April 25, 1983.

3. George Holcomb, agent of the University of Minnesota Agricultural Extension Service, letter to agricultural agents in Southwestern Minnesota, October 19, 1981.

4. In three memos to AEFS lawyers Howard Cox and Louis Ainsworth, Commissioner Mark Seetin of the Minnesota attorney general's office spelled out his various concerns about AEFS's compliance with the law, December 1, December 23, and December 29, 1981.

5. Sandy Johnson, "Jerusalem Artichoke Production Questioned," Sioux Falls *Argus Leader*, December 9, 1981.
6. Jim Ruen, "The Gamble Behind the Jerusalem Artichoke," *The Farmer*, January 2, 1982.
7. John Archer, director of Division of Securities, "Order to Cease and Desist," to AEFS, March 5, 1982; and John Archer, "Order Vacating Order to Cease and Desist and Opportunity for Hearing and Administrative Complaint," to AEFS, March 18, 1983.
8. Richard Dwire, *State of Minnesota v. Fred Hendrickson*, partial transcript, vol. 2, 223.
9. Louis Ainsworth, letter to fellow company attorney Howard Cox, December 23, 1981, found in company papers in author's possession.
10. Louis Ainsworth, letter to AEFS, December 30, 1982.
11. Louis Ainsworth, memo to AEFS, December 20, 1982.
12. AEFS's test before the Minnesota attorney general revolved around the following five questions, not a single one of which it could satisfactorily answer. "1) What is the present state of affairs with respect to the market or use of the artichoke? 2) Where does the research and development of these markets stand, and how much of that effort is being supported by AEFS? 3) How far down the road would [is] commercial production in these areas, assuming that research and development ... are favorable? 4) [What are] the major inhibiting factors in these markets such as the low price of gasoline, the low price of corn and other feed stock, the easy availability of alternative feedstocks and the present limitation of the supply of Jerusalem artichokes? 5) [What is] the feasibility of growers doing much processing on the farm?" Louis Ainsworth, letter to Richard Dwire, December 16, 1982.
13. Jack Nissenbaum, interview with author, January 10, 1992.
14. Richard Dwire, *State of Minnesota v. Fred Hendrickson*, vol. 2, 226.
15. Ibid., 227.
16. In *Hyper-Growth: The Rise and Fall of Osborne Computer Corporation* (Berkeley, Calif.: Idthekkethan, 1984) Adam Osborne and John Dvorak describe the failure of Osborne Computer Corporation because of the astronomical growth it underwent from 1981 to 1983.
17. The most famous American pyramid scheme was the ingenious Ponzi scam of the 1920s. Immigrant Charles Ponzi offered investors a 50 percent return on their investments in less than two months merely by paying earlier investors with money from later investors. Stefan Kanfer, "Pigs Always Get Slaughtered," *Time*, February 6, 1990, 53.
18. Richard Dwire, *State of Minnesota v. Fred Hendrickson*, vol. 2, 220.
19. Wesley Buckle, phone interview with author, August 11, 1990.
20. Mark Hughes, telephone interview by AEFS investigator Vincent Carraher, employed by Dwire's defense firm, Thompson and Lundquist, September 27, 1983, found in author's company records.
21. Linda Julian, interview with Carraher, September 27, 1983. Kimberly Wornson, Dwire's secretary, confirmed much of Julian's opinions. She stated that, while James Dwire was not easy to work for because he often changed his plans, ideas, and schedules, he was "honest and fair." She offered further: "I began to feel that things were moving too fast. A lot of the times people were hired with no experience. ... Policy changed, they tried to rewrite the policy book, things often became confusing." She said that Fred Hendrickson contributed

very little. "[He] did not provide any direction or guidance, even though he had a law background." Kimberly Wornson, letter to investigators, September 27, 1983.

22. Richard Skorczewski, interview with Carraher, September 27, 1983.

23. Jim Menk, interview with Carraher, September 29, 1983.

24. Warren Anderson, interview with Paul Glorvigen, February 19, 1988. Anderson was also interviewed by the author, December 2, 1991. Also of interest is his letter to AEFS, December 11, 1982, in author's company files.

25. Larry Gauthier, interview with attorney general investigator Gregg LeCuyer, July 20, 1983.

26. For a description of the Laidlaws and their relations to Kramer, who contradicted them significantly in his interviews with the author, see their testimonies to the multi-county grand jury investigation re: AEFS, October 15–29, 1984, 213–46, 247–88. These testimonies as well as documents pertaining to Kramer's and AEFS's economic relations with the Laidlaws fill a large loose-leaf notebook in his files.

27. Bonnie Laidlaw, *Jerusalem Artichokes: Recipes for All Seasons* (Minneapolis: Little Lamb Chokes, Division of AEFS, 1983).

6. Killing off the Goose That Laid the Golden Egg

1. Definitions found in Alexander Henn, *Corporations*, 3d ed., (St. Paul: West Publishing, 1983), 582–83, 599–644, passim.

2. Ibid., 626.

3. *American Jurisprudence*, 2d ed., vol. 18B (Rochester, N.Y.: The Lawyers Corporative Publishing Co., 1985), section 1689, 542, and section 1711, 566.

4. Mark Dunnell, *Minnesota Digest*, vol. 4B (St. Paul: Butterworth Legal Publishers, 1987), 223.

5. Ibid., 224.

6. Fred Hendrickson, letter to James Dwire, October 28, 1982, hand delivered on October 29, 1982, author's company papers. For an example of Hendrickson's desire to regulate his and Dwire's relation to AEFS, see his preliminary draft, November 9, 1982, company files.

7. Tim Ribbens, audit for AEFS, March 18, 1983, Lyon County Court records.

8. Also see "Withdrawals by Principals," Grand Jury Investigation re: AEFS, Exhibit 12, October 15, 1984. See federal bankruptcy court's extensive audit of AEFS by Touche Ross & Co. examiner's report, September 2, 1983, 10–17.

9. For Hendrickson's and Dwire's borrowings from AEFS, see the Touche Ross & Co. examiner's report, September 2, 1983. Supplementing the audit numbers are the monthly and special reports by Vekich and Cox (author's company files) as well as extensive prosecutorial evidence generated for indictment and trials of Dwire, Hendrickson, and Kramer, court files.

10. Fred Hendrickson, letter to tax accountant Doug Amen, October 14, 1983, Hendrickson's files.

11. The Touche Ross & Co. audit reported that Dwire rented 717 acres to AEFS for $143,340 annually and 150 acres to Dwire, Inc., for $30,000 annually; Hendrickson rented 214 acres to AEFS for $42,860 annually, 12.

12. Fred Hendrickson, memo to AEFS, July 15, 1982, Hendrickson's files.

13. Fred Hendrickson, interview with author, April 21, 1991. Subchapter S describes a corporation that operates as a partnership and is taxed upon the dis-

tribution of profits to partners rather than both profits and dividends, as is the case of a corporation under Subchapter C.

14. Fred Hendrickson, deposition by Edward Bergquist, *Bankruptcy Trustee of the Estate of AEFS v. James Dwire, Fred Hendrickson, et al.*, June 14, 1984, 99.

15. According to Hendrickson, the money sent to Grow Force Fertilizer was to be used on his and Dwire's farms and sold to other growers, ibid., 100–101. Dwire testified that it was to be resold to AEFS, *State of Minnesota vs. Fred Hendrickson*, vol. 4, 801–2. Also of use to understand this transaction so revealing of Hendrickson and Dwire's relations, see "The Escrow Agreement," April 20, 1983, and Howard Cox's letter to Dean Hubbard, Bank of Seattle, January 6, 1983. This two-page letter found in the company files accompanied the checks and set forth terms of the escrow account, court files.

16. Fred Hendrickson, interview with author, April 21, 1991.

17. Paul Laidlaw, testimony, Grand Jury Investigation re: AEFS, October 1984, 234.

18. James Dwire, letter to Vekich-Arkema, March 29, 1983.

19. Ibid.

20. This transaction was not recorded at the Lyon County Court. At the time of AEFS's bankruptcy, Dwire produced a backdated lease between himself and AEFS. According to the terms of the lease, AEFS had signed a ten-year lease at $10,000 a month. Upon acceptance of the lease, according to bankruptcy court, "James Dwire was paid the amount of $220,000, which represented monthly rentals for the first twelve months and the last ten months of the lease. The lease was accepted by Fred Hendrickson, corporate secretary." Apparently, Dwire also considered putting his name on the main corporate office building, since in his files there is an original contract of sale made out to him. In his files there was an identical contract made out to AEFS except that it was dated six months later.

21. *State of Minnesota v. Fred Hendrickson*, vol. 4, 786. In the same testimony he suggests that several attorneys told him to own things in his own name, ibid., 744.

22. Touche Ross & Co. examiner's report, ledger entry, 5–8.

23. Ibid., 7.

24. Paul Laidlaw, testimony, Grand Jury Investigation re: AEFS, October 15, 1984, 230.

25. Bonnie Laidlaw, testimony, Grand Jury Investigation re: AEFS, October 15, 1984, 269.

26. Ibid., 277.

27. Touche Ross & Co. examiner's report, ledger entry, 7.

28. Paul Laidlaw, testimony, *State of Minnesota v. Lowell Dale Kramer*, March 22, 1988, vol. 2, 379.

29. "Withdrawals by Principals," Grand Jury Investigation re: AEFS. For Hendrickson's first expenses and advances, see his letter to Dwire re: "expense submission of September 19, 1981," October 2, 1981, company files. Also see his "Memo of Understanding on Personal Draws for Fred Hendrickson," September 19, 1981, and his confidential memo to James Dwire, March 30, 1982, in which he details amounts of money he "absolutely" needed for past and present promises and transactions.

30. Bonnie Laidlaw, testimony, Grand Jury Investigation re: AEFS, October 15, 1984, 281–2.

31. Hendrickson, memo to Dwire, July 7, 1982, company papers.

32. Hendrickson, memo to Dwire, July 19, 1982, company papers.
33. Fred Hendrickson, letter to James Dwire, August 12, 1982.
34. Fred Hendrickson, letter to James Dwire, October 28, 1982, 5 pp.
35. Fred Hendrickson, letter to James Dwire, October 28, 1982, 2 pp.
36. Fred Hendrickson, letter to James Dwire, November 11, 1982.
37. Ibid.
38. L. D. Kramer, memo to AEFS, June 30, 1983.
39. L. D. Kramer, memo to James Dwire, August 31, 1982.
40. "Withdrawal by Principals," Grand Jury Investigation re: AEFS, exhibit 12.

7. Folding up the Tent

1. Jim Nichols, telephone interview with author, May 1991.
2. Ben Steensma, interview with author, May 9, 1991.
3. Tom Fabel, former deputy attorney for the Minnesota attorney general's office, interview with author, March 25, 1990.
4. The *Farmer* article, "Jerusalem Artichoke Firm Under Investigation," February 19, 1983, charged that AEFS was conducting a pyramid scheme, its officials were engaged in fraud, and charges were pending against them. AEFS tried to block the publication of the article in Ramsey County court. Failing to do so, AEFS initiated a summons against the Webb Company. The Webb Company replied in *AEFS, Inc. v. Webb Company*, March 9, 1983. Since AEFS was overwhelmed with rescission requests, the case proceeded no further.
5. Michael Vekich testimony, *State of Minnesota v. Lowell Dale Kramer*, March 1988, vol. 4, 965.
6. Howard Cox, letter to AEFS, December 29, 1982, company files.
7. For Kramer's efforts to make Challenge Fund an independent financial agency, see Michael Vekich, letter to AEFS, May 5, 1983. Kramer himself confirmed their plans to remove AEFS from sales by selling off rights to state organizations, interview with author, June 1, 1991.
8. Howard Cox, letter to Michael Vekich, May 11, 1983.
9. Jim Newes, Joint Omnibus Hearing, *State of Minnesota v. James Dwire, Fred Hendrickson, and L. D. Kramer*, August 1986, 67–71.
10. Ibid., 55.
11. Ibid.
12. Ibid., 70.
13. Ibid., 101.
14. Daryle Uphoff, interview with author, June 11, 1991.
15. Mr. and Mrs. Arthur Erickson, letter to AEFS, May 24, 1983, files of the Minnesota attorney general.
16. For an overview of the prosecution's case against Kramer, see Kasal's opening statement, his cross-examination of Kramer, and his closing statement, *State of Minnesota v. Lowell Dale Kramer*, 1988, vol. 1, 203–20, and vol. 6, 1235–1318, 1327–64.
17. L. D. Kramer, interview with author, October 1, 1990.
18. Jim Nichols, interview with author, May 1991.
19. Newes, Joint Omnibus Hearing, 83–84.
20. L. D. Kramer, interview with author, June 1, 1991.

21. L. D. Kramer's "Time Line," a chronology in loose-leaf binder prepared for his trial, in Kramer papers.

22. Ibid.

23. It appears that Dwire and Kramer only retroactively determined the price and the amount of seed taken from AEFS, since the Stotts note was made part of the second of two different settlement statements, drafted two days apart from each other, on August 1 and August 3, found in company papers. The first statement, tailored around the Stotts note, credited to AEFS 800,000 pounds of seed at a conveniently discounted 80 cents a pound, while debiting AEFS for payment of $7,600 to Louis Veit for Kramer's partnership with him. This transaction—which of course satisfied Veit—did not explicitly credit AEFS with the seed that Kramer gave to Veit. Also, the statement questionably debted AEFS for charges by Hillcrest Leasing, Kramer and Associates, Tim Kramer, Robert Vekich ($20,000), and others, who might have had a claim against Challenge Fund but certainly not against AEFS. The second statement, which was unsigned, omitted these charges but deducted $60,000 for spoiled seed. Although both statements were found in a court-authorized search of Kramer's office, neither statement appeared in AEFS books, nor was any other statement found or known to exist that described seed taken from AEFS for the Challenge Fund and Kramer's partnerships. (The absence of any statement in AEFS records was confirmed by the head of distribution, Ken Bostrom, interview with author, June 4, 1991.) In a lengthy interview on May 30, 1991, Kramer claimed that Dwire, who reduced the August 3 note by 10 percent for spoilage of the seed, took it with him but failed to enter it into AEFS books. However, casting suspicion on the authenticity of the transaction, "a company memo" by Kramer indicates that as of September 26, 1983, both of Stotts's notes were counted among the $2,800,000 in unplaced notes. Later Kramer offered both of Stotts's notes and all his other notes to satisfy the bankruptcy court's claims against him. Kramer files contain a full loose-leaf volume on Stotts.

24. All Challenge Fund growers, except Tom Stanfield, who sent Challenge Fund $12,000, ignored Challenge Fund billings, claimed the seed they had originally received was spoiled or didn't grow, or told Challenge Fund to come and get its useless seed back before they plowed it into the ground.

25. At one point Kramer and Associates assigned eight notes: two notes for $75,000 went to Hillcrest Leasing; a note of $125,000 was given to Kramer's secretary, A. J. Youngberg; $200,000 in notes went to his brother, Wendall Kramer; and a $25,000 note went to his sons, Tim and Dale.

26. These explanations for AEFS's failure were voiced in Kramer's interviews with the author, October 1, October 8, and November 29, 1990, and June 1, 1991.

27. L. D. Kramer, interview with author, June 7, 1991.

28. Ibid.

29. Ibid.

30. The agreement, found in company papers, offered Dwire and Hendrickson 25 percent each of Stotts's thousand-acre farm in exchange for a thousand acres of seed and their serving as individual securers of 50 percent of Stotts's bank debt of $1.4 million. Hendrickson contended that it was AEFS's relationship to Stotts, in which he was not a central player, that more than anything else convicted him of theft by swindle.

31. Fred Hendrickson, letter to Edward Bergquist, October 10, 1983, Hendrickson files.

32. Fred Hendrickson, letters to James Dwire, June 24 and 25, 1983.
33. Hendrickson's emphasis, ibid.
34. Ibid.
35. Fred Hendrickson, letter to James Dwire, July 8, 1983.
36. Fred Hendrickson, letter to James Dwire, July 19, 1983. In a July 5, 1983, letter to Kramer, Hendrickson sought to make Kramer assure Dwire's response to "the Grow Force matter" and to have him repay his $50,000 consulting fee. Kramer replied he did help with the initial transaction, but since his company, Kramer Associates, no longer had a contract with AEFS, he would look into the matter only for "an hourly rate of $100 per hour, plus out-of-pocket expenses," July 12, 1983, company files.
37. Ibid.
38. Ibid.
39. Hendrickson, letter to Jerry Knapper, July 19, 1983.
40. Hendrickson, letter to Edward Bergquist, October 18, 1983.
41. Daryle Uphoff, interview with author, June 11, 1991. Also, see settlement agreement between Fred Hendrickson and Edward Bergquist, August 26, 1986, and Hendrickson's correspondence with Uphoff, especially his financial statement of April 1, 1984, and his letter to Uphoff on April 24, 1984.
42. James Dwire, telephone interview with author, September 22, 1991.
43. A farmer and his son murdered two bankers in nearby Ruthton, Minnesota, in September 1983 and fled to Paducah, Texas, where the son turned himself in to police and the father was found dead. Incidentally, Dwire even added spice and intrigue to this story. Several months after the murder, Dwire and his friend from Lynd, Louis Taveirne (the boyfriend of the father's wife), went to the site where the father's body was found and supposedly discovered a suicide note by the father confessing his guilt for the murder of the two bankers. The suicide note was incontrovertibly false. For a fuller discussion of the murders and the events associated with them, see Joseph Amato, *When Father and Son Conspire: A Minnesota Farm Murder* (Ames: Iowa State University Press, 1988).
44. Jerry Knapper, interview with author, September 21, 1991.
45. In addition to the Laidlaws testimony to the multicounty Grand Jury Investigation re: AEFS in 1984 and testimony at the Hendrickson and Kramer trials in 1988, Kramer files contain a loose-leaf volume on the Laidlaws, and company files contain contracts signed between the Laidlaws, AEFS, and Kramer. Additional materials were generated by the Paul and Bonnie Laidlaw bankruptcy case, United States Bankruptcy Court, District of Minnesota, March 1, 1988, and their civil action against Kramer, *Laidlaws v. L. D. Kramer et al.* in Fourth Judicial district, 1984.
46. L. D. Kramer, interview with Vincent Carraher for Dwire's defense attorney, Thompson & Lundquist, n.d., and Kramer, interview with author, October 1, 1990.
47. Kramer, interview with Carraher.
48. Kramer, interview with author, October 1, 1990.
49. John DeLanghe, interview with author, summer 1991.
50. "Alleged Unusual Transactions," an entry in the Touche Ross & Co. bankruptcy case re: AEFS, 1983, 16.
51. Burt and Gelene Johnson, interview with Gregg LeCuyer, attorney general's office, June 15, 1983. Their memos and records are found in company files

and Kramer files. Five other distribution centers did not respond to the bankruptcy auditors.

52. Gregg Bittner, letter to Minnesota attorney general, May 9, 1983.

53. For example, see Wayne and Marlene Smith, letter to Fred Hendrickson, June 23, 1983.

54. Kenneth Barker, letter to growers, July 30, 1983. Covenant Christian Farmers had a three-person board comprised of former AEFS employee Kenneth Barker, the pastor of Hendrickson's church and a follower of Pastor Pete; the Reverend Neil Rhodes of Open Bible Ministries; and farmer and church member Paul Paulson.

55. Dan Fisher, letter to Fred Hendrickson and James Dwire, July 22, 1983.

56. Fred Hendrickson, letter to Dan Fisher, February 22, 1984.

57. Examiner's report, bankruptcy case re: AEFS, exhibit B. For A.N.W. Seed Corp.'s legal problems, with which AEFS was deeply entangled, see file of *State of Washington v. A.N.W. Seed Corporation*, which was still under appeal as recently as 1990.

58. At their first meeting, the Minnesota Artichoke Growers Association elected Ralph Welcome of Stacy, Minnesota, as their president, listened to Harry Norton propose small cooperatives of ten to twenty growers entering alcohol production, and hired former colorful Granite Falls attorney Swen Anderson to represent MAGA at the forthcoming bankruptcy hearing in July.

59. For the South Dakota Jerusalem Artichoke Growers Association, see minutes of meeting of "National Meeting of AEFS, Inc.," June 1, 1983, and "Choke Growers Say They'll Have Last Laugh," *West Central Tribune* [Willmar, Minn.], April 19, 1983.

60. Robert Engbricht, letter to Fred Hendrickson, February 2, 1984.

61. Steensma was president and treasurer, and Alton Mjolsness of Felton, Minnesota, was vice president. Former AEFS company officer Harry Norton of Manitoba, Canada, was manager, and former district sales manager Cal Maxwell served as vice president and secretary. See Prospectus, National Alternative Crop Growers Cooperative, Inc., District of Columbia, July 26, 1983, 12 pp.

62. National Alternative Crop Growers Cooperative, Inc., "Order to Show Cause," State of South Dakota Department of Commerce, Division of Securities, October 28, 1983.

63. Ben Steensma, interview with author, January 5, 1991.

64. Pat Derner, interview with author, January 20, 1992.

8. The County Attorney and His Investigator

1. AEFS, Inc. Order for Conversion, U.S. Bankruptcy Court, District of Minnesota, September 13, 1983.

2. Touche Ross & Co. examiner's report, submitted to U.S. Bankruptcy Court, District of Minnesota, September 1983, exhibit B, 5. A useful short survey of AEFS's condition as exposed by the bankruptcy hearing was offered by attorney Chris Carlson's lengthy letter, July 11, 1983, to his client, the South Dakota's Jerusalem Artichoke Growers Association.

3. Touche Ross & Co. examiner's report, exhibit G, 28.

4. See chapter 7, note 51.

5. Edward Bergquist, interview with author, May 9, 1991, and telephone interviews with author, June 1, 1991, and September 1992.

6. Daryle Uphoff, interview with author, June 11, 1991, Uphoff, who granted me full access to his files, also responded to questions in two telephone calls in the fall of 1991 and another call on September 24, 1992.

7. The initial preparations for these cases are found in Uphoff's stored files.

8. Uphoff, interview, June 11, 1991.

9. See chapter 7; Touche Ross & Co. examiner's report, September 2, 1983, 10, 15, and exhibit 5; and White Lightning, plaintiff against AEFS, Uphoff files.

10. Trustee Final Report (File 9), AEFS, U.S. Bankruptcy Court, District of Minnesota, St. Paul, May 23, 1983–September 15, 1989, and author's interviews with Bergquist.

11. Trustee Final Report, Final Disbursement of AEFS, and the lists of secured and unsecured creditors.

12. Ibid.

13. James Dwire, *State of Minnesota v. Fred Hendrickson*, vol. 4, 814.

14. Hendrickson was assigned so comparatively little debt because he cooperated with Bergquist and Uphoff.

15. These larger unsigned notes, found in company papers, never brought forward in the defendants' case, done on the same day, on the same paper, and with the same typewriter, appear to be an effort on someone's part to regularize their relations with AEFS at a single swoop.

16. Edward Bergquist, "unemployment application of James Dwire," November 30, 1983.

17. L. D. Kramer, letter to the Reverend H. Rhode, August 2, 1983.

18. L. D. Kramer, tax returns for 1986, found among Kramer files.

19. Fred Hendrickson, Proof of Claims for Wages and Proof of Claim as Creditor, both dated January 21, 1984, part of U.S. Bankruptcy Court file.

20. Fred Hendrickson, letter to Daryle Uphoff, April 24, 1984, with attachments including notice of default on property payments and a financial report, Hendrickson files and court papers.

21. Fred Hendrickson, letter to Daryle Uphoff, February 20, 1984.

22. Rolland Henkoff, "Oh, How the Money Grows at ADM," *Fortune*, October 1990, 105–14.

23. Minister Ray Crouse of the Assembly of God Church of Hutchinson was found guilty of theft from a widow. No sooner had her husband died than the Reverend Crouse, who had cared for the aging couple, moved into her house, obtained power of attorney over her affairs, and removed $30,000 worth of bonds, money, and coins from her house and took them to his house and the church. Crouse contended that the husband had given him the bonds before he died. The Reverend Herman De Rhode, district superintendent of the Minnesota Assemblies of God (1964–1989), took this prosecution of one of his successful ministers personally and informed Kasal that he would use all influence to make sure he was defeated in any election Kasal chose to run. Ray Crouse, matter of McLeod County Grand Jury, May 1980.

24. Peter Kasal, interview with author, July 16, 1991.

25. Jim Newes, interview with author, June 11, 1991.

26. Biographical information on Peter Kasal was based primarily on interviews with him on February 23, 1990, and July 16, 1991, as well as telephone interviews on June 28 and July 7, 1991.

27. Kasal, interview, July 16, 1991.

28. Jim Newes, interview with author, September 16, 1991.

38. Presentence Investigation Report of Fred Hendrickson, prepared by state officer Andrew Doom for Judge Richard Kelly, April 4, 1988.

39. Fred Hendrickson and George Hendrickson, interview with author, October 14, 1990.

40. Fred Hendrickson, interview with author, April 4, 1991.

41. Ibid.

Conclusion: The Planets Went Astray

1. "Crop Watch," *The Farmer*, February 2, 1991. According to the article, "current buyers are a California firm that sells fresh 'chokes and a Georgia company that makes pickles and relishes."

Sources

The primary sources for this work were legal and public documents. These documents were generated by the Minnesota attorney general's inquiry into American Energy Farming Systems, 1981 to 1983; federal bankruptcy proceedings against AEFS in 1983; McLeod County's investigation of AEFS; the state of Minnesota's indictments; and the legal investigations of James Dwire, Fred Hendrickson, and L. D. Kramer, which all began in 1982 and concluded in trials for Hendrickson and Kramer in 1988.

Lyon County Court is the court of record. Indexed materials in four large boxes include some of the original aborted multicounty grand jury materials; Lyon County's criminal complaints; preliminary motions and appeals; Dwire's plea bargain; transcripts and evidence from the trials of Hendrickson and Kramer; and materials generated by appeals in advance of and after the trials.

McLeod County investigator Jim Newes put at my disposal all the materials that he had gathered and prepared first to indict and then to try the three men. These materials included oral interviews of AEFS employees and growers; reports on undercover visits to AEFS sales meetings; video and audio sales tapes; subpoened bank records; a nearly complete collection of company records and checks; the evidence used during the aborted multicounty grand jury hearing; and graphs and charts used to illustrate what the county determined were illegal transactions.

I was also given access to Kramer's defense materials, found in the Mankato office of Blue Earth public defender Calvin

Johnson, which were wonderfully organized, thanks to Kramer's efforts. The collection of documents, housed in approximately sixty loose-leaf binders, contains, in addition to trial materials, a large array of company records; a nearly complete record of Kramer's work schedule and salary; documents associated with his multiple and complex transactions with AEFS, subsidiaries of AEFS, and individual partnerships; records of companies he created, including Challenge Fund, Hillcrest Leasing, and Remark; five large, invaluable books of interviews of prosecution and defense witnesses; and Kramer's time line of AEFS's history and his relation with it.

Hendrickson generously gave me access to his unorganized personal and company papers. Of unique interest, these papers include more than a dozen audio tapes of his discussions with and advice to his attorneys; materials having to do with appeals of his conviction and disbarment; his very important correspondence with Dwire and with AEFS; his communications on behalf of Bio-Markets of America; his files on alternative energy; and his proposals, prospectuses, and charters for a dozen other companies he created or planned to create prior to and after AEFS. Also, he gave me a complete set of the twenty-five videocassettes of the company's first annual convention.

Douglas Blanke, former head of the consumer division of the Minnesota attorney general, permitted me access to a significant collection of documents accumulated in the course of his office's investigation of AEFS for consumer fraud and other charges. The collection—twenty-one large legal boxes (sixteen of which deal with rescission announcements and responses)—contains investigatory interviews of AEFS salespeople and growers; a remarkably thorough collection of expert scientific, technological, engineering, and horticultural opinion about the Jerusalem artichoke and AEFS's capacity to process and market the crop; grower complaints against AEFS; a useful collection of newspaper clippings, articles, and other material pertaining to the Jerusalem artichoke and AEFS; and AEFS's evidence attempting to prove the legitimacy of the crop and the company.

The federal bankruptcy court in St. Paul, ably served by clerk Grace Young, holds a useful collection of files related to AEFS's bankruptcy. The most valuable parts of the collection—

comprised of ten bound files in addition to legal notifications—are the transcript of the extensive bankruptcy hearings, a complete list of creditors, and the very extensive examiner's report undertaken by Touche Ross & Co.

Court-appointed trustee Edward Bergquist of Minneapolis generously shared his opinions with me, as did Minneapolis attorney Daryle Uphoff, who served as counsel for unsecured creditors. Also, Uphoff opened his files to me, comprised of four large legal boxes, which contain the materials he generated in the course of his search to locate and to recover—by court action if necessary—AEFS assets.

Additional legal materials were found at the South Dakota Consumer Protection Division. Its head, Debra Bollinger, not only gave me access to the materials regarding AEFS's violation of the state's security law but also gave me my first lesson on white-collar crime. Special aide to the Iowa attorney general Chuck Rutenbeck—charged with examining agricultural fraud—provided interesting comments on rural crime and mailed me interesting materials on this subject. Individuals from attorney general offices in Wisconsin, North Dakota, Indiana, and Washington sent me material on AEFS and successor organizations.

At many stages of my research, newspaper articles proved immensely helpful. Cited in individual chapter notes, the most important articles provided information about the promise of the Jerusalem artichoke, other plants of promise, the character of AEFS, Kramer's background, the pending attorney general investigations, the bankruptcy proceedings, the grand juries, the trials, and Hendrickson's disbarment.

Interviews, many of which are cited in notes, played an indispensable role in uncovering the many hidden parts of the story. They helped me understand the history of alternative energy and crop development; the makings of a horticultural hysteria; the inner workings of a contemporary company; the lives and the backgrounds of several individuals; and the complex, secret, and illegal transactions. In truth, this story couldn't have been written without my interviews and those of others.

A few important interviews were conducted by senior seminar student Rudolph Curtler, who wrote an interesting paper on

AEFS's exploitation of religion. In addition to accompanying me on interviews with McLeod County prosecutor Peter Kasal and his investigator, Jim Newes, Curtler conducted worthwhile interviews with sales trainer Ron Mann and AEFS employee Lola Boe.

McLeod County investigators Linda Shamla, Richard Moisan, and Jim Newes carried out many personal and phone interviews while investigating the company and its practices. The transcripts of these interviews were useful. Also, investigator Gregg LeCuyer of the Minnesota attorney general's office—whom my daughter Felice and I interviewed—carried out numerous useful interviews regarding the integrity of the crop and the company. Investigator Vincent Carraher carried out numerous interviews for Dwire's defense attorney, John Lundquist of Minneapolis. Investigator Paul Glorvigen did many interviews for Hendrickson's public defender, John Scholl, and Kramer's public defender, Calvin Johnson. The transcripts of these interviews were found in Kramer's files of trial witnesses.

My own interviews numbered approximately one hundred. Most of these interviews were conducted by telephone. Some of the interviewees insisted on confidentiality. This was especially the case with former acquaintances and business associates of Dwire's, Hendrickson's, and Kramer's. Accordingly, for the sake of consistency, I deleted in my notes the names of almost all sources who commented on Dwire's life in Marshall prior to AEFS, Hendrickson's pre-AEFS days in Rapid City, and Kramer's role in Glenwood, Minnesota, in the 1960s, even if these individuals did not request confidentiality. Exceptions to this rule are found in the notes to chapters 1, 2, and 4.

Hendrickson and Kramer themselves generously met with me on several occasions for long periods of time, and they freely responded to my questions on the phone. Both men critically and constructively read the biographical chapters on themselves. Dwire was equally responsive in a lengthy telephone interview with me.

Also, I conducted lengthy phone interviews with recently deceased Richard Dwire, James Dwire's brother, and Jerry Knapper, James Dwire's brother-in-law and head of AEFS sales.

Ronn Mann, who trained AEFS sales personnel, met with me on several occasions, as did Richard Spencer, head of AEFS research. James Menk, who managed AEFS during its bankruptcy, and James Anderson, who served as one of Dwire's attorneys, both met with me. John Peterson, Pastor Pete's son and Hendrickson's secretary; Karen Hirmer, AEFS secretary; Ken Bostrum, distribution head; and Pat Derner, who worked for Fred Hendrickson in market development, all spoke with me on the telephone. Others associated with the company who spoke with me on the phone included Marshall regional farmers Louis Veit and John DeLanghe and eastern South Dakota grower George Fish. Salesman John Dreckman, an early grower and transporter of Jerusalem artichokes, spent several hours with me. I had several face-to-face and telephone interviews with Ben Steensma, also an early AEFS grower, who became president of a successor organization to AEFS, the National Alternative Crop Growers Cooperative. Steensma gave me access to the complete files of the Chemurgic Council, which were given to him by the auctioner at AEFS's bankruptcy sale.

AEFS science consultants L. T. Fan of Kansas State University, Larry Tieszen of Augustana College, Al Rusk of Southwest State University, and Pat Derner of Milford, Iowa, all spoke with me.

Other scientists sympathetic to AEFS who spoke to me included Wesley Buchele of Ames, Iowa, and Wendell Peden, a Rapid City, South Dakota, veterinarian. Independent crop developer and speculator Thomas Reichert of Edina, Minnesota, who lost thousands of tons of his Jerusalem artichokes to AEFS, spoke to me at length on two separate occasions about his hopes for the Jerusalem artichoke and his relations with AEFS, as did Warren Anderson, a lawyer for the Minnesota Jerusalem Artichoke Growers.

Many scientists spoke to me on the telephone and, in several instances, followed up our conversations by sending me materials on the Jerusalem artichoke and alternative crops. Among these scientists were Tom Lukens of the Golden State Bulb Growers in Watonsville, California, who was a pioneer in promoting the Jerusalem artichoke in the late 1970s; John Pesek, head of agronomy at Iowa State University; Luther Waters, head of the department of horticulture science at Ohio State University, who worked for the Minnesota attorney general's office; James Duke of the U.S. Department of Agriculture; James Brown of the Arizona Jojoba Grower Processors; Daniel Putnam, professor of alternative crops at the University of Minnesota; Noel Vietmeyer of the National Academy of Science; and the widely published Anson Thompson of the U.S. Department of Agriculture in Phoenix, Arizona. Homer Socolofsky of the department of history at Kansas State University sent me his unpublished essay on government efforts to develop sorghum sugar in the nineteenth century.

Especially important and lengthy interviews were given by Kramer's attorney Calvin Johnson of Mankato; Hendrickson's attorney John Scholl of Worthington; Johnson and Scholl's investigator, Paul Glorvigen; and Jim Nichols, former commissioner of the Minnesota Department of Agriculture. Attorney Kevin Stroup of Clarkfield, Minnesota, helped me understand several important legal distinctions, and attorney Tom Fabel of Minneapolis, formerly a chief officer at the Minnesota attorney general's office, opened an important research door for me and also clarified why the attorney general did not pursue a criminal investigation of AEFS.

Former McLeod County prosecutor Peter Kasal granted me two lengthy interviews and responded to telephone questions. Former McLeod County investigator Jim Newes not only provided me with sources for this study but also, with his keen wit, provided insights into the complex world of law.

A diverse corpus of secondary literature, as indicated by chapter notes, supplemented and offered insight into the array of subjects addressed in this book. For the Jerusalem artichoke as a plant and as a crop, see Victor Boswell, *Growing the Jerusalem Artichoke*, U.S. Department of Agriculture Leaflet No. 116 (Washington, D.C.: U.S. Government Printing Office, 1936); James Duke, "Helianthus Tuberosus," unpublished paper, July 1987; Roy Sachs et al., "Fuel Alcohol from Jerusalem Artichoke," *California Agriculture* (Sept.-Oct. 1981), 4–6; D. N. Shoemaker, *The Jerusalem Artichoke as a Crop Plant*, U.S. Department of Agriculture Technical Bulletin No. 33 (Washington, D.C.: U.S. Government Printing Office, 1927) 1–32; U.S. Department of Agriculture, *Experiment Station Work-IV*, Farmers Bulletin No. 73 (Washington, D.C.: U.S. Government Printing Office, 1908); U.S. Department of Agriculture, *Growing the Jerusalem Artichoke*, Leaflet No. 116, (Washington, D.C.: U.S. Government Printing Office, 1936); and D. L. Wipe and Lori Wilfahrt, "Today's Weed: Jerusalem Artichoke," *Weeds Today*, Early Spring 1982, 14–16.

For alternative crops in general and a few examples, see the publications of the Council for Agricultural Science and Technology, Ames, Iowa, especially "Development of New Crops: Needs, Procedures, and Options," Report No. 102 (October 1984); University of Minnesota Center for Alternative Crops and Products, *BioOptions* 1, no. 1 (Summer 1989) and ff.; James Brown, "The Jojoba Industry, A 15 Year Commercial Perspective" (Unpublished keynote address paper presented at the Eighth International Conference on Jojoba and Its Uses, Asunción, Paraguay, June 17–22, 1990); Ged Davis, "Energy for Planet Earth," *Scientific American* 263, no. 3 (September 1990): 55–62; D. A. Dierig, A. E. Thompson, and D. T. Ray, "Relationships of Morphological Variables to Rubber Production in Guayule," *Euphytica* 44 (1989): 259–64; Jules Janick, *Horticultural Science* (San Francisco: Freeman, 1963); John Haldren, "Energy in Transition," *Scientific American* 260, no. 3 (September 1990): 157–63; Ronald Henhoff, "Oh, How the Money Grows at ADM," *Fortune*, October 8, 1990, 105; David Pimental et al., "Perennial Grains: An Ecology of New Crops," *Interdisciplinary Science Review* 11, no. 1 (1986): 42–49; Dennis Farney, "Meet the Men Who Risked Their Lives to Find New Plants," *Smithsonian*, June 1980, 129–40; William Lockeretz, "Agricultural Diversification by Introduction of an Unfamiliar Crop: The U.S. Experience with the Soybean," unpublished paper, September 1987; Gary Ritchie, ed., *New Agricultural Crops* (Boulder, Colo: Westview, 1979); and Anson Thompson, "New Nature Crops for the Arid Southwest," *Economic Botany* 39, no. 4 (1985): 436–53.

For a history of the relationship between human society and plants, see Edgar Anderson's seminal *Plants, Man and Life* (Berkeley: University of California Press, 1967); A. Richard Crabb, *The Hybrid-Corn Makers: Prophets of Plenty* (New Brunswick, N.J.: Rutgers University Press, 1947); Alfred Crosby, *The Columbian Exchange: Biological and Cultural Consequences of 1492*

(Westport, Conn.: Greenwood, 1972), and *Ecological Imperialism: The Biological Expansion of Europe, 900–1900* (New York: Cambridge University Press, 1986); Henry Hobhouse, *Seeds of Change: Five Plants that Transformed Mankind* (New York: Harper & Row, 1986); Sidney Mintz, *Sweetness and Power: The Place of Sugar in Modern History* (New York: Penguin, 1985); Simon Schama, *The Embarrassment of Riches: An Interpretation of Dutch Culture in the Golden Age* (Berkeley: University of California Press, 1988); N. W. Simmonds, ed., *Evaluation of Crop Plants* (New York: Longman, 1976); Jack Weatherford, *Indian Givers: How the Indians of the Americas Transformed the World* (New York: Crown, 1988); and Charles Wilson, *New Crops for the New World* (New York: Macmillan, 1945).

For suggestive works on the alcohol fuel movement in the first half of the twentieth century and the search for alternative fuels, see *Proceedings of the Dearborn Conference of Agriculture, Industry and Science: Dearborn, Michigan, May 7 and 8, 1935* (New York: The Chemical Foundation Inc., 1935); *Proceedings of the Second Dearborn Conference of Agriculture, Industry and Science: Dearborn, Michigan, May 12, 13, 14, 1936* (New York: The Chemical Foundation, Inc., 1936); William Hale, *Prosperity Beckons: Dawn of the Alcohol Era* (Minneapolis: Butan, 1936); The Washington Gasahol Commission, *The American Artichoke: The Weed that Whips OPEC!* (Ephrata, Wash.: The Washington Gasahol Commission, 1981); and Herman Withe and Paul Kalachow, *Food for Thought* (Indianapolis: Indiana Farm Bureau, Inc., 1942).

For a study of the myths, beliefs, and ideologies that disposed AEFS salespeople and growers to lend such energy and faith to the promise of AEFS, see Nicole Biggart, *Charismatic Capitalism: Direct Selling Organizations in America* (Chicago: University of Chicago Press, 1989); Nicholas Cords and Patrick Gerster, *Myth and the American Experience*, vol. II (New York: Glencoe, 1973); Gilbert C. Fite, *American Farmers: The New Minority* (Bloomington: Indiana University Press, 1984); Richard Hafstadter, *The Age of Reform* (New York: Vintage, 1955); Richard Hofstadter, *Anti-Intellectualism in American Life* (New York: Vintage, 1963); Richard Hofstadter, *The Paranoid Style in American Politics and Other Essays* (New York: Vintage, 1967); Lewis

Lapham, *Money and Class in America: Notes and Observations on Our Civil Religion* (New York: Weidenfeld & Nicolson, 1988); Charles Latz, ed., *Farming the Lord's Land: Christian Perspectives on American Agriculture* (Minneapolis: Augsburg, 1980); and Daniel Yergin, *The Prize: The Epic Quest for Oil, Money and Power* (New York; Simon & Schuster, 1991).

For studies of the energy crisis, see Lester Brown, *Building a Sustainable Society* (New York: Norton, 1981); Lester Brown, Christopher Flavin, and Colin Norman, *Running on Empty* (New York: Norton, 1979); J. A. Duke et. al., *Handbook of Agricultural Energy Potential of Developing Countries*, 4 vols. (Boca Raton, Fla.: CRC Press, 1987); Martin Melosi, *Coping with Abundance: Energy and Environment in Industrial America* (Philadelphia: Temple University Press, 1985); W. Palz and P. Chartier, eds., *Energy from Biomass in Europe* (London: Applied Science Publishers, 1980); and U.S. National Alcohol Fuels Commission, *Fuel Alcohol: An Energy Alternative for the 1980s* (Washington, D.C.: U.S. Government Printing Office, 1981).

To understand the farm crisis and its impact on the region, see Joseph Amato, *When Father and Son Conspire: A Minnesota Farm Murder* (Ames: Iowa State University Press, 1988); Julie Bleyhl, "Farm Financial Analysis" (unpublished report for the Minnesota Farmers Union, December 5, 1985); Osha Gray Davidson, *Broken Heartland; The Rise of America's Rural Ghetto* (New York: The Free Press, 1990); Gilbert Fite, *American Farmers: The New Minority* (Bloomington: Indiana University Press, 1984); Minnesota Department of Agriculture, *Minnesota Farm Financial Survey, 1985*, February 3, 1986; Dan Morgan, *Merchants of Grain* (New York: Penguin, 1980); William Pratt, "Midwest Farm Protest—Then and Now," in *Plowing Up a Storm: A History of Midwestern Farm Activism* (Nebraska Educational Television Network, 1985), 21–25; Mike Meyers, "Propping up the Farm," special issue of the *Minneapolis Star and Tribune*, August 11 and 12, 1985; Jonathan Rauch, "The Great Farm Gamble," *National Journal*, March 29, 1986, 13–16.

Of particular interest for the examination of evangelical religion, see "Assemblies of God Church," *Encyclopedia Americana* vol. 2 (Danbury, Conn.: Gralier, 1989): 527; Charles Farah, "America's Pentecostals: What They Believe: Speaking in

Tongues Isn't Everything," *Christianity Today* 3 (October 16, 1987): 22; Francis FitzGerald, "Reflections: Jim and Tammy," *The New Yorker*, April 23, 1990, 45–87; Randy Frame, "Assemblies of God Celebrates 75 Years," *Christianity Today* 33 (September 22, 1989): 45; Jeffrey Hadden and Anson Shupe, *Televangelism: Power and Politics on God's Frontier* (New York: Henry Holt, 1988); Miles Austin, *Don't Call Me Brother: A Ringmaster's Escape from the Pentecostal Church* (Buffalo, N.Y.: Prometheus, 1989); and Harold Smith, "America's Pentecostals: Where They Are Going," *Christianity Today* 31 (October 16, 1987): 27.

For an appreciation of the multiple legal questions and possible types of criminality involved in AEFS and the trials of its owners and consultant, see *American Jurisprudence*, 2d ed., vol. 18B (Rochester, N.Y.: The Lawyer Corporative, 1985); Gregory Couch and Anne Michaud, "New Found America Emerges from Ashes of Regulatory-Troubled Entity," *Los Angeles Times*, August 25, 1991; Shanler Cronk, *Criminal Justice in Rural America* (Knoxville, Tenn.: National Institute of Justice, 1981); Mark Dunnell, *Dunnell's Minnesota Digest*, 3d ed. (St. Paul: Butterworth Legal, 1987); Herbert Ddelhertz and Thomas Overcast, eds., *White-Collar Crime: An Agenda for Research* (Lexington, Mass.: Heath, 1982); Harry Henn and John Alexander, *Laws of Corporations and Other Business Enterprises*, 3d ed. (St. Paul: West, 1983); Arthur Leff, *Swindling and Selling* (New York: The Free Press, 1976); Ronald Ostrow and Robert Rosenblatt, "S & L Crisis' New Focus: Neil Bush," *Star Tribune Newspaper of the Twin Cities*, July 15, 1990; and *Scoundrels & Scalawags* (Pleasantville, N.Y.: Reader's Digest, 1968).

Index

Ainsworth, Louis, 93–95, 137
Amaranth, xxv, 21–22
American Energy Farming Systems (AEFS); in bankruptcy court, 154–59; and buyers, 72–74; as a Christian company, 89–90, 98; contracts of, 70; corporate philosophy, 56–57; filing for bankruptcy, 124, 127–37; first convention of, 53–56; and "Hyper-Growth," 96–97; management of, 97–124; Minnesota attorney general's investigation of, 92–95, 126–27; theft from, 109–20, 127–37
Amway, 25, 45
Anderson, Warren, 99–100
Aquanalysis, Inc., 46. See also Dorband, Wayne
Assemblies of God, 78

Bakker, Jim and Tammy, 26–27, 52, 78, 198
Bergquist, Edward, 139, 141–42, 157–58
Bio-Markets of America, Inc., 95, 114, 128
Bittner, Greg, 69–70
Blue Water Harvester, Inc., 39
Boe, Kim, 40, 48, 108, 153

Challenge Fund, 120, 128, 133–37

Challenge Homes, 77, 81–87
Chubey, B. B., 22, 54
Clark, Mary Jo, 55

D & G Excavating, Inc., 36, 39
Dearborn conferences, 6–8
Derner, Pat, 75, 97, 152
Dorband, Wayne, 39, 45–46, 54, 93, 97, 145–46, 157
Dwire, Allen, 30–34
Dwire, Inc., 30–31, 35–36, 38–40, 48, 108, 113–16
Dwire, James, 24–25, 29–48ff, 96–97, 102–3, 179–80, 183–84; companies formed by, 113, 116–17; criminal proceedings against, 161–71
Dwire, Richard, 31–32, 144

Energy Crisis, 9–11
Erickson, Vince, 22, 147, 159

Falwell, the Rev. Jerry, 52, 197
Fan, L. T., 45, 54, 101
Farm crisis, 11–12
The Farmer, 91, 127, 140
Ford, Henry, 6
Freedom News, 64, 71

Gauthier, Larry, 100
Guayule, xxvi–xxvii

Hale, William, 5–6

Index

Hendrickson, Fred, 15–28, 101ff, 138–42, 185–93; criminal proceedings against, 161–74
Hixon, Ralph, 5
Hughes, Mark, 97–98

Jerusalem artichoke, 1–4, 22–23, 46–47; in France, 46–47, 62, 65; price of, 105; selling of, 61–65, 67–70; as source of alcohol fuel, 13
Jim Dwire Construction, 39
Johnson, Calvin, 174–75
Johnson, Fred, 4–6, 8–9
Jojoba xxvi–xxvii
Julian, Linda, 98, 143, 145

Kasal, Peter, 130, 137, 161–78
Kilthau, Lyle, 23, 24, 54, 150–51, 157
Knapper, the Rev. Jerry, 27, 41, 42, 52, 54, 62, 65–67, 101, 141, 146
Kramer, the Rev. Lowell Dale, 52, 54–55, 77–78, 103–4, 118–24, 133–37, 179–83; criminal proceedings against, 161–69, 174–76

Laidlaw, Bonnie and Paul, 54, 103–5, 115, 118–19, 146–48
Lukens, Tom, 22, 91
Lynd Redi-Mix, Inc., 36, 39

Maiz, Betty, 55
Mann, Ron, 67–69, 146
Marshall Evangelical Free Church, 41, 89, 144
Maxwell, Calvin, 55–56, 151
Menk, Jim, 99, 146
Messersmith, Bob, 90, 140
Minnesota Jerusalem Artichoke Association, 99

National Alternative Crops Growers Cooperative, 151–52
National Farm Chemurgic Council, 6-7, 152

Newes, Jim, 129, 160, 162, 164–78
Nichols, Jim, 125–26, 134, 137

O'Reilly, Pat ("Family Farmer"), 145, 151

Peden, Wendell, 54
Peterson, Richard ("Pastor Pete"), 25–26, 41, 89
Philip, South Dakota, 15–16
"Prayer Power." *See* Peterson, Richard ("Pastor Pete")

Reichert, Thomas, 22, 91, 148–49, 155, 159
Roberts, Oral, 26, 52, 79, 179
Rusk, Alvin, 23–24, 43, 45, 65, 101

SL&C Partnership, 39
Scholl, John, 171–73
Sheenan, Don, 54
Skorczewski, Richard, 40, 98–100
Skrien, Paul, 90, 145, 146
Soybeans, xxv, 12–13
Spencer, Richard, 45, 65, 89, 93, 97, 101, 145
Steensma, Ben, 71–72, 126, 151–52
Sunchokes. *See* Jerusalem artichoke
Sunflowers, xxvi

Tieszen, Larry, 45, 97, 140, 145
Trilateral Commission, 27

University of Minnesota Agricultural Extension Service, 90-91
Uphoff, Daryle, 141–42, 156–57

Van Dyke, Les, 71–72
Van Zee, Andy, 65, 70–71, 150
Vekich, Michael, 108–9, 127–28

Webb Press. *See The Farmer*

Zink, Esther, 55

Joseph Amato is a professor of history at Southwest State University, Marshall, Minnesota. He earned a B.A. degree from the University of Michigan; an M.A. from the University of Laval, Quebec, Canada; and a Ph.D. from the University of Rochester, New York. He is the author of several books, including *Guilt and Gratitude: A Study of the Origins of Contemporary Conscience; Death Book: Terrors, Consolations, Contradictions, & Paradoxes*; and recently, *Victims and Values: A History and a Theory of Suffering*.

Professor Amato is one of the founders and definers of Southwest State University's Rural Studies Program. He not only has directed and taught in the program since its inception but also has helped win major and minor grants for its development. He is the founder of the recently formed Society for the Study of Local and Regional Study. In addition, he has supported the idea of rural studies with his writings, which include a variety of articles and reviews and the books *Countryside: Mirror of Ourselves, When Father and Son Conspire: A Minnesota Farm Murder*, and the forthcoming *Decline in Rural Minnesota*.

In addition to promoting and publishing books and articles on southwest Minnesota through the university and Crossings Press, he has written a history of Southwest State University, *A New College on the Prairie*. He also has written a study of the Belgian farmers of his region, *Servants of the Land*, which will be the subject of a documentary by Belgian public television. He recently has written a set of articles on rural decline for the Minnesota League of Cities.